# TEACHING ECONOMICS TO UNDERGRADUATES: ALTERNATIVES TO CHALK AND TALK

# TEACHING ECONOMICS TO UNDERGRADUATES: ALTERNATIVES TO CHALK AND TALK

Edited by

*William E. Becker* and *Michael Watts*

**Edward Elgar**
Cheltenham, UK • Northampton, MA, USA

*4/2/00*

Published by
Edward Elgar Publishing Limited
Glensanda House
Montpellier Parade
Cheltenham
Glos GL50 1UA
UK

Edward Elgar Publishing, Inc.
6 Market Street
Northampton
Massachusetts 01060
USA

A catalogue record for this book
is available from the British Library

**Library of Congress Cataloguing in Publication Data**
Teaching economics to undergraduates : alternatives to chalk and talk
   / edited by William E. Becker and Michael Watts.
      Includes index.
      1. Economics—Study and teaching (Higher)—United States.
   I. Becker, William E.   II. Watts, Michael.
   HB74.8.T4 1999
   330'.071'173—dc21                                    98–48149
                                                           CIP

ISBN 1 85898 972 8 (cased)

Printed and bound in Great Britain by Biddles Ltd, Guildford and King's Lynn

# CONTENTS

# FIGURES AND TABLES

## FIGURES

## TABLES

# FOREWORD

## William J. Baumol

We dismal scientists may well seem conspicuously unqualified to lay claim to any special insights into the educational process. Practitioners of our discipline have been charged with incoherence, excessive abstraction and employment of language and analytic tools that are best calculated to prevent effective communication. But whatever truth there may be to these charges, there is a very different side to the matter. For there are economists who have, at the same time, been in the vanguard in thinking about educational methods and, more particularly, in subjecting these methods to systematic empirical testing – in finding whether the pudding does indeed possess proof. I am confident this contribution will, in time, be recognized as the major advance in educational analysis that it surely is. There are, of course, others besides economists who have sought to base their educational practice on empirical evidence. But it is arguable that the concerned economic researchers have gone further along this path than has any other group.

One result has been that the profession has come up with a rich body of ideas for improvement in the educational procedures that is well worth learning about. This book undertakes to provide at least a broad sampling of the requisite information. The eleven essays that are contained in the volume have been edited and assembled by two specialists outstandingly qualified for the task. Moreover, the authors of the individual essays include some of the most experienced and accomplished contributors to the field. The qualifications of these authors alone are enough to ensure the merits of the book and the wide attention it deserves.

The subjects dealt with cover a considerable range. They encompass particular teaching devices: cooperative learning, market experiments, the Internet, Monte Carlo techniques, and use of case methods, sports and literature as a framework for course design. In addition, the book deals with broader topics, such as the teaching of economics to the two sexes, and the teaching of quantitative economics. In spanning this range the volume will provide two types of assistance to the teacher of economics to undergraduates. First, it will offer novel approaches that can enliven the process and increase the effectiveness with which knowledge and analytic skills can be imparted to the students. Second, it can stimulate the thought of the instructors themselves about the logic that should guide their teaching process.

I have often suggested to my colleagues that investigation of the means that make for effective communication is as much a respectable and difficult intellectual endeavor as is research on the substance of the materials the teaching is intended to impart. Yet many of the academic economists I have known have devoted themselves almost exclusively to research and their own absorption of the results of the research carried out by others, giving little consideration to the best ways to transmit these materials to their students. The conventional chalk and talk procedures some of them have employed with so little consideration constitutes neglect of the opportunity to contribute most effectively to the educational process.

This book may well help to stimulate some reform in this arena. Certainly it can help to make such reform more effective and easier to carry out. It is a substantial contribution to the teaching of economics as well as to the pertinent research.

# PREFACE

This volume covers a range of innovative teaching techniques and examples aimed at engaging students in the learning processes. Selection of material was based on a review of the past ten years of the *Journal of Economic Education* and other scholarly sources to find approaches and topics that have the greatest potential for adoption by other instructors. We asked authors to provide detailed, "hands-on" demonstrations to make it clear to other economics instructors how their approaches can be used in different courses and classroom situations at the undergraduate level.

The chapters in this book are thus intended to be something of a teaching cookbook or guide for economics teachers. Our opening chapter presents a brief history of economic education in higher education and reviews current practices in undergraduate teaching of economics. The remaining 11 chapters demonstrate alternatives to the lecture and chalkboard approach that dominates the teaching of economics. These chapters are grouped into three sections: "Active and Cooperative Learning," "Writing, the Internet, and Discovery Through Sampling" and "Examples from the World Around Us." Each of these chapters includes a list of Do's and Don'ts to guide instructors through the successful implementation of activities.

## ACTIVE AND COOPERATIVE LEARNING

Robin Bartlett provides a careful literature review and rationale for "Making Cooperative Learning Work in Economics Classes." She also provides numerous examples of activities that have been used in a variety of undergraduate classes, and several innovative ways to deal with the potential problems of this approach, such as free riding by some members on student teams.

Maureen Lage and Michael Treglia discuss "Gender and Active Learning." They review earlier studies that have tried to explain why women are under-represented in the economics profession and course enrollments, and gender-related differences in student performance in undergraduate economics courses. They then examine how active learning approaches can be used to eliminate these "gender gaps," and provide several activities and general strategies that can be used to help accomplish that goal.

Charles Noussair and James Walker discuss one of the most popular recent developments in economics: the use of experiments in research and teaching. In their chapter on "Student Decision Making as Active Learning: Experimental Economics in the Classroom," Noussair and Walker stress the instructional benefits that arise from classroom experiences in which students become active participants and decision makers in the learning process. They point out that experiments can be used to let students experience a variety of economic phenomena, including incentives, equilibria, and market failures. Experiments allow instructors to demonstrate the effects associated with changes in a single variable, holding all else constant.

## WRITING, THE INTERNET, AND DISCOVERY THROUGH SAMPLING

W. Lee Hansen's chapter on "Integrating the Practice of Writing into Economics Instruction" discusses how to use several different kinds of writing assignments in individual courses, and systematically across different courses in the economics curriculum. Hansen argues that by doing this, students will develop proficiencies in finding and using sources of economic data and analysis, as well as better expository skills. Those skills are expected to be of value both to individual students and their future employers, and in that way, these assignments demonstrate the usefulness of economics coursework to students.

Kim Sosin reviews "Using the Internet and Computer Technology to Teach Economics." She examines recent developments and directions in this rapidly evolving area, and discusses at length classroom uses of the Internet. She provides two specific web projects, designed for instructors with different levels of experience and comfort in using this kind of instructional technology. She also provides a listing of useful Internet sites.

Peter Kennedy argues for a specific course reform and teaching approach in his chapter on "Using Monte Carlo Studies for Teaching Econometrics." He begins the course with a careful discussion and handouts through which students discover the concept of a sampling distribution. He then uses Monte Carlo studies to characterize sampling distributions, and throughout the course gives students assignments in which they explain how to conduct Monte Carlo studies designed to investigate several important econometric issues.

## EXAMPLES FROM THE WORLD AROUND US

Undergraduate student exposure to sports is pervasive. Local TV news and newspapers devote from one-sixth to one-third of their time and space to sports. In their chapter, "Using Sports to Teach Economics," John Siegfried and Allen

R. Sanderson share numerous examples from sports to illustrate both common sense and counterintuitive analyses and propositions from economics. They provide examples from both men's and women's sports to use with different topics covered in undergraduate economics courses.

Michael Watts' chapter on "Using Literature and Drama in Undergraduate Economics Courses" provides an extensive list of literary passages dealing with economic concepts and themes, and sample discussion questions to use with those passages. He suggests that inserting one passage early in the course can increase discussion and student participation throughout the course. A few formal assignments featuring these readings in most undergraduate courses adds variety to traditional presentations, and engages many students who are less comfortable discussing more technical material on these topics.

William Zahka's chapter discusses how to use "Acceptance Speeches by the Nobel Laureates in Economics" as classroom assignments in different undergraduate courses. He points out several features of these speeches that make them especially well suited for classroom use, and then classifies the speeches by content and level of rigor, to make it easier for instructors to find the most appropriate speeches for their own classes.

Rendigs Fels and Stephen Buckles began promoting the use of the case method to teach introductory economics courses more than 20 years ago, and published one of the first case-based textbooks in economics. Here, in his chapter on "Using Cases as an Effective Active Learning Technique," Buckles provides an updated rationale for using the case method in economics, and several examples of using cases in undergraduate courses.

William Becker's chapter extends the Fels and Buckles case approach to the teaching of statistics and econometrics courses offered by an economics department. In "Engaging Students in Quantitative Analysis with the Academic and Popular Press" he provides examples of this approach as featured in his textbooks. He also shows how data and examples from these sources complement student assignments in computer labs and on written problem sets.

## ACKNOWLEDGMENTS

The quality of this book was raised markedly through the editorial assistance of Suzanne Becker, who also serves as the assistant editor of the *Journal of Economic Education*. She is both skilled with the English language and familiar with the economic education literature. The authors of the chapters in this volume benefited from this expertise.

Julie Marker assisted in the preparation of this manuscript, as she does with each issue of the *Journal of Economic Education*. We gratefully acknowledge Julie's patience, precision, and promptness in the production of camera-ready copy. Julie has made us all look better in print.

Final art work was prepared by Graphic Services at Indiana University under the direction of Susie Hull, to whom we are also grateful.

Finally, financial support for the development of this book was provided by the Calvin K. Kazanjian Foundation and the National Council on Economic Education. Our home institutions of Indiana University and Purdue University also provided support. The University of South Australia provided support while Becker was visiting during the months of June through August in 1997 and 1998. We gratefully acknowledge that assistance, without which this volume would not have been possible.

William E. Becker
Michael Watts

# LIST OF CONTRIBUTORS

Robin L. Bartlett, Professor of Economics, Denison University; Editorial Advisory Board, *Journal of Economic Education*; and Chair, American Economic Association Committee on the Status of Women

William J. Baumol, Director, C.V. Starr Center for Applied Economics, New York University; and Professor Emeritus, Princeton University

William E. Becker, Professor of Economics, Indiana University; Adjunct Professor, School of International Business, University of South Australia; and Editor, *Journal of Economic Education*

Stephen Buckles, Professor of Economics, Vanderbilt University

W. Lee Hansen, Professor Emeritus, Department of Economics, University of Wisconsin – Madison

Peter Kennedy, Professor of Economics, Simon Fraser University; and Associate Editor, *Journal of Economic Education*

Maureen J. Lage, Associate Professor of Economics and Women's Studies Affiliate, Miami University of Ohio

Charles Noussair, Associate Professor of Economics, Krannert School of Management, Purdue University

Allen R. Sanderson, Senior Lecturer in Economics, The University of Chicago; and Senior Research Scientist, National Opinion Research Center (NORC)

John J. Siegfried, Professor of Economics, Vanderbilt University; Adjunct Professor of Economics, University of Adelaide; and Secretary, American Economic Association

Kim Sosin, Professor of Economics and Co-Director of Center for Economic Education, University of Nebraska at Omaha

Michael Treglia, Global Health Economist, Eli Lilly and Co.

James Walker, Professor of Economics and Associate Director, Workshop in Political Theory and Policy Analysis, Indiana University

Michael Watts, Professor of Economics and Director, Center for Economic Education, Purdue University; and Associate Editor, *Journal of Economic Education*

William J. Zahka, Professor of Economics, Widener University

# CHAPTER 1

# TEACHING ECONOMICS:
# WHAT WAS, IS, AND COULD BE

**William E. Becker**

**Michael Watts**

There are some 2,875 post-secondary educational institutions in the United States, approximately half of which (1,470) are two-year institutions offering the associate degree. Of the remaining 1,405 institutions, 640 offer the bachelor's degree, 530 offer the bachelor's and master's, and 235 offer doctorate degrees (Becker 1997, 1349). With this institutional diversity – and the sheer numbers of courses, instructors, and students – one might expect great differences in the way undergraduate students are taught. But at least in the case of economics that is not the case.

Instead, over the past decade some authors of best selling books condemning general instructional practices in American colleges and universities saw fit to single out undergraduate economics instruction as an example of what is wrong with U.S. universities (e.g., Anderson 1992). That special condemnation may be overdone, but it is not groundless. Cashin (1990) reports on a national data base showing that economics is consistently one of the lowest ranked disciplines on undergraduate student ratings of both courses and instructors.[1]

In the 1980s there was a worldwide movement to improve post-secondary instruction through the use of teaching methods designed to have students actively and cooperatively involved in the learning process. In the United States, the Harvard Assessment Seminars represented the most prestigious effort in that direction (Light 1990, 1992). Yet academic economists generally did not participate in that work. Only two of the 100 scholars involved in the Harvard Assessment Seminars taught economics, and both of them taught in Harvard's Kennedy School of Government, not in the Department of Economics. Only one had a Ph.D. in economics (Becker 1997, 1351). Results from our national survey (Becker and Watts 1996) show most academic economists have not kept pace with the changing instructional methods in higher education.

That is particularly unfortunate because the American Economic Association, and other professional associations of economists that have followed the AEA's lead, have a long history of interest in and support for effective teaching of economics. Before viewing current teaching practices, it is worthwhile to consider briefly this part of the history of economic education in the United States.

## I. ATTENTION GIVEN TO TEACHING BY ACADEMIC ECONOMISTS

In 1891 the first president of the American Economic Association (AEA), Francis Walker, expressed his personal satisfaction with popular interest in economics, noting "it is a great thing to have the whole nation at school in political economy." At that time, Walker felt that dissatisfaction with material conditions and debates over many public policy issues were "making every man and every woman an economist," although he hastened to add that "The economists who are thus being made are ... just now pretty poor ones" (p. 20). Nearly 80 years later, the future Nobel laureate George Stigler said much the same thing:

> (T)hat the public does concern itself most frequently with economic questions ...is a true and persuasive reason for its possessing economic literacy. ...The public has chosen to speak and vote on economic problems, so the only question is how intelligently it speaks and votes. (1970, p. 7)

Stigler was certainly not sanguine about the public's level of economic literacy, which raises the question: Why was more not accomplished between 1891 and 1970? There were, in fact, sporadic attempts to improve the teaching of economics during the eight decades between these comments. While Walker was serving as president, the AEA established a standing Committee on the Teaching of Political Economy, which issued reports on "commercial" education for 15 years. In 1915, the AEA established a Committee on Secondary Education in Economics, and through the 1920s resumed a series of roundtable discussions on teaching general economics, in addition to the continuing committee work on secondary and collegiate teaching. But by 1950, when Lawrence Leamer published "A Brief History of Economics in General Education" it was shown that economists who were working and occasionally writing in this area almost always failed to find out what had been written by previous authors, resulting in frequent repetition and little real progress. Leamer called for the development of a cumulative body of literature on teaching economics, but that plea was largely unheeded for two decades. In 1967 Keith Lumsden wrote, "(T)he bulk of the evidence we have tells us that we, as scientists, are not being very scientific about our teaching, especially at the elementary level; we are not applying our professional standards to ourselves as teachers." (p. v)

In 1969 *The Journal of Economic Education* (*JEE*) was first published, initially by the National Council on Economic Education (NCEE – then known as the Joint Council on Economic Education) in cooperation with the AEA's current standing Committee on Economic Education, which was established in 1956.[2] Ten years later, enough studies had been published in the *JEE*, the annual *Papers and Proceedings* volume of the *American Economic Review*, several edited volumes, and a handful of other outlets, to warrant a review article on "Research on Teaching College Economics: A Survey" in the *Journal of Economic Literature* (*JEL*) (Siegfried and Fels 1979). The standards for research on teaching economics and the volume of such research increased dramatically from 1969 to 1979, and that pattern has continued since then, based on several standard measures. For example, a number of other *JEL* review articles in economic education have been published (most recently Becker 1997), and the *JEE* has dramatically improved its position in the ranking of journals based on out-of-journal citation counts (Laband and Piette 1994).

In 1982, the *JEE* broadened its mission to include an instruction section featuring articles dealing with innovative teaching methods, and a section providing overviews of new content developments in the various subfields of the discipline, in addition to theoretical and empirical articles evaluating the effectiveness of different teaching methods and materials. Other economic journals (including the *American Economic Review*, the *Journal of Political Economy*, the *Review of Economics and Statistics*, *Economic Inquiry*, and the *Southern Economic Journal*) have periodically published economic education research and instruction articles as well, although that seems to be largely a function of particular editors' interests, often ending when those editors complete their terms at the various journals. As a result, only the *JEE* and the annual *AEA Papers and Proceedings* issues have a long, sustained history of publishing research and instructional articles on economic education.

In 1995, we published a review article dealing with innovative instructional approaches in undergraduate economics (Becker and Watts 1995). We were impressed with the wide variety of methods developed by economists from many different kinds of schools for use in many different courses. But in a subsequent study (1996), we surveyed a national sample of economists teaching undergraduate courses. Our results were clear and striking – very few economists have taken the time or trouble to teach using any method other than traditional lectures presented at the front of the room, or any technology other than the chalkboard.

In short, by training and inclination, the vast majority of academic economists fall into the instructional habit of "chalk and talk" as graduate students or as young assistant professors, and they are very rarely willing or able to break that habit.[3] That pattern may reflect an efficient equilibrium for economists, given pressures to conduct research or other claims on their time, and the start-up costs of learning how to use new teaching methods or assignments. But relative declines in the numbers of students majoring in economics during the late 1980s and early 1990s, findings about students' dissatisfaction with economics courses and instructors compared to other subject areas, and the simple question of whether most economics instructors really have a comparative advantage in lecturing instead of using other teaching methods, all suggest that the equilibrium may be one established by convenience, custom, and inertia rather than efficiency or, especially, by what represents effective teaching practices in today's undergraduate curriculum.

There is recent evidence that in other subject areas class discussion and other forms of active learning – not extensive lecturing – are the most prominent forms of instruction in U.S. higher education (Sax et al. 1996, 13). Are economists and economics really different enough to make the prevalence of classroom lectures in economics a reasonable outcome, particularly because students don't seem to endorse what economics teachers are doing, compared to their ratings of other courses and teachers?

## II. CURRENT PRACTICES IN TEACHING ECONOMICS

That there is little variation in teaching practices employed in undergraduate economics courses can be seen in the results of our 1996 national survey, with responses from 628 instructors (Table 1.1). Note that across all of the different types of courses (introductory, intermediate theory, statistics and econometrics, and other upper division), and at all of the different Carnegie classifications of schools, the median response for the amount of class time spent lecturing was the response that represented 83 percent, except in upper division elective courses at doctoral schools, where the median response was 50 percent. The median response for class time use of the chalkboard was always 83 percent.

## Table 1.1: Teaching Methods, Examples, and Assignments

| | Median (and Mean) Responses by University Type | | | | |
| | Research | Doctorate Granting | Masters | Liberal Arts | Associate Institutions |
|---|---|---|---|---|---|
| **Introductory** | | | | | |
| Lecture time | 83(78) % | 83(68) % | 83(73) % | 83(72) % | 83(73) % |
| Guest Lectures | 0(3) % | 0(3) % | 0(3) % | 0(2) % | 0(3) % |
| Class Time Use of | | | | | |
|   Chalkboard[a] | 83(60) % | 83(65) % | 83(68) % | 83(57) % | 83(65) % |
|   Overhead[b] | 6(28) % | 0(17) % | 6(25) % | 6(17) % | 22(30) % |
|   Computer labs | 0(3) % | 0(5) % | 0(6) % | 0(4) % | 0(4) % |
|   Coop learning | 0(8) % | 6(15) % | 6(16) % | 0(11) % | 6(19) % |
| Classroom Experiments | 0(5.6) % | 0(4.1) % | 0(4.9) % | 0(4.3) % | 0(10.1) % |
| Games & Simulations | | | | | |
|   Computer | 0(1.2) % | 0(2.7) % | 0(2.6) % | 0(0.8) % | 0(2.9) % |
|   Other | 0(1.9) % | 0(3.3) % | 0(3.7) % | 0(3.2) % | 0(7.6) % |
| Examples from | | | | | |
|   Literature | 0(9) % | 6(8) % | 6(11) % | 6(5) % | 6(15) % |
|   Sports | 6(11) % | 6(11) % | 6(11) % | 6(11) % | 6(21) % |
| Assigned Materials | | | | | |
|   Textbooks | 83(78) % | 83(75) % | 83(77) % | 83(74) % | 83(73) % |
|   Workbooks | 6(36) % | 6(31) % | 22(35) % | 22(32) % | 22(37) % |
|   Class notes[c] | 6(30) % | 6(33) % | 6(30) % | 6(26) % | 22(37) % |
|   Problem sets[c] | 50(48) % | 22(37) % | 22(38) % | 22(34) % | 22(29) % |
|   Popular press | 22(25) % | 22(33) % | 6(28) % | 22(24) % | 22(30) % |
|   Academic pubs. | 0(3) % | 0(3) % | 0(5) % | 0(3) % | 0(4) % |
| Class Size | 100(162) | 30(31) | 40(45) | 45(67) | 30(30) |
| Number[d] | 100 | 96 | 120 | 77 | 60 |
| | | | | | |
| **Theory** | | | | | |
| Lecture Time | 83(74) % | 83(66) % | 83(73) % | 83(74) % | 83(83) % |
| Guest Lecturers | 0(2) % | 0(3) % | 0(2) % | 0(2) % | 6(6) % |
| Class Time Use of | | | | | |
|   Chalkboard[a] | 83(71) % | 83(65) % | 83(71) % | 83(69) % | 83(83) % |
|   Overhead[b] | 6(16) % | 0(15) % | 6(16) % | 0(7) % | 6(6) % |
|   Computer labs | 0(4) % | 0(12) % | 0(6) % | 0(4) % | 0(0) % |
|   Coop learning | 0(10) % | 6(20) % | 6(13) % | 0(9) % | 22(22) % |
| Classroom Experiments | 0(3.8) % | 0(2.9) % | 0(4.1) % | 0(5.1) % | 5.5(5.5) % |
| Games & Simulations | | | | | |
|   Computer | 0(0.6) % | 0(5.0) % | 0(3.2) % | 0(0.4) % | 5.5(5.5) % |
|   Other | 0(1.1) % | 0(3.7) % | 0(2.3) % | 0(2.2) % | 5.5(5.5) % |
| Examples From | | | | | |
|   Literature | 0(7) % | 0(6) % | 6(11) % | 6(4) % | 6(6) % |
|   Sports | 6(8) % | 6(8) % | 6(8) % | 6(9) % | 22(22) % |
| Assigned Materials | | | | | |
|   Textbooks | 83(76) % | 83(77) % | 83(74) % | 83(77) % | 22(22) % |
|   Workbooks | 6(25) % | 6(27) % | 6(22) % | 6(24) % | 0(0) % |
|   Class notes[c] | 14(31) % | 6(32) % | 6(24) % | 6(22) % | 83(83) % |
|   Problem sets[c] | 50(52) % | 22(37) % | 22(39) % | 22(39) % | 6(6) % |
|   Popular press | 6(25) % | 22(33) % | 6(24) % | 6(18) % | 50(50) % |
|   Academic pubs. | 6(12) % | 6(16) % | 6(12) % | 0(10) % | 6(6) % |
| Class Size | 40(50) | 20(20) | 25(24) | 30(30) | 5(5) |
| Number[d] | 103 | 70 | 98 | 59 | 2 |

## Table 1.1: Teaching Methods, Examples, and Assignments (cont'd)

| | Median (and Mean) Responses by University Type | | | | |
|---|---|---|---|---|---|
| | Research | Doctorate Granting | Masters | Liberal Arts | Associate Institutions |
| **Statistics/Econometrics** | | | | | |
| Lecture Time | 83(79) % | 83(73) % | 83(71) % | 83(67) % | 83(83) % |
| Guest Lectures | 0(0) % | 0(2) % | 0(1) % | 0(0) % | 0(2) % |
| Class Time Use of | | | | | |
| Chalkboard[a] | 83(66) % | 83(70) % | 83(69) % | 83(64) % | 83(83) % |
| Overhead[b] | 6(23) % | 0(10) % | 6(20) % | 0(7) % | 0(2) % |
| Computer lab | 22(34) % | 22(29) % | 22(34) % | 22(30) % | 6(11) % |
| Coop learning | 0(15) % | 6(23) % | 6(22) % | 0(10) % | 22(35) % |
| Classroom Experiments | 0(2.5) % | 0(5.1) % | 0(5.8) % | 0(3.7) % | 5.5(20.2) % |
| Games & Simulations | | | | | |
| Computer | 0(4.3) % | 0(0.6) % | 0(7.2) % | 0(6.1) % | 0(7.3) % |
| Other | 0(0) % | 0(1.2) % | 0(1.9) % | 0(1.1) % | 0(0.0) % |
| Examples From | | | | | |
| Literature | 0(2) % | 0(3) % | 0(7) % | 0(5) % | 6(4) % |
| Sports | 6(7) % | 6(10) % | 6(9) % | 6(9) % | 6(11) % |
| Assigned Materials | | | | | |
| Textbooks | 83(80) % | 83(75) % | 83(75) % | 83(69) % | 83(83) % |
| Workbooks | 0(16) % | 0(18) % | 0(15) % | 0(22) % | 50(44) % |
| Class Notes[c] | 6(31) % | 6(33) % | 22(34) % | 22(33) % | 83(83) % |
| Problem sets[c] | 83(64) % | 50(46) % | 50(51) % | 50(50) % | 6(18) % |
| Popular press | 0(9) % | 0(11) % | 0(10) % | 0(9) % | 0(7) % |
| Academic pubs. | 0(19) % | 0(9) % | 0(7) % | 3(14) % | 0(0) % |
| Class Size | 30(37) | 19(20) | 25(25) | 22(23) | 25(22) |
| Number[d] | 52 | 35 | 61 | 37 | 4 |
| | | | | | |
| **Upper Division** | | | | | |
| Lecture Time | 83(74) % | 50(61) % | 83(68) % | 83(68) % | 83(83) % |
| Guest Lectures | 0(4) % | 6(6) % | 6(6) % | 6(5) % | 3(3) % |
| Class Time Use of | | | | | |
| Chalkboard[a] | 83(68) % | 83(62) % | 83(62) % | 83(65) % | 83(83) % |
| Overhead[b] | 6(19) % | 0(10) % | 6(17) % | 0(11) % | 3(3) % |
| Computer labs | 0(7) % | 0(8) % | 0(8) % | 0(7) % | 0(0) % |
| Coop learning | 0(11) % | 6(20) % | 6(18) % | 6(19) % | 25(25) % |
| Classroom Experiments | 0(3.9) % | 0(3.8) % | 0(4.8) % | 0(3.5) % | 2.8(2.8) % |
| Games & Simulations | | | | | |
| Computer | 0(2.4) % | 0(4.7) % | 0(4.9) % | 0(1.8) % | 2.8(2.8) % |
| Other | 0(1.9) % | 0(3.5) % | 0(4.0) % | 0(2.9) % | 2.8(2.8) % |
| Examples From | | | | | |
| Literature | 0(7) % | 6(6) % | 6(9) % | 6(7) % | 28(28) % |
| Sports | 6(7) % | 6(8) % | 6(8) % | 6(8) % | 36(36) % |
| Assigned Materials | | | | | |
| Textbooks | 83(68) % | 83(70) % | 83(72) % | 83(70) % | 53(53) % |
| Workbooks | 0(16) % | 0(10) % | 0(20) % | 0(11) % | 42(42) % |
| Class notes[c] | 6(31) % | 6(30) % | 6(26) % | 6(23) % | 42(42) % |
| Problem sets[c] | 50(43) % | 6(28) % | 22(33) % | 22(33) % | 3(3) % |
| Popular press | 22(28) % | 22(34) % | 22(29) % | 6(26) % | 53(53) % |
| Academic pubs. | 22(41) % | 22(33) % | 6(25) % | 22(31) % | 3(3) % |
| Class Size | 30(35) | 15(18) | 20(20) | 20(26) | 15(14) |
| Number[d] | 159 | 87 | 108 | 85 | 4 |

a. Written during class only  b. Prepared acetates only
c. Instructor prepared  d. Number providing class size information

What isn't happening in the classroom is cooperative learning (except for associate schools where four instructors claimed to be teaching elective upper division courses, the highest median response is 6 percent of class time), computer labs (in statistics and econometrics courses the highest median response is only 22 percent, in all other courses the median response at all types of school is zero), classroom experiments or games and simulations (the median response is always zero, except at associate schools in categories with very few instructors, as noted above, where the median response still rises only as high as 5.5 percent), examples from literature (the highest median response is 6 percent) or sports (where the highest median response is also 6 percent, except for the associate schools where only two instructors report teaching intermediate theory courses).[4]    Even the lecture-supporting, low-technology overhead projector is rarely used beyond the introductory courses.  Because the amount of lecture time doesn't drop off in the other types of classes, this presumably reflects smaller class sizes on the one hand, but less positively it probably also indicates that publishers aren't providing as many or as well-prepared transparency masters for instructors to use in these classes.  It certainly does not provide evidence that instructors are putting much effort into preparing their own transparencies to use in class, or even that they are reproducing visuals and data exhibits from other sources, at least in this format.

Considering the instructional materials that teachers assign at these different types of schools and in the different types of courses, the data are again remarkable more for the homogeneity in the responses, rather than their variance.  The median response for assigning a textbook is again 83 percent in all cases except at the upper-division theory and elective courses at associate schools, where the sample size is extremely small.  Workbooks are assigned by a median of 22 percent of instructors in introductory courses at all but the research and doctoral schools, but beyond that workbooks are rarely assigned.  Other kinds of reading and homework assignments (including class notes, problem sets, and readings from the popular or financial press, or from academic journals), are not widely assigned except for problem sets in introductory and econometrics and statistics courses.  Term papers and other formal writing assignments are assigned in less than a fourth of the upper-division field courses, and much less often than that in all other types of courses.

Admittedly, there is only limited evidence that the nonlecture methods are more effective in raising student test scores or grades, and then perhaps mainly for certain groups of students (e.g., see Light 1990 and 1992; Johnson, Johnson, and Smith 1991; and Robin Bartlett's chapter in this volume).  But in most of the articles we reviewed on innovative and active-learning approaches, there was at least anecdotal evidence, and in many cases there were data from student course and instructor evaluations, indicating that students preferred these approaches.  Furthermore, in some cases – perhaps most notably in the "writing across the curriculum" papers described in Lee Hansen's chapter in this volume – students are also developing other important skills that will help them function more effectively in the labor market or graduate school, even though those skills are not always measured by exam scores, and often not even in course grades.

Student preferences certainly aren't the only measure of instructional effectiveness and value, but they do count for something, *ceteris paribus*, and together with student grades[5] it seems plausible that they are related to future enrollments in upper-division economics courses. With respect to effective teaching methods, in 1979, in the first review article on economic education research published in the *Journal of Economic Literature,* Siegfried and Fels concluded that "Different students learn economics in different ways. The best teaching strategy provides alternative learning methods" (p. 953). We reinforced that conclusion in 1995, saying that "Great orators should lecture. The rest of us should consider using a variety of teaching methods to actively engage our students and reduce the amount of time we spend lecturing to audiences that are often captive in the short run, but all too willing and able to vote with their feet in the long run..." (p. 699).

Using alternative teaching approaches clearly isn't the norm in undergraduate economics classes today, but the chapters in this volume make it clear that it could happen, and does in exceptional cases.

## NOTES

1. That demonstrates that economics is a relatively unpopular course in the undergraduate curriculum, but it does not demonstrate that economics instructors are less effective in improving student understanding or on numerous other instructional margins. Why economics courses receive relatively low student rating is open to debate. Becker (1997) argues that sample selection problems have been relatively ignored in studies aimed at trying to asses the relationship between students evaluations of instruction and such things as class size, instructor gender, and grades. Grades are often relatively low in economics courses, compared to other subjects (Sabot and Wakeman-Linn 1991).

2. There is still a direct advisory link between the AEA Committee and the *JEE*, and the *JEE* continues to receive financial support from the NCEE, although it is now published by Heldref Publications, a division of the Helen Dwight Reid Educational Foundation.

3. Other surveys on the teaching of undergraduate economics were published by Siegfried et al. (1996) and by Benzing and Christ (1997). With Cynthia Lay Harter of Duquesne University, we have investigated the determinants of why the few economics instructors in our national survey used teaching methods other than traditional lectures, and different kinds of class assignments (1998). We found that class size, instructor gender, the percent of work time devoted to teaching, and the Carnegie school

classification were significant explanators in some, but not all, of these instructional choices. Still, the general picture to note is one of little experimentation and even less variance in the actual use of available instructional methods and materials.

4. Space constraints do not allow us to report complete findings, but to the list of things not being used at any substantial level we can also add: computer-generated displays, VCR tapes/films, 35mm slides, audio cassettes, team teaching, guest lecturers, laboratory assignments, studies of the lives or work of eminent economists, and database searches.

5. On the relationship between course grades and course completion and enrollments in subsequent economics courses, see Sabot and Wakeman-Linn (1991); Anderson, Benjamin, and Fuss (1994); Dynan and Rouse (1997); and Horvath, Beaudin, and Wright (1992).

## REFERENCES

Anderson, G., D. Benjamin, and M. Fuss. 1994. The determinants of success in university introductory economics courses. *Journal of Economic Education* 25 (Spring): 99-119.

Anderson, M. 1992. *Impostors in the temple: The decline of the American university*. New York: Simon & Schuster.

Becker, W. E. 1997. Teaching economics to undergraduates. *Journal of Economic Literature* 35 (September): 1347-73.

_____ and M. Watts. 1995. Teaching methods in undergraduate economics. *Economic Inquiry* 33 (October): 692-700.

_____ and _____. 1996. Chalk and talk: A national survey on teaching undergraduate economics. *American Economic Review* 86 (May): 448-53.

Benzing, C. and P. Christ. 1997. A survey of teaching methods among economics faculty. *Journal of Economic Education* 28 (Spring): 182-88.

Cashin, W. 1990. Students do rate different academic fields differently. In M. Theall and J. Franklin, eds. *Student ratings of instruction: Issues for improving practice*. New Directions for Teaching and Learning, no. 43 (Fall) San Francisco: Jossey-Bass,: 113-21.

Dynan, K. and C. Rouse. 1997. The underrepresentation of women in economics. *Journal of Economic Education* 28 (Fall): 350-68.

Harter, C. L., W. E. Becker, and M. Watts. 1998. Who teaches with more than chalk and talk? Working paper.

Horvath, J., B. Q. Beaudin, and S. P. Wright. 1992. Persisting in the introductory economics course: An exploration of gender differences. *Journal of Economic Education* 23 (Spring): 101-08.

Johnson, D. W., R. T. Johnson, and K. A. Smith. 1991. *Cooperative learning: Increasing college faculty instructional productivity*. ASHE-ERIC Higher Education Report No. 4. Washington, DC: School of Education and Human Development, George Washington University.

Laband, D. N. and M. J. Piette 1994. The relative impacts of economics journals: 1970- 1990. *Journal of Economic Literature* 32 (June): 640-66.

Leamer, L. E. 1950. A brief history of economics in general education. *American Economic Review* 40 (December): 18-33.

Light, R. J. 1990. *The Harvard assessment seminars*. Cambridge, MA: Harvard University School of Education and Kennedy School of Government, First Report.

_____. 1992. *The Harvard assessment seminars*. Cambridge, MA: Harvard University Graduate School of Education and Kennedy School of Government, Second Report.

Lumsden, K. G., ed. 1967. *New developments in the teaching of economics*. Englewood Cliffs, New Jersey: Prentice-Hall.

Sabot, R. and J. Wakeman-Linn. 1991. Grade inflation and course choice. *Journal of Economic Perspectives* 5 (Winter): 159-70.

Sax, L. J. et al., 1996. *The American college teacher: National norms for the 1995-96 HERI faculty survey*. Los Angeles: Higher Education Research Institute, UCLA.

Siegfried, J. J. and R. Fels. 1979. Research on teaching college economics: A survey. *Journal of Economic Literature* 17 (September): 923-69.

_____ et al. 1996. How is introductory economics taught in America. *Economic Inquiry* 34 (January): 182-92.

Stigler, G. J. 1970. The case, if any, for economic education. *Journal of Economic Education* 1 (Spring): 77-84.

Walker, F. A. 1891. The tide of economic thought. *American Economic Association Publications* (First Series).

CHAPTER **2**

# MAKING COOPERATIVE LEARNING WORK IN ECONOMICS CLASSES

**Robin L. Bartlett**

To be able to effectively use cooperative learning groups in economics classes, it is important to understand where they are located along the whole continuum of available teaching techniques, and to know the distinctive features of cooperative learning groups, as opposed to groups in general. At one end of the learning environment continuum are individual learning environments. Typically, in this environment, students come to class, take notes, and talk to no one. The professor may, or may not, know students by their names. Classes may be large (several hundred students) or small (25 or fewer students). There are very few interactions among students and between the students and the instructor. Nonetheless, in this environment, some students learn. Students may learn passively by listening to an instructor give a lecture, or students may learn actively by interacting with the instructor or material through the use of discussion questions, reaction papers, or individual presentations (Bonwell and Eison 1991; Meyers and Jones 1993). The defining characteristics of individual learning environments are that students are solely responsible for their own learning and the instructor and text are the sole authorities (Bruffee 1993). Most economics classes can be characterized as individual learning environments as documented by Becker and Watts (1995, 1996).

Although many economics instructors assign students to work in groups for class presentations, papers, or other projects, groups are not necessarily cooperative learning groups, and do not always operate as effectively and efficiently as most economics instructors would like. At this midpoint of the learning environment continuum, students may gather for study or work sessions and find that one student has done all the preparation and ends up teaching the material to other, less-prepared students. In that case, the one student who is teaching is actively engaged in learning, but the other students who are listening and taking in the material are still learning passively.

## I. THE PLACE OF COOPERATIVE LEARNING

Putting students in unstructured groups without goals, procedures, and assigned roles to accomplish an educational task is like putting five students on a basketball court and telling them to score as many points as possible. Without assigned roles and a game plan, a group of students is just a group of students. Some groups may figure out how to organize and produce results on their own. More often than not, however, unstructured groups are disasters waiting to happen. To avoid such disasters, as with athletic teams, everyone needs to know his role and how to interact with everyone else on the team. With adequate coaching on individual skills and a game plan, a team achieves more than what any one individual achieves alone. Many a team sweatshirt has sported the letters TEAM on the back with the words: "Together Everyone Achieves More" written under them.

Cooperative learning groups (Bennett, Rolheiser-Bennett, and Stevahn 1991; Bruffee 1993; Cooper, Robinson, and McKinney 1994; Johnson and Johnson 1989; Kagan 1994; Sharan 1990; and Slavin 1990) are structured groups. Usually, they are composed of two to six students. Instructors may assign students to groups after taking into account a student's individual capabilities and talents. For example, an instructor may decide to put a very good student in a group with average students. Putting students together who have had some economics with students who have not may make sense also. Or, she may decide to randomly assign students to a group. Well-defined educational tasks and student roles are assigned to facilitate the group's work. Typically, students find times to meet outside of class by organizing evening study sessions or early morning discussion breakfasts. The instructor also develops evaluation schemes and monitors group activities.

The essential element of a cooperative learning group experience is that students are responsible for their own learning as well as that of other members of their group. Each student has a role to play, and the instructor provides the game plan or sequence of activities for the groups to do. Although the students learn from each other, the instructor and the text are still predominantly the authorities in the class. Keenan and Maier (1994) developed several cooperative learning exercises for Introductory Economics and favorably assessed them.

Cooperative learning in teams as employed by Bartlett (1995) is a variation of individual learning groups that takes into account the fact that some students prefer to learn alone and others prefer to learn in a group. In my courses, students work alone or as a member of a team. Teams voluntarily form any time and remain together for the duration of the course. Teams perform all of the assignments and even take all tests as a unit. Any interaction with the instructor is as a team. The only safety value, or out for students who are unhappy with their team, is the final. A team member may take the final individually if he so chooses. Students who chose to learn alone earn a grade based upon their own performance on various assignments. Students who chose to be on a team receive a grade based upon the performance of one of their teammates on the same assignments. The teammate who performs any given assignment is randomly selected, to reduce free riding problems. The task could be taking a quiz, answering a problem set question, or taking an exam for the team. Although the educational task for the teams is still defined by the instructor and the responsibility of various roles is discussed, the roles that individual students play are negotiated with other team members. The team game plan, how the team is going to go about accomplishing its goal, is also defined by the students themselves.

At the other end of learning environment continuum are learning communities (Gabelnick, MacGregor, Matthews, and Smith 1990; Wells, Chang, and Maher 1990). A learning community in economics classrooms is established in one of two ways. First, in an individual classroom, the instructor and students become co-learners in the tradition of Paulo Freire (1983). Instructors and students are both (although not necessarily equally) responsible for student learning. Instructors come with an expertise in economics, but the knowledge of economic events that students bring to the class is equally valued and validated. The authority of the instructor and text is shared with the economic experiences of the students themselves. In essence, the cooperative learning group expands to include the instructor.

Second, the classroom is extended beyond the individual classroom to include more faculty, students, courses, and even the surrounding community. Within an institution, several courses and their faculty may be combined. Students may be assigned to small cooperative groups of two to six students with similar interests. For example, students register for two courses concurrently. The advantage of linking two courses is the simultaneous development of theoretical course content and technical skills. At Denison

University, the Economics Department has a lecture/laboratory curriculum where students register concurrently for a traditional economic theory or field course and a laboratory course. The former course focuses on theoretical concepts and the latter course focuses on developing computational and computer skills (Bartlett and King 1990). Courses may also revolve around a common theme. A group of students enrolls in several courses and participates in an additional seminar intended to assimilate the material. Or, as at the Evergreen State College, four faculty and students cover a whole year's worth of course work as a unit. Service-learning is a classic example of going beyond the institution into the community. McGoldrick (1998) has her students write a 15-page paper. The focus of the paper is either a topic not covered in class or the experiences gained from working 15 hours in the community on a related task.

The defining elements of learning communities are that the boundaries inside and outside the individual classroom are removed. Students either include the instructor in their group, or the walls of the individual classroom are expanded and mutual learning takes place. In the first case, the authority is shared and in the second case, expanding the boundaries of the classroom may, or may not, result in shared authority between students and instructors. Given the reconfigurations, the authority of instructor, student, and community around the institution is shared.

## II. COOPERATIVE LEARNING IN DETAIL

Over the past two decades, Johnson and Johnson (1989), along with collaborators (Johnson, Johnson, and Holubec 1993; Johnson, Johnson, and Smith 1991b), pioneered the concept of cooperative learning. The purpose of a cooperative group is to ensure that every individual within the group develops his academic and social skills to the maximum. The research reviewed by Johnson, Johnson, and Smith (1991b), Sharan (1990), and Slavin (1990) on the effects of cooperative learning environments suggests that this is indeed the case. Cooperative learning environments have been shown to be better learning environments than individual ones. Students learn more and learn more effectively. Students become more involved in the subject matter and tend to have lower attrition rates. Other researchers (Anderson and Adam 1992; Bartlett 1996; Baxter Magolda 1992; Belenky et al. 1986; Cooper, Robinson, and McKinney 1994; Ginorio 1995; Kleinsmith 1993; Maher and Tetreault 1994; Moses 1991; Sandler, Silverberg, and Hall 1996; Tobias 1990 and Treisman 1992) also suggest that cooperative learning groups are more conducive for learning by women and students of color. Finally, there is some evidence to suggest that cooperative learning techniques help mitigate stereotypes (Miller and Harrington 1990; Slavin 1990, Chapter 4).

## Types of Cooperative Learning Groups

Three basic types of cooperative learning groups exist: formal, informal, and base. Members of **formal** cooperative learning groups are selected by the professor and exist for as long as is necessary to perform a specific assignment – for example, to write a research paper or to prepare a class presentation. If an instructor assigns a group of students to investigate the administration's fiscal policy or a local school board's financial options for a new school building, they work together until they complete that task.

**Informal** groups are short-term and are used to clarify or reinforce points made in a lecture or following a classroom exercise. Informal cooperative learning groups may be formed when an instructor stops after 10 minutes of lecturing on the determinants of demand and allows students to check their notes with other students sitting around them, or when an instructor asks students to respond to her question by first thinking about it, writing down a response, and then sharing it with a neighboring student. Informal groups may or may not be formed by the students themselves. Selected students may be those sitting in reasonable proximity or may be identified by numbering off.

**Base** groups are formed for the duration of the course and students work on all class assignments as a group whether they are problem sets, exams, or presentations. Students not only find academic support in these groups, but also social support. At some institutions, base groups can also be formed for all courses for the duration of a student's college career. Base groups are formed by the instructor, by the students themselves, or by the educational institution.

## Student Roles

Within a cooperative learning group, each student plays one or more roles. Assigned roles help to keep the group on task. One student serves as the **recorder**, writing down the group's discussion and editing the group's response. At a later date, that same student may serve as the **checker**, making sure that everyone in the group understands the nuances of the discussion and the group's answer. One way for a student to check on everyone's understanding is to ask a student to give his understanding of the group's answer or to repeat what he heard a previous student say. Another student is the **encourager**, helping to motivate and supporting individual participation efforts. The encourager draws everyone into the conversation and makes sure that each student contributes. Another member serves as the **elaborator**, making connections between the different members' comments. The elaborator may also try to make connections between the current discussion and course lectures. The **clarifier** corrects mistakes in other students' remarks and the **summarizer** restates the major findings or conclusions of the group. The group also designates a **runner**. The runner is the go-between with other groups or with the instructor. Finally, the group needs an **observer**, a student who observes the group process and provides feedback and suggestions at the end of each work session. Some of these eight possible roles are easily combined – e.g., runner and summarizer.

## The Elements of Cooperative Learning

Cooperative learning has five elements: positive interdependence, face-to-face interactions, individual accountability, social skills, and group processing. To ensure that cooperative learning works as planned, each of the five elements must be present. *Positive interdependence* exists when each student's success is dependent on the success of other students in her group. Positive interdependence is facilitated by having a common goal, shared resources, shared rewards, and complementary roles. A student works with the other members of her group to solve problems, research an issue, or study for a test. An instructor develops and distributes different materials to different students, forcing students to share and cooperate. Individual talents and abilities are developed. The success of one student depends on the success of all.

*Face-to-face interaction* occurs when a student actively promotes the learning of another student by providing encouragement, concern, and more importantly, feedback. For students to have face-to-face interactions with each other, time for interactions needs to be set aside in class or arranged outside of class. Depending upon the type of academic institution within which an economics instructor works, finding times for group meetings may be more or less problematic. Students in economics courses taught in large urban research-oriented universities may have more difficulty finding times to meet outside of class than at smaller residential colleges. As a result, the instructor may have to set aside class time or even to set aside an entire class for students to have meetings. Setting aside lecture time for cooperative groups, however, does not necessarily mean that less material is covered. Students still cover the same amount of material, but the mix of in-class and out-of-class time usage changes.

The third element of cooperative learning is *individual accountability*. Various evaluation and grading schemes are used to ensure that each student takes the group's task and their role in the accomplishment of that task seriously. The activities of informal groups are rarely evaluated or graded. A student in a formal group, however, might receive the grade she deserves on a test and additional bonus points if the other members of her group reach a minimum performance level. An instructor could average all the group member's grades or give the group the grade of one randomly selected student. Group grades could be totaled. The permutations on these themes are endless. The point is that a student receives feedback on the performance of other individuals in the group as well as her own. Peer pressure is brought to bear on those who are not willing to pull their weight in the group or who are not doing their best.

Cooperative learning is also intended to develop a student's *social skills*. Assigning roles helps students interact in a programmed way and alerts them to the importance of process and group dynamics. Ice-breaking exercises are used to help students initially get to know each other, to discover each others' talents, and to develop a level of trust. In smaller classes, instructors can take a few minutes out of their first class for students to interview another student in the group and then introduce him to the rest of the group or class. Introductions by other students take the spotlight off individual students who for some reason may feel awkward about introducing themselves. Introductions bring all students into the class conversation. In larger introductory economics classes, instructors can ask each student to get out a piece of paper and to write down all the things she can remember about a penny. After five minutes, ask students to pair up with another student and compare notes and continue the process. After a few more minutes, have them join up with another pair and try to construct a list with 19 attributes of a penny. After five more minutes, have them take out a penny, examine it, and compare their list with the penny. Ask which group got 19 (Scearce 1992). This exercise allows students to meet all the students sitting around them and establish some familiarity and comfort with them.

Developing *group processing skills* is the final element. To see how a group works together give them a puzzle or problem to solve. For example, put introductory students into a group of six and ask them to examine Figure 2.1 and then work with the other members of their group to determine the number of triangles in the figure. In order to get the better students to teach the less prepared students, every member of the group has to be able to explain the group's answer to the entire class. When a group feels that everyone understands the answer sufficiently to explain it to the whole class, the group raises its collective hand. The instructor has the group count off from one to six and then rolls a die. The selected student comes to the front of the class and begins to explain. At this point the rest of the class can comment on the accuracy of the student's presentation. If at any time the student falters, he returns to his group and works some more. This exercise illustrates to students how important it is to pay attention and listen to peers.

For students to learn to feel safe in their groups and to trust others, a discussion about basic civility and giving space to talk and be heard with the entire class is helpful before such exercises. To develop group skills and facilitate the group's efforts, the group observer should go over the group's work at the end of each session and highlight things that each member did well and ask each member of the group for suggestions that would help with the group's work.

### Figure 2.1: Counting Triangles

This is a team effort. Everyone on your team must be able to count the number of triangles in the picture below. As soon as your team feels confident that every member of your team can explain to the group how many triangles there are and how to count them, have the whole team raise their hands and be prepared to have one member of the team randomly selected to explain your answer to the class.

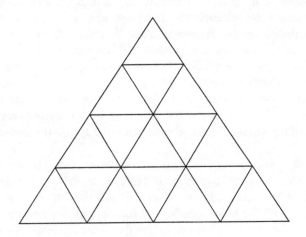

## III. COOPERATIVE LEARNING DESIGNS AND EXAMPLES

Over the past ten years college instructors have begun incorporating cooperative learning into their courses (Johnson, Johnson, and Smith 1991a), particularly in the humanities (Bruffee 1993) and into economics (Keenan and Maier 1994). Instructors in the sciences use group learning, particularly in labs, to a much greater extent than do instructors in the social sciences. The way students interact with each other within a cooperative learning group varies by design. There are several basic designs for cooperative learning activities and several variations on each activity depending upon the goals and creativity of the instructor. The following are examples of cooperative learning exercises that have been developed and used in introductory and advanced undergraduate economics courses by the author.

## Think-Pair-and-Share

These exercises are used to develop and reinforce students' understanding of recently discussed material. After an instructor discusses the differences between a change in demand and a change in the quantity demanded, he asks his students to demonstrate the effect of a growing interest in mountain bikes on the price and quantity of in-line skates in the market. Each student is asked to first develop her own answer to the question and then to share it with another student. After the first student shares her answer, the second student gives his explanation. They both then develop a composite or agreed upon answer to the question. Think-Pair-and-Square cooperative learning groups go a step farther by having the first pair of students present its answer to a second pair of students. Both pairs then work on the answer. The answer can be recorded and submitted for evaluation or verbally shared with the larger group in a debriefing session.

*Example One — Lecturing 10 Minutes at a Time.* This is an informal cooperative learning technique that can be used in large or small economics courses. This technique is useful when basic skills or content material need to be understood before students can move on to the next idea. This exercise is appropriate when introducing students to definitions of markets, aggregate income accounting, various financial instruments, or other economic terms or ideas with which they are not familiar.

**Needed:**   One 60 minute timer with a loud bell

**Process:**   Set the timer for 10 minutes and begin lecturing as usual. When the bell of the timer rings, ask students to turn to another classmate and compare their notes for one or two minutes. Have them look for points that need clarification. Instruct them to work with their classmate to help formulate any questions they may have. After two minutes, entertain questions. Once all of the questions have been answered, set the timer for another 10 minutes and proceed. It is very important not to continue lecturing when the timer goes off and not to answer questions immediately when students raise their hands. They can tell you what their question is but do not answer it until all the students have a chance to look over their notes and compose any questions they may have. Otherwise, students will stop looking at their notes and listen to your answers. This is a particularly good technique for first and second year students in introductory economics courses. A natural content break may seem more logical, but it may take more than 10 minutes to get a concept across and by then some of the students are lost.

The advantages of this technique are straightforward. The instructor has immediate feedback on where students are with the material just presented. It saves time in the long-run. If students do not understand a critical concept at the beginning of the class, the remainder of the class will not be wasted by building on a concept that is either not understood, or worse yet, misunderstood. In addition, students who are not great note takers can catch up by filling in missing pieces. Good notes will help students study for tests later.

*Example Two — Working with a Concept.* Students in economics courses are often presented with concepts that need to be applied to be learned. At the introductory level, the effect of changes in the various determinants of the demand for oranges or some other commodity or service will not register in their minds until they have a chance to work with the concept by applying it to an example. To give students this opportunity, the instructor may ask her students to think about what happens to the demand for oranges when the *New England Journal of Medicine* publishes a study that finds eating an orange a day can add ten years to a person's life expectancy. Each student takes a minute to think about the answer and then she turns to the student next to her and explains it. In turn, that student explains his answer to her. The instructor can then solicit answers from the various groups. In advanced courses, the instructor may let the pairs form foursomes and so on until the students feel they have adequately addressed the question.

The advantages of this exercise are similar to those in example one. Allowing students to regularly interact helps students to feel connected. For students who feel different in economics classes, for example, because of their color, religious heritage, or age, making connections with other students is particularly difficult and this is one way to build interactions. Much of the work on improving the performance of women and students of color in the classroom underscores the significance of making such connections.

## Jigsaw

This exercise requires more preparation on the part of the instructor. Each group is given part of the information necessary to understand or analyze an economic issue or problem. One group may have one or two pieces of economic data. Another group has different pieces of information. The individual groups work on understanding the information that they have and then meet with another group to teach them about their information and to learn the information the second group possesses. The different pieces of the puzzle are compiled and put together until everyone has the requisite information to do the analysis.

The jigsaw is a good cooperative learning exercise for more advanced level economics courses. This technique can be used in lower level courses, but given the amount of time and energy that goes into gathering the information and creating questions, the more background students have in economics the better.

*Example One — Macro.* An example of this would be an assignment where students are to determine the effect that a change in the political make-up of Congress or the White House will have (or had) on aggregate economic activity, particularly on gross domestic product (GDP) and prices.

**Needed:** Aggregate economic data

A watch or clock

**Process:** Divide the class into four groups. Have students collect aggregate economic information from the *Wall Street Journal* for several economic series. The first group will follow personal income, consumer credit, retail sales, and consumer confidence to monitor the consumer sector of the economy. The second group follows construction spending, housing starts, and inventories to evaluate activity in the investment sector. The third group collects information on the trade gap, key exchange rates, and the federal budget deficit to observe spending in these sectors. The last follows GDP, prices, and unemployment. First, have each group meet and examine any movements in the data they are watching. Then have the consumer and investment groups pair off to brief each other on their respective information bases. Similarly, for the third and fourth groups. After these two groups have shared their information, have students from groups one and three share their information and similarly with two and four. Then pair groups one and four and two and three. Once all of the groups have shared their information, the individual groups caucus and put all the information together and use the economic theory that they have learned over the term to analyze all the economic data they have collected. Each group then presents their analysis. After all the presentations the other groups have an opportunity to critique the analysis of each group. The instructor can evaluate each group's work. A variation on this activity would be to let all four groups try to come up with a consensus. For this exercise to work efficiently it is helpful to assign students roles in their groups.

*Example Two — International.* This jigsaw cooperative learning technique is used in an International Economics class at Grinnell College. The class had Introductory Economics as its prerequisite.

**Needed:** Appropriate international data

A watch or clock

**Process:** Class is divided into five groups based upon the sections of the room in which they were sitting. Each group is given the same information from a recent issue of the *International Statistics Yearbook.* The five groups of about six to eight students are given different questions: 1) Based upon the concept of purchasing power parity did the Canadian dollar become overvalued between 1988 and 1989? 2) What were real interest rates in the United States and Canada in 1988 and 1989? 3) Based on nominal interest rate parity, how would you predict the 1989 value of the Canadian dollar? 4) What do 1988 and 1989 national income account figures suggest is the Canadian marginal propensity to import? 5) How do Canadian balance of payments figures reflect capital flow incentives? The groups are given 15 minutes to work through their assigned question and then a spokesperson for each group reports on its findings. When the five pieces of information are written on the blackboard by the instructor, the students are asked if economic theory can explain the changes in data that occurred. If so, how so? If not, why not?

## Consensus Building

This technique is particularly good for classroom discussions of an economic issue. Students are put into groups to answer questions or to react to readings. Once the group comes to a consensus answer, the recorder writes down the group's response and waits for her opportunity to present it to the larger class. After hearing the individual group reports, the class engages in an informed discussion and converges upon a class consensus answer.

This technique is most productively used in advanced courses or senior seminars where students need to decide what the relevant theory is and how to apply it and what the relevant facts are and how to select them. Traditional case studies can be used and modified to become cooperative learning exercises. The first activity below is an actual case that a class had the opportunity to analyze. It provides a way to start and sustain good discussions.

*Example One – A Divorce Case*. This case analysis resulted when a group of attorneys approached the instructor to work on a plaintiff's divorce case. The instructor was teaching an advanced level economics course on Women in the Labor Force and was halfway through the semester when the opportunity arrived. Not having the time to do the case herself, she volunteered her students. The students were excited to have a real opportunity to put their computer and economic skills to work. Their task was to determine the economic impact of divorce, with any identifying names and references omitted, on the resulting reconstituted families and to offer a remedy.

**Needed:**   Background material on the plaintiff

W2 forms for several years
copies of tax returns for several years
the current household's assets and debts
the current household's monthly expenses
copies of checking, savings, and other financial accounts

**Process**:   The class was divided into four teams and given the above background information on the case. The lawyers asked the students to go beyond the normal settlement as instructed by Ohio law (where a household's assets and liabilities are divided in half and the absent parent pays $35/child/week in child support) to determine the impact of the divorce on the plaintiff – a woman with four children between the ages of one and 10 – and to suggest a remedy.

To do this, each team was to calculate the intact family's standard of living relative to the poverty level and those of the two reconstituted families after the divorce. Each team was to decide on what numbers to use and how to present the case. First, students needed to determine the appropriate income, or incomes, for the intact household, what inflation rate to use to project future income streams, and how far into the future their projections should go.

Second, students had to find data on poverty levels and determine the appropriate one for each of the families. Then students calculated the ratios of the family's income to the appropriate poverty level to determine how well-off each family was – before and after the divorce. These calculations allowed them to determine who was made better or worse off by the divorce and how much money needed to be transferred from one family to the other. The groups calculated a settlement – how much money was to be transferred from one reconstituted family to another and for how long. The end result was to have each family equally bearing the impact of the divorce. Neither family would be made better or worse off than the other. The groups worked for a week during class time. The first period during the second week, they reported their calculations and argued them before the class. The brief of the class was used as evidence in the court hearings that took place the next month.

To determine the input of various students into the process, the following evaluation form was handed out after the completion of the case (Figure 2.2).

## Figure 2.2: Sample Group Evaluation Form

Group Evaluation Form

1. Please list below the names of each member of your group (putting your own name first):

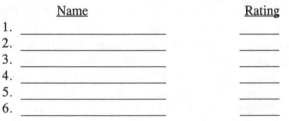

2. Next to your name, rate your contribution to the team's effort on a scale of 1 to 4 (where 1 = I did very little to 4 = I did a great deal of work on the case).
3. Now, next to each member of your team's name, rate their contribution to the team's effort on a scale of 1 to 4 (where 1 = did very little to 4 = did a great deal of the work on the case).
4. Did any member of the team make an outstanding contribution to the group's effort? (Yes / No) Describe his/her contribution.

Students took grading themselves and each other very seriously. Several wrote more about the team's work than anticipated. Their evaluations were the sole source of information for grading this assignment. Responses on student evaluations at the end of the term suggested that students worked harder because a family (in particular, a woman and her four children) was depending on them.

*Example Two — Additional Reading.* Another cooperative learning technique is to assign extra reading such as government reports, histories, or even novels in a course and have in-depth discussions of the material and have students come to consensus about what the major issues or points were in the reading. For example, expecting students in a Women in the Labor Force class to discuss the history of Asian American women in the United States would fall flat without proper preparation.

**Needed:**   Reading material other than the textbook
One 60 minute timer with a loud bell

**Process:**   Assign students 40-50 pages to read before class. When the period starts ask them to get in their discussion groups to answer several questions for the first 20 minutes of the class. For example, students may be asked to compare the social, economic, and religious institutions that Japanese women left in Japan at the turn of the century and those that they found in the United States when they migrated. The recorder writes down the group's response. After 20 minutes, the summarizer is asked to report briefly on the group's major findings. Summarizers from other groups are asked to make any additions or corrections to the first group's list. The process continues with a different group being the first to report on the next question. Once all of the questions are answered, a discussion ensues until a consensus is reached. At the end of the class, the question and answer sheets are picked up and given to the secretary for typing and duplication.

At the beginning of the next discussion class, the typed question and answer sheets from the previous discussion are distributed with the group's name and its members printed at the top of the handout for identification. These sheets are distributed along with the evaluation sheet for students to grade the contribution of other students. In this particular class exercise, student evaluations are the determining factor for grades on class participation.

## Cooperative Writing

This is the fourth basic cooperative learning activity. It takes a variety of forms, from pairing up to prepare a critique of the work of another student, or a group paper. In one format, a student reads another student's paper and writes comments and suggestions for improvement using a feedback form provided by the instructor. The student who wrote the paper then revises and submits the paper to the instructor for evaluation. Attached to the final paper is a copy of the original paper and the other student's feedback form. Students are graded for their work on their own paper and for their work on another student's paper.

An instructor can assign a short two-page paper in any economics class to let students explore an application of a basic concept. For example, a principles instructor can have students read the *Wall Street Journal* or *The Economist* and find an article that illustrates a particular microeconomic principle such as the impact of human rights policies on the manufacturing of sneakers or a macroeconomic concept such as the pros and cons of using gross domestic product versus gross national product as a measure of a nation's output. Students can write a response or their own analysis of the author's presentation. Before handing it in to the instructor another student reads the student's work for clarity, quality of the analysis, and presentation. The student incorporates the feedback of the reviewer and then hands in the original paper, the revised paper, and the other student's comments and suggestions. Writing allows students who are more verbally oriented an opportunity to show their understanding of economics in their preferred way and for students more graphically comfortable to develop written skills. Much has been written on the impact of writing on cognitive development.

Groups can also write papers on the concepts and issues brought up in any economics course. For example, a group could take the same material on the impact of human rights policies on the production of sneakers and write a paper. In order for a group to write this paper, the group should first outline the paper and then divide up the work. In the outline of the paper, the students may want to identify whether this is a demand or supply problem, how human rights policies intervene in the market, what is the impact of this intervention in the market, and what are some alternative solutions to the problem of not using slave or prison labor to manufacture sneakers. The group then divides up the sections and assigns one section to each member. The group begins with each student writing for 10-15 minutes on his own section. They should write nonstop. After 10-15 minutes, each student's section is passed on to the student sitting to his right and that student reads it and makes comments, corrections, and suggestions. After another 10-15 minutes, the papers are passed to the right again. The process is repeated until every student has read the section of every other student in the group. With this process, each student gets feedback on his own work and also obtains an understanding of the work of his fellow students. One student can be designated to type up a final draft of the group paper and hand it in the next day.

Individual instructors can modify these activities depending upon the desired educational outcome, the number of students in a class, and the amount of time that can be devoted to the effort. The key point is that the role of the instructor is no longer one of covering the material but one of specifying the educational task, explaining its significance to the students, deciding upon group structure, monitoring group activity, and evaluating group efforts.

*Example One — An Economic Report.* In economics courses, students have opportunities to write solid, analytical pieces. Instead, economics students tend to be more adept at shifting curves on a graph or solving a system of equations. However, using team writing in a course is another way to determine how well students understand the economics behind the problem versus how well they have mastered the mathematical techniques. This activity can be used when students are asked to do a two or three page analysis of a *Wall Street Journal* article on the impact of the tobacco settlements on the stock prices of the major producers or an analysis of the macroeconomics economic news.

**Needed:**  Wall clock and 60 minute timer
            A pad of paper for each student
            Different colored pens

**Process:**  Each student comes to the class with his data gathered, sources read, and/or ideas crystallized. Divide students into teams of four to eight members depending upon how many major paragraphs there will be in the paper. Set the timer for 15 minutes and ask the groups to outline their analysis and divide up the paragraphs to be written among themselves. When the timer rings, ask each member of the group to begin writing his paragraph of the paper. Set the timer for another 10 minutes. When the bell rings, have each student pass his paragraph to the student on his right. Instruct each student to carefully read over the other student's work and make corrections, connections, and suggestions. Set the timer for another 5 minutes. When the bell rings, instruct each student to pass the paragraph he was reading to the student on his right and proceed by setting the timer again. Have students continue passing paragraphs to the right and setting the timer until every member of the team has had a chance to read and write a critique every other student's paragraph.

If there are six students on a team, it should take 45 minutes to write and prepare critiques of six paragraphs. Now each student takes the paragraph she originally wrote and rewrites it incorporating the suggestions of the other students and with the knowledge of what is in each of the other paragraphs. The timer is set for the last 5 minutes. By the end of 50 minutes, each student will have made a significant contribution to the start of a short paper and a cooperative writing experience has occurred. The six paragraphs can be handed in for comments. Ninety minute classes will allow for larger groups and/or longer papers. Instructors may get groups to start writing their papers in this fashion and finish them outside of class, or devote two sessions to the activity.

Groups are graded on the quality of the final product. Cooperative written papers are often better than individually written papers. There are several other advantages of this technique. First, students are required to write during the whole class whether they are in the mood or not. The exercise shows them that the hardest part of writing papers is getting started. Under these conditions they get a substantial start and feedback within a relatively short period of time. Students also learn that even if the time is not just right for writing and maybe they are not fully ready, that something can still be accomplished. Students leave the class with a better understanding of what they understand and what yet needs to be done. Using writing in an introductory economics course, where writing is least likely to be used, is also a way to attract the very capable students in the other social sciences and even the humanities to the field. Some students may shy away from economics not because they do not find it of interest, but because of the way the ideas are expressed. Finally, for those students who are adept at mathematics, developing their facilities with language will help them express the analysis.

## Permutations on a Theme

The number of variants on the four basic cooperative learning designs are unlimited. Below are two examples of cooperative learning groups that grew out of using teams in introductory economics and intermediate macroeconomic theory.

*Example One — Mini-Lectures.* This particular technique can be an informal or formal cooperative learning activity and is helpful in introductory or intermediate economics courses when application is necessary to facilitate reaching higher levels of economic understanding. Students may be at a point in the class where they are familiar with a basic economic concept, and now need to apply it in order to learn it.

**Needed:**   A 2'×4' easel pad for each team

Colored markers - a different color for each team

Masking tape or bulletin board pins

A die

One 60 minute timer with a loud bell

An assistant (student or otherwise) to type up group answers

**Process:**   On the first (and second) day of the week for a class that meets two (or three) days a week, lecture on a basic introductory or intermediate theory topic; such as the determinants of market structure. On the second (or third) day, divide the class into groups of six students for the duration of the course. Assign a role and a number from one to six to each student in each group. Give an easel pad and a different colored marker to each group. Groups should use the same color marker for the remainder of the course. Thus, there will be a red group, blue group, etc. Color consistency helps groups compare their answer to those of other groups and helps the assistant identify different groups' work.

Pass out a question or a set of questions to each group at the beginning of each mini-lecture class. Instruct the students that one member of each group will be randomly selected to lecture to the class, therefore everyone should practice the answer with the group before the time period is up. Now set the timer to give the groups 15-20 minutes to develop their lecture. The group's recorder writes down the group's basic ideas on the sheet of paper. When the

15-20 minutes are up, randomly select a student from each group to give a mini-lecture to the class. For example, roll the die, and if a two should turn up, all students with the number two will answer the questions. The randomly selected student proceeds to the front of the class with the sheet of paper torn from the easel pad. The student tapes the sheet of paper to the blackboard or pins it to a bulletin board. Using easel pad paper eliminates the time necessary to rewrite the answer on the board. The student takes five minutes to lecture to the class on the group's response to the question. Other group members are not allowed to help the randomly selected student during her or his presentation. After the student has completed the group's answer, one or two questions or requests for clarification may be entertained from other students.

To ensure that students put in the necessary effort, group responses are evaluated. One way to do this is to use a "check," "minus," or "plus" grading system. A "check" means that the randomly selected student did an adequate job lecturing on the answer. A "minus" means that the lecture was either confusing or incorrect. And a "plus" means that the student who presented the group's response had a good understanding of the material and presented it well. It is important that students understand that they are lecturing to the class and not just answering a question for the instructor. The number of "checks," "minus," and "pluses" earned over the course can be used for a class participation grade. Letter grades can also be assigned.

This technique keeps students on top of the material and maximizes what they get from traditional lectures. Students learn that it is easier to be prepared and attend a lecture than it is to read the material themselves. Moreover, because any one of them could be randomly selected to lecture on the group's discussion, each student pays close attention. When students are evaluated on how well they respond to the question and present the material, they are more likely to take each other seriously and work hard in their groups.

*Example Two — Team Problem Sets and/or Test Taking*. Instructors of economics often give problem sets as homework, preparation for a test, or for extra credit. The following exercise is easily incorporated into introductory or intermediate courses. This exercise is for instructors who want their students to work more traditional problem sets.

**Needed:**   A die, coin, a deck of cards, or other objects such as numbered ping pong balls in a fish bowl

**Process:**   Assign a problem set for students to work on outside of class. On problem set day, students come prepared to demonstrate to other students how to solve the assigned problems. Proceed as with mini-lectures, dividing the class into groups. For each problem, a student is randomly selected to go to the blackboard and demonstrate to the class how his group arrived at its answer. The "check," "plus" and "minus" grading system is easily employed once again to evaluate student answers. Students who average "checks" get a "B" for class participation, and so forth.

If an instructor is allowing students the option of taking the course alone or as a team, the group acts as a unit or team for the above problem set exercises and for test taking as well. The same random selection process is used to decide which team member will take the test for all of them. Students may have a preference, however, about when that selection process takes place. For example, if a student is randomly selected before the test and the other members of the team leave the room, she has more pressure than if each member of the team takes the test and the random selection process takes place afterwards. It is hard to tell which option students prefer, or which is more desirable, therefore it is best to let students decide whether it is better for them to assume all the pressure while taking the test, or to know how well they did and not be chosen.

## IV. ISSUES IN COOPERATIVE LEARNING ACTIVITIES

The first issue that comes to mind when talking about cooperative learning versus the traditional lecture mode is what are the tradeoffs? Instructors are afraid that less material is covered. However, the same amount of material can be covered using either technique, but how it is covered is very different. There are also some start-up costs for the instructor. Just as it took two to three years to feel comfortable developing and giving lectures, it will take two to three years for an economics instructor to develop the skills and familiarity with the various cooperative learning techniques used in the classroom. Therefore, an instructor should move gradually by adding one cooperative learning technique at a time. As the instructor's comfort and confidence with the technique grows, more techniques can be used simultaneously.

Then there is the question of how to put students in groups. The selection process depends upon what the instructor wants to achieve. For informal cooperative learning exercises, the characteristics of groups are probably not very important. However, for more formal learning exercises, the instructor may want to put a diverse group of students together. There is some evidence that same-sex groups do better than mixed-sex groups. Better prepared students will teach and learn more by doing so, and less well-prepared students will study more to do their share. Because the stakes are high for cooperative learning teams, students should be allowed to form their own groups. Several ice-breaking exercises can be done at the beginning of the term to facilitate getting to know each other.

In individual learning environments, students may be evaluated using objective tests or by more complicated educational tasks such as group presentations. In a cooperative learning environment, a student, however, is not only evaluated on how well she performs on tests and other assignments, but also on how well other members of her group perform. Grades are assigned using either absolute or relative grading schemes. With an absolute standard, a student's success does not depend on the success or failure of other students in the class. An economics instructor awards an A to any student who gets 90 percent of the questions on a test correct or successfully completes 90 percent of an assignment. With a relative standard, students compete against other students. Student performance is evaluated by economics instructors grading "on the curve." Whereas students still work independently, their success or failure depends on the relative success or failure of other students. Here, an economics instructor might award an A to only the top 5 percent of her class. Much of the cooperative learning literature argues for an absolute standard; yet, some would argue that there is very little difference between the two.

A fourth problem is how much weight the cooperative learning component has in determining the student's final grade. It is difficult to weigh the cooperative learning component heavily without knowing how much an individual contributed to the group's success. At the same time, not counting the cooperative component heavily in the grading process lessens a student's motivation and increases a student's willingness to free-ride.

Finally, course and instructor evaluation forms are geared toward the standard college lecture course. Students will find cooperative learning new, and they may be slow to appreciate it. Because students are accustomed to the standard lecture format of most economics classes, they may initially resist moving to a cooperative learning format. It is hoped they will find cooperative learning economics classes more engaging and eventually more instructive as students in other disciplines have. Despite the issues that have yet to be thought through to make cooperative learning work in economics classes, the more diverse student body of the 21st century demands that economics instructors begin the process. Students are voting with their feet for courses of study that are multidisciplinary and more cooperative. Economics instructors need to respond to that vote.

## V.    DO'S AND DON'TS

Although a list of specific Do's and Don'ts for each of the above examples could be compiled, it would be repetitive; the following is a composite list.

- Do be sure that instructions for assignments are clear and that students know exactly what they are to do. The instructions should include which student is going to do what, how long the group has to do the exercises, and what the group is expected to produce.
- Do make sure that students know why they are doing the task. Students are more motivated to work when they know why they are being asked to perform certain tasks.

- Do decide how groups will be formed before coming to class. It is less potentially awkward for students and their peers if the instructor asks them to pair off or number off rather than just get in groups.
- Do walk around the room during the exercises, and listen to student conversations. It is difficult to know what is going on in the groups if the instructor spends her time reading while students are working. The pieces of conversations the instructor picks up while walking around the room help to monitor students' progress and interactions.
- Do give students enough time to reflect on the material or perform the task. When instructors use cooperative learning techniques where students will have to speak in front of their peers, it is important that they have time to be prepared and comfortable with their preparation. Students who do not feel that they had enough time will feel nervous and dislike the whole experience.
- Do give comments or suggestions when needed to facilitate the group process. Sometimes a group will get stuck on a problem. A few words from the instructor may put them on the right track and avoid undo frustration.
- Do keep time allocations. In order to keep the process moving along it is important not only to allocate an appropriate amount of time for a task, but to keep to it. If the instructor starts letting students have an extra five minutes here and there, students may not work as hard.
- Do use colors to identify teams and build rapport. If the same group of students is always referred to as the red team other students begin to identify them as such and vice versa. Building team identity is important for building team cohesiveness. The more the students are committed to the teams success, the more success the team will have.
- Do encourage students to give constructive feedback and to make helpful suggestions to other students. Students can provide other students with very helpful comments and suggestions. It is easier for them to spot errors in someone else's work than it is in their own.
- Do make encouraging comments. Students respond positively to encouraging comments that suggest they can work through a task or that the instructor has confidence in their abilities to perform a task. Negative comments are discouraging to students.
- Don't feel you have to solve the problem for the group. Students can work through substantive and group dynamic issues. Cooperative learning exercises give students an opportunity to learn from others and develop social skills.
- Don't answer a question the minute you are asked. If you have asked the class to work on something, reserve questions until the end of the allotted time. If you answer questions immediately, students will listen to the other

student's question and your answer and will not reflect on the material for themselves or formulate their own questions.

- Don't be too quick to bail students out. If a group member gets stuck, randomly pick a student from another group and let that student give the answer a try.

## VI. CONCLUSION

Cooperative learning groups are a workable alternative or supplement to the traditional economics classroom. The chalk and talk method of conveying economics works well for some students, but there are some students who need more connection with other students and with the material to make the learning environment conducive for them. Cooperative learning activities are fun for students. There is excitement in the room and interaction – student to student and student to instructor. Moreover, students are connecting with the material in very tangible ways catering to students with a variety of learning styles. Reticent students are also more likely to have an opportunity to practice asking questions to a classmate before asking them before the whole class and facing possible ridicule. Students who find themselves at the margin are structured into the class making it easier for them to feel comfortable. A more exciting, stimulating, and comfortable classroom cannot help but facilitate the learning of economics.

## REFERENCES

Anderson, J. A., and M. Adams. 1992. Acknowledging the learning styles of diverse student populations: Implications for instructional design. In L. B. Border and N. Van Note Chism, eds. *Teaching for diversity* No. 49. San Francisco: Jossey-Bass Publishers: 19-33.

Bartlett, R. L. 1996. Discovering diversity in introductory economics. *Journal of Economic Perspectives* 10 (Spring): 141-53.

_____ . 1995. A flip of the coin – A roll of the die: An answer to the free-rider problem in economic education. *Journal of Economic Education* 26 (Spring): 131-9.

_____ and P. G. King. 1990. Teaching economics as a laboratory science. *Journal of Economic Education* 21 (Spring): 109-12.

Baxter Magolda, M. 1992. *Knowing and reasoning in college: Gender-related patterns in students' intellectual development*. San Francisco: Jossey-Bass Publishers.

Becker, W. E. 1997. Teaching economics to undergraduates. *Journal of Economic Literature* 35 (September): 1342-73.

_____ and M. Watts. 1995. A review of teaching methods in undergraduate economics. *Economic Inquiry* 33 (October): 692-700.

_____. 1996. Chalk and talk: A national survey on teaching undergraduate economics. *American Economic Review* 86 (May): 448-53.

Belenky, M. F., B. M. Clinchy, N. R. Goldberger, and J. M. Tarule. 1986. *Women's ways of knowing: The development of self, voice, and mind.* New York: Basic Books.

Bennett, B., C. Rolheiser-Bennett, and L. Stevahn. 1991. *Cooperative learning: Where heart meets mind.* Bothell, WA: Professional Development Associates; and Toronto, Ontario: Educational Connections. Distributed in the U.S. by Interaction Book Company, 7208 Cornelia Drive, Edina, MN 55435.

Bonwell, C. C., and J. A. Eison. 1991. *Active learning: Creating excitement in the classroom,* ASHE-ERIC Higher Education Report No. 1. Washington, DC.: The George Washington University, School of Education and Human Development.

Bruffee, K. A. 1993 *Collaborative learning: Higher education, interdependence, and the authority of knowledge.* Baltimore, MD: The Johns Hopkins University Press.

Cooper, J. L., P. Robinson, and M. McKinney. 1994. Cooperative learning in the classroom. In D. F. Halpern and Associates, eds. *Changing college classrooms.* San Francisco: Jossey-Bass Publishers.

Freire, P. 1983. *Education for critical consciousness.* New York: Continuum Press.

Gabelnick, F., J. MacGregor, R. S. Matthews, and B. L. Smith. 1990. Learning communities: Creating connections among students, faculty, and disciplines. In R. Young, ed. *New directions for teaching and learning.* San Francisco: Jossey-Bass Inc., Publishers: 19-37.

Ginorio, A. B. 1995. *Warming the climate for women in academic science.* Washington, DC: Project for the Status and Education of Women, Association of American Colleges.

Johnson, D. W. and R. T. Johnson. 1989. *Cooperation and competition: Theory and research.* Edina, MN: Interaction Book Company.

_____, _____ and E. J. Holubec. 1993. *Circles of learning: Cooperation in the classroom.* Edina, MN: Interaction Book Company.

_____, _____ and K. A. Smith. 1991a. *Active learning: Cooperation in the college classroom.* Edina, MN: Interaction Book Company.

_____, _____ and _____. 1991b. *Cooperative learning: Increasing college faculty instructional productivity.* ASHE-ERIC Higher Education Report No. 4. Washington, D.C.: George Washington University, School of Education and Human Development.

Kagan, S. 1994. *Cooperative learning.* San Juan Capistrano, CA: Kagan.

Keenan, D. and M. H. Maier. 1994. *Economics live!: Learning economics the collaborative way.* New York, NY: McGraw-Hill, Inc.

Kleinsmith, L. J. 1993. Racial bias in science education. In D. Schoem et al., eds. *Multicultural teaching in the university.* Westport, Connecticut: Praeger, 180-90.

Maher, F. A., and M. K. Thompson Tetreault. 1994. *The feminist classroom: An inside look at how professors are transforming higher education for a diverse society.* New York: Basic Books.

Maier, M. H. and D. Keenan. 1994. Cooperative learning in economics. *Economic Inquiry* 32 (April): 358-61.

McGoldrick, K.   1998.   Service-learning:   An application for economics students. *Journal of Economic Education* 29 (Fall): 365-76.

Meyers, C., and T. B. Jones.   1993.   *Promoting active learning:   Strategies for the classroom.*   San Francisco:   Jossey-Bass Publishers.

Miller, N., and H. J. Harrington.   1990.   A situational identity perspective on cultural diversity and teamwork in the classroom.   In S. Sharan, ed.   *Cooperative learning: Theory and research.*   New York, NY:   Praeger Publishers: 39-75.

Moses, Y. T.   1991.   *Black women in academe:   Issues and strategies.*   Washington, DC:   Project for the Status and Education of Women, Association of American Colleges.

Sandler, B. R., L. A. Silverberg, and R. M. Hall.   1996.   *The chilly classroom climate:   A guide to improve the education of women.*   Washington, DC.: Association of American Colleges.

Scearce, C.   1992.   *100 Ways to Build Teams.*   Palatine, Il.:   IRI/Skylight Training and Publishing.

Sharan, S.   1990.   *Cooperative learning:   Theory and research.*   New York, NY: Praeger Publishers.

Slavin, R. E.   1990.   *Cooperative learning: Theory, research, and practice.*   Needham Heights, MA:   Allyn and Bacon (A Division of Simon and Schuster, Inc.).

Tobias, S.   1990.   *They're not dumb, they're different:   Stalking the second tier.* Tucson, AZ:   Research Corporation.

Treisman, U.   1992.   Studying students studying calculus:   A look at the lives of minority mathematics students in college.   *The College Mathematics Journal* 23 (5):   362-72.

Wells, G., G. L. M. Chang, and A. Maher.   1990.   Creating classroom communities of literate thinkers.   In S. Sharan, ed.   *Cooperative learning:   Theory and research.* New York, NY:   Praeger Publishers:   95-121.

CHAPTER **3**

# GENDER AND
# ACTIVE LEARNING

### Maureen J. Lage

### Michael Treglia

In gaining knowledge and comprehension of a subject, individuals take information and make it a part of themselves. Learning is thus a very personal experience. However, recent research on education shows that learning occurs most successfully in social situations. Active engagement with other learners is a characteristic of educational experiences that are reported to be highly personally fulfilling (Light 1990). At the same time, other researchers have found there are gender-related distinctions in achievement in undergraduate economics courses. In particular, the performance of women in economics courses has been below that of males. Further, women have been, and remain, underrepresented in the field of economics (Ferber and Nelson 1993). Lumsden and Scott (1987), among others, have suggested the traditional organization of economics classes may impart a gender bias against women. In other words, the design of the classroom setting can be an important component in creating an environment that fosters both successful learning and women's persistence in economics.

One aspect of the classroom environment over which individual instructors have a great amount of control is the teaching method. However, recent surveys reveal the use of only a few techniques by the overwhelming majority of economics teachers. Becker and Watts (1996) report that the median amount of time spent lecturing in all undergraduate courses was 83 percent. They also report 83 percent as the median amount of time the chalkboard was used for presentation of graphs and text.[1]

In contrast to the similarity of teaching techniques used within academic economics, typical populations of undergraduate students are composed of individuals who are drawn from a distribution of learning styles. For instance, experiential learning theory posits two primary dimensions to the learning process that delineate types of learning abilities (Kolb 1981). The first dimension spans the concrete experiencing of events to their abstract conceptualization. The second dimension ranges from reflective observation of experiences to active experimentation with theories in problem solving. These two dimensions give rise to four types of learning styles that appear to be related to gender and ethnicity. Women and people of color tend to take in information through concrete experiences and process it through active experimentation. In contrast, Euro-American males and Asians show tendencies to take in information through abstract conceptualization and process it through observation and reflection (Bartlett 1996). The latter tendencies seem to be conducive to success in traditional economics classes. For instance, in a typology of academic fields, economics is included with subjects such as the natural sciences and mathematics that are characterized by the predominant use of learning abilities from the abstract-reflective category (Kolb 1981).

As a second example of diversity in learning styles, gender has been shown to be related to the Thinker (T) – Feeler (F) dimension of the Meyers Briggs Type Indicator (MBTI) that refers to decision-making. Sixty percent of males prefer an analytical mode of cognition (T-type) while sixty percent of females prefer a narrative mode (F-type).[2] This percentage breakdown may reveal different "dominant decision-making preferences between the genders that may aid understanding of the ways males and females learn and act." (Gabelnick and Pearson 1989, 123). However, while an individual may learn in a culture whose norm is different from the individual's temperament, learning is accomplished best in a culture that is congruent with the individual's preferences.

A typical lecture-based class offers a limited opportunity to effectively reach all students because they absorb and process information in a variety of ways. The emphasis in the lecture is on passive learning (Siegfried et al. 1991). Whereas note taking is the primary activity during these classes, there is little opportunity for active experimentation with the ideas and information presented. Furthermore, any discussion that occurs in the typical lecture-based class is usually of an adversarial nature where points are debated and defended (Belenky et al. 1986).

In addition to the manner in which the material is presented, it should be recognized that what material is covered also has important implications for successful learning. For instance, women may prefer 'connected knowing,' i.e., an orientation that emphasizes material that is related to peoples lives, working with others, and a joining of minds (Bartlett 1996). Indeed, Belenky, et al. (1986, 4) observed that "women often feel alienated in academic settings and experience 'formal' education as either peripheral or irrelevant to their central interest and development." Traditional introductory economics may be particularly weak in presenting material that is seen as being of relevance to the conduct of young women's lives. Despite the fact that "gender topics" may be particularly well suited for having students relate economic theory to their own lives, textbooks for introductory economics courses have traditionally ignored these issues (Feiner 1993).[3]

The above findings on: 1) the incongruity between a single teaching style that is used by a majority of economics teachers, but possession of diverse learning styles by students; and 2) a classroom environment that, through the use of traditional textbooks and choice of topics, may be adverse to the affective domain for half the student population are pieces of evidence that point in the direction of discouraging women from the study of economics. Statistics on the percentage of women as economics majors, economics degree holders, and professional economists, respectively, can be used to support the above argument. For instance, the National Center for Education Statistics (1995) reports that by 1992-93, women received approximately 30 percent of the B.A. degrees in economics, 30 percent of the M.A. degrees, and only 23 percent of the Ph.D. degrees. Although the share of women in graduate programs has remained fairly constant since the late 1980s, the share of undergraduate economics majors who are female has declined over the past ten years to approximately 30 percent (CSWEP 1996).

Can anything be done to stimulate interest in economics among underrepresented groups and improve on the above statistics? We describe ways to change the classroom environment to make it more hospitable to individuals with diverse learning styles. Specifically, we discuss the implementation of active learning techniques. At the outset, it should be noted that improving the classroom climate for a particular group of students does not necessarily imply the climate is becoming worse for other groups. Lage and Treglia (1996) show that, at least at one institution, changes in the classroom that are consistent with the recent scholarship on women can lead to improved performance for all students.

## I. ACTIVE LEARNING

Although the phrase 'active learning' has not been given a complete definition, Bonwell and Eison (1991) list the following characteristics that are often associated with this style of learning and pedagogy: 1) students are involved in more than simple listening; 2) less emphasis is placed on transmitting information and more on developing student's skills; 3) students are involved in higher-order thinking (e.g. analysis, synthesis, and evaluation); and 4) greater emphasis is placed on students' exploration of their own attitudes and values. The use of learning techniques that embody these characteristics enables a teacher to reach a variety of students with diverse means of absorbing and processing information (Kolb 1981; Bartlett 1995).

A large amount of educational research has recommended the use of active learning in the classroom (Chickering and Gamson 1987; Cross 1987; among others). More recently, researchers in the field of economic education have also discussed the benefits of such methodology. Siegfried et al. (1991, 209) state that the traditional method of lecturing limits students intellectual stimulation for the subject and that "effective learning *requires* active participation by students." (Emphasis added.) Becker and Watts (1995, 1996) argue that while great lecturers should continue to lecture, "The rest of us should consider using a variety of teaching methods to actively engage our students" (1995, 699).

There are a variety of ways to incorporate active learning into the classroom. Some methods include writing, case studies, discussion, cooperative learning, debates, and role-playing. In addition, McGoldrick (1998) has recently suggested that service learning is an effective method to actively engage students.[4] In the following sections, we provide examples of two distinct methods of active learning, cooperative learning and classroom discussion, while paying particular attention to the gender implications of these models.

## II. COOPERATIVE LEARNING

Cooperative learning is "the instructional use of small groups so that students work together to maximize their own and each other's learning." (Johnson et al. 1991, iii). A wide range of literature, including Losee et al. (1995) and Sandler et al. (1996), has illustrated that women perform better in a cooperative and collaborative environment.[5] As Madison (1995, 158) summarizes, "The literature is consistent; women are more comfortable working in collaborative environments than competitive environments, and they are more successful and more persistent when they are comfortable." Despite this evidence, cooperative learning is rarely used in principles and intermediate economics courses (Becker and Watts 1996).

Consider the topic of the comparative advantage of nations and gains from trade. In a traditional principles lecture course, the instructor might define comparative advantage, absolute advantage, and specialization, then construct a numerical example, calculate the per-unit opportunity costs and show how two nations could be made better off by specializing and then trading with each other. In contrast, we have typically used this topic as an excellent way to introduce cooperative learning into the classroom environment. The class is started with the instructor giving a lecture of *no more than ten minutes* during which the main point is to give to students the above three definitions. The students are then divided into small groups and given a worksheet (see Appendix 3.A) containing a carefully constructed problem of comparative advantage. The worksheet must be completed in class. Rather than watching an instructor go through the example, the students actively engage with the material and with the others in their group. As the students are completing the worksheet, the instructor is moving throughout the class, giving encouragement and responding to any questions that arise.[6]

After the groups have completed the assignment, a group is chosen at random and then an individual within the group is selected to present the group's answer. The answer includes an explanation as to *how* the group arrived at the conclusion. Before moving on to the next question, the instructor ensures that all groups agree with the answer provided. If a group gives an incorrect answer, typically another group will have come up with the correct answer and will volunteer. If, however, all groups have an incorrect answer, the instructor informs the class that the answer is incorrect and asks the groups to rework the question.

When implementing cooperative learning in the classroom it is important to remember that, in general, women may be less likely to participate than male students (Banks 1988). One method of facilitating equal participation is Bartlett's (1995) suggestion of rolling a die to choose a member of the group to present the group's answer. Because of this randomization, the group must ensure that *all* students in the group understand the answers and are prepared to present them to the class. Although Bartlett used this method as a means of eliminating free riding, it also ensures roughly equal participation across genders (if the groups themselves are gender balanced; see below). Alternatively, one could assign roles to students to ensure active participation by all.[7]

## III. DO'S AND DON'TS: FOR EXERCISES

This list of Do's and Don'ts will help in the construction of cooperative learning exercises.

- Do keep groups relatively small.
- Do anticipate and counteract the free-rider problem in groups.
- Do keep groups relatively gender-balanced. For example, if a group consisted of one woman and three men, the woman might find it difficult to have her opinion heard.
- Don't reinforce gender stereotypes. For example, if students are assigned roles to facilitate participation, assign the role of recorder to a male group member.
- Do encourage students to assist each other. For example, the random selection of a group member to discuss answers encourages group members to work together so that each is prepared to answer questions.
- Do prepare follow-up questions for groups that finish earlier than others.
- Do set up the classroom so students can easily work together. For example, having chairs that students can move into their groups is preferred.

- Don't have students look to the instructor for the "correct" answers. Under such circumstances, students may not listen to anyone but the instructor. If one group does not have the correct answer, have a different group present their answers and explanations.
- Do walk by groups as students are working on their assignments. During this time the instructor can answer questions and informally monitor groups.
- Do spend some class time prior to implementing cooperative learning on group dynamics.
- Do individually (and privately) talk to group members who are dominating their group about letting other students participate.

## IV. GENDER TOPICS FOR CLASSROOM DISCUSSION

In addition to paying careful attention to the method of instruction in the classroom, it is also important to consider what topics are covered in the economics curriculum. It has been documented that, at least at the principles level, traditional textbooks have largely ignored women as subjects of economic study (Feiner 1993). Further, Ferber and Nelson (1993) argue that women have been mostly absent as subjects in all fields of economics. Gender bias may even occur in the economist's definition of a research problem (see the *Guidelines for Recognizing and Avoiding Racist and Sexist Biases in Economics*, reprinted in Feiner 1993; and Blank 1993). The preceding facts do not bode well for stimulating interest in economics for female students when it is recognized that women tend to learn best when they can relate material to their own lives (Bartlett 1996; Baxter Magolda 1992). As mentioned above, these pieces of data may help explain the relatively low number of women in the economics profession.

One way to address the concerns outlined above is to supplement the traditional textbook with outside readings. Bergmann (1987, 393) argues eloquently for the role of "women's issues" in the teaching of economics: "Both female and male students will find them interesting and important. Students recognize that these issues have affected their parents' lives and will affect their own – their career prospects, their chances to enjoy affluence, and their everyday domestic arrangements." Some possible topics she suggests incorporating into the curriculum include the economics of marriage, women's wages, the increase in female labor-force participation, and the place of housewives in the economy. Additional topics for study are given in Feiner (1994), Lage and Treglia (1996) and Bartlett (1996).

Given the above, in our own classes we have typically chosen to incorporate outside readings on "gender issues" as discussion topics.[8] Although perhaps obvious, it is crucial that the subject of the discussion be interesting to both the instructor and the students. In addition, as Bonwell and Eison (1991, 23) state, "good reading selections must be complex enough to engender different points of view regarding the issues or problems presented. If they contain a little controversy, so much the better." We have found that Bergmann's suggestions for incorporating topics on the economics of gender clearly fits this bill.

It is, of course, imperative that students have read the material in order to have a successful discussion. If the reading assignment is relatively short, the instructor may consider allowing the students to read the assignment in class. The loss of class time is compensated by the improved classroom discussion that follows. For longer assignments the instructor may give a brief quiz prior to discussion to ensure that students come to class prepared. Alternatively, the instructor may require the students to turn in a brief (one paragraph) writing assignment explaining the material. Making this assignment the "price of admission" to the class may also help ensure students are prepared for discussion.[9]

Once the reading has been selected, the instructor should carefully construct a set of questions that will frame the discussion. This is, arguably, the most difficult part of any discussion. There are a variety of ways to organize discussion questions.[10] McTighe (1985) organizes questions in correspondence with Bloom et al.'s (1956) levels of cognitive learning. Within this framework, *knowledge questions* are the most basic. These simply ask students to recall facts from the reading. *Comprehensive questions* require students to organize facts while *application questions* ask students to use the facts. Further along Bloom's scale are *analysis questions* that require students to combine ideas in order to form a new prediction. Finally *evaluative questions* ask student to combine two or more items based upon defined criteria in order to render opinions, judgments, and/or decisions.

Again, consider the example of the comparative advantage of nations and the gains from trade. Students initially complete the group exercise (previously discussed) that had them work through a numerical example of how nations benefit from exchange with each other. Although this lesson gives students an understanding of the mechanics involved in applying the underlying concepts, students typically still have trouble relating this topic to their everyday lives. In contrast, many students have had some direct contact with a two adult household or have an expectation of being part of such a family in the future. An outside reading that supplements the traditional coverage of the above topic is Chapter Three in Blau and Ferber (1992), "The Family as an Economic Unit: The Division of Labor Between Husband and Wife." The chapter explains the concepts of comparative advantage, specialization and trade, as well as going over the advantages and disadvantages of this model when applied to a "traditional" marriage. Discussion questions (provided in Appendix 3.B) have students review the basic concepts. Students are then asked to change the assumptions of the model and make new predictions. Finally, the model is extended to the analogous situation of nations trading with each other. Working through the questions in this fashion, students are able to make a connection between an abstract economic concept and their own lives.

## V.  DO'S AND DON'TS: FOR CLASSROOM DISCUSSION

This list of Do's and Don'ts will help in leading successful discussions.

- Do provide guidelines for class discussion.  For example, students might be assigned Chapters 9 and 10 from McGill and Beaty (1993) which discuss the skills necessary for working effectively in group settings.
- Do write questions as specifically as possible.
- Do ask questions in a logical order.
- Do ask questions at various cognitive levels.
- Do encourage students to ask questions.
- Do give students ample time to respond to questions.
- Do limit the instructor's role to guiding the discussion.
- Don't provide the "correct" answers.
- Do wait an equal amount of time for both male and female students to give answers before moving on to another student.
- Do use questions that encourage participation.  For example, use questions that ask students if they have made similar observations during their lives.
- Don't allow the discussion to be dominated by any one or few individuals, including yourself.
- Do try to ensure equal participation across gender.
- Do ask women and men questions of equal difficulty.
- Don't single out women (or members of minorities) to speak out as representatives of that group.

## VI.  CONCLUSION

The underrepresentation of women in both the economics classroom and the profession has long been noted.  Although students are typically drawn from a distribution of learning styles, in which gender and race are conditioning variables, the traditional organization of economics classes seems to be geared toward a particular learning style that is most often associated with Euro-American males and Asians.  Thus, the classroom design may fetter both women's performance and desire to persevere in the discipline.  However, teaching style is an element of pedagogy over which individual instructors possess a great deal of control.  Cooperative learning, group discussion, and other forms of nonhierarchical classroom activities foster engagement among students and between students and faculty.  These techniques offer possibilities for enhancing the persistence of women in economics as well as leading to improved performance for students with diverse learning styles.

## Appendix 3.A:  Worksheet — Comparative Advantage and Gains from Trade*

Print Your Name_____
                          (Last)                              (First)

Social Security Number _____ Section _____

You are given the following information about Japan and Brazil's PPFs:

| | Japan | | Brazil | |
|---|---|---|---|---|
| Possibility | Coffee | Computers | Coffee | Computers |
| A | 0 | 1,000,000 | 0 | 80,000 |
| B | 50,000 | 500,000 | 40,000 | 40,000 |
| C | 100,000 | 0 | 80,000 | 0 |

1.  Graph each nation's PPF.  What does the shape of their PPF tell us about the per-unit opportunity cost?

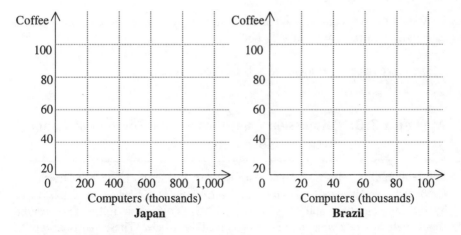

2. Per-unit opportunity cost is calculated as the number of the goods given up divided by the number of goods gained (with units given by the good given up).  Given this formula, what is Japan's per-unit opportunity cost of producing coffee (i.e., how many computers does Japan have to give up in order to gain one additional unit of coffee)?  What is Brazil's per-unit opportunity cost of coffee?  Show your work.

3.  A country is said to have a **comparative advantage** in the production of the good for which it has a lower per-unit opportunity cost.  Given this definition, which country has the comparative advantage in coffee production?

4. What is Japan's per-unit opportunity cost of producing computers? What is Brazil's per-unit opportunity cost of producing computers? Which nation has the comparative advantage in computer production?

5. Assume that each country specializes in producing the good that they have the comparative advantage in (i.e., produces *only* the good in which they have a comparative advantage). How much coffee would Japan produce? How many computers would Japan produce? How much coffee would Brazil produce? How many computers would Brazil produce?

6. Assume that Japan and Brazil decide to trade with each other. (Note: Assume each country is specializing, as in question 5.) Specifically, the terms of trade are set at 5 computers per unit of coffee and the two countries agree to trade 175,000 computers for 35,000 units of coffee. After trade, how much coffee and how many computers does Brazil end up with? After trade, how much coffee and how many computers does Japan end up with? Show your work.

Graph each of these points on the PPFs you drew in question 1. Have both these nations benefited from trade? Explain.

7. Would the two countries agree upon terms of trade equal to 20 computers for each unit of coffee? Why or why not?

* Space provided for student work is omitted here.

## Appendix 3.B:   Discussion Questions — The Division of Labor between Husband and Wife*

Before attending class read "The Family as an Economic Unit: The Division of Labor Between Husband and Wife," in *The Economics of Women, Men, and Work*, by Francine D. Blau, and M.A. Ferber, 1992, 34-48. The following questions should help to guide your thinking as you read the article. These questions will be discussed in class and you will be expected to explain your answers.

1. What are the economic benefits to forming a family that are described in the reading?

2. What are the disadvantages of the "traditional" division of labor within the family that are described in the reading?

3. For each of the economic benefits to forming a family, on a scale from zero (low) to ten (high), what weights would you assign to signify the relative importance you place on that factor?

4. For each of the disadvantages of the "traditional" division of labor within the family, on a scale from zero (low) to ten (high), what weights would you assign to signify the relative importance you place on that factor?

5. If the assumption that women have a comparative advantage in housework was changed to an assumption that men have a comparative advantage in housework, what would you predict would be the structure of a "traditional" family?

6. Do you anticipate forming a "traditional" family? Which of the factors discussed above influence your decision? Are there any additional factors?

7. From the textbook and the worksheet we learned that two nations can each be made better off by producing the good in which it has a comparative advantage and then trading with the other nation. Given the disadvantages of the traditional division of labor within a family, can you think of any analogous reasons why nations may *not* want to trade with each other?

* Space provided for student work is omitted here.

## NOTES

* Attendance at the AEA Teacher Training Workshop, the NSF sponsored conference on "Improving Introductory Economics by Incorporating the Latest Scholarship on Race and Gender," and the IAFFE sponsored conference on "Getting Real and Making Connections: Exploring Alternative Pedagogies" has helped clarify our thinking on these topics. We thank Marianne Ferber for providing guidance to the literature on women in economics and the editors for comments that substantially improved the chapter.

1. It has also been suggested that gender-related performance differentials may be related to the widespread use of a particular assessment instrument. Siegfried and Kennedy (1995) found that multiple-choice questions account for about two-thirds of total assessment. It has been widely recorded that males perform better than females on standardized tests. However, the gender-related differences in performance disappeared or were reversed when essay questions were used (Lumsden and Scott 1987).

2. The other three scales of the MBTI do now show any significant variation by gender. (Gabelnick and Pearson 1989).

3. Bergman (1987) argues that 'gender topics' will be interesting to all students, not just women.

4. The Corporation for National and Community Service defines service learning as "[A] method under which students ... learn and develop through active participation in thoughtfully organized service that: is conducted in and meets the needs of a community and is coordinated with an institution of higher education and with the community; helps foster civic responsibility; is integrated into and enhances the academic curriculum of the students ...; and includes structured time for the students to reflect on the service experience." (Adapted from *A service-learning guide for faculty*, University of Richmond, 1997). Although beyond the scope of this chapter, McGoldrick (1998) provides excellent descriptions of how to incorporate service learning into the economics curriculum. In addition, she explains how service learning is consistent with feminist pedagogy and hence, may be of particular value to female students. As she states, service learning "encourages a basis for discussion consistent with feminist pedagogical goals. This is accomplished by taking the subject material authority away from the instructor and giving students ownership of the development and application of economic theory, providing a common experience among the students, and exposing students to the realities of the theory." (McGoldrick 1996, 8).

5. Many of the characteristics of successful cooperative learning exercises are consistent with common themes of feminist pedagogy. Specifically, the use of nonhierarchical classrooms; having the class produce and share knowledge together; and encouraging active participation (Shrewsbury 1993; Sandler et al. 1996).

6. The classes we teach typically have forty or fewer students. The classrooms have movable chairs, which facilitates student interactions.

7. For example, Johnson, et al. (1991) suggest that students in the group each be assigned one of the following roles: summarizer, accuracy checker, elaborator, researcher, encourager, recorder, and observer.

8. In principles of microeconomics for example, we devote two weeks to discussion of outside readings related to gender issues. As a result, we have omitted coverage of long-run adjustment in the special cases of increasing, and decreasing, cost perfectly competitive industries, as well as special topics on unions. Other instructors may choose different topics to de-emphasize.

9. If using this strategy, it is important that the "admission price" does not deter students from attending class. We have typically handled this issue by making it clear that what is covered during discussion classes will also be covered on exams. Alternatively, the instructor could make class participation an explicit component of the grade in the course.

10. Bonwell and Eison (1991) contains a thorough discussion on constructing discussion questions.

## REFERENCES

Banks, T.L. 1988. Gender bias in the classroom. *Journal of Legal Education* 38 (March / June): 137-46.

Bartlett, R.L. 1996. Discovering diversity in introductory economics. *Journal of Economic Perspectives* 10 (Spring): 141-53.

_____. 1995. A flip of the coin - A roll of the die: An answer to the free-rider problem in economic instruction. *Journal of Economic Education* 26 (Spring): 131-9.

Baxter Magolda, M.B. 1992. *Knowing and reasoning in college: Gender-related patterns in students' intellectual development*. San Francisco: Jossey-Bass.

Becker, W.E. and M. Watts. 1996. Chalk and talk: A national survey on teaching undergraduate economics. *American Economic Review Proceedings* 86 (May): 448-53.

_____ and _____. 1995. Teaching tools: Teaching methods in undergraduate economics. *Economic Inquiry* 33 (October): 692-700.

Belenky, M.F., B.M. Clinchy, N.R. Goldberger, and J.M. Tarule. 1986. W*omen's ways of knowing: The development of self, voice, and mind*. New York: Basic Books Inc.

Bergmann, B.R. 1987. Women's roles in the economy: Teaching the issues. *Journal of Economic Education* 18 (Fall): 393-407.

Blank, R.M. 1993. What should mainstream economists learn from feminist theory? In M.A. Ferber and J.A. Nelson, eds. *Beyond economic man: Feminist theory and economics*. Chicago: University of Chicago Press: 133-43.

Blau, F.D. and M.A. Ferber. 1992. *The economics of women, men, and work*. Englewood Cliffs, New Jersey: Prentice-Hall.

Bloom, B., M. Englehart, E. Furst, W. Hill, and D. Krathwohl, eds. 1956. *Taxonomy of educational objectives (cognitive domain)*. New York: David McKay Co.

Bonwell, C.C. and J.A. Eison. 1991. *Active learning: Creating excitement in the classroom*, Washington, D.C.: The George Washington University, School of Education and Human Development.

Chickering, A.W. and Z.F. Gamson. 1987. Seven principles for good practice. *AAHE Bulletin* 39 (March): 3-7.

Committee on the Status of Women in the Economics Profession. 1996. 1995 Annual report. *CSWEP Newsletter* (Winter): 1-10.

Cross, P.K. 1987. Teaching for learning. *AAHE Bulletin* 39 (April): 3-7.

Feiner, S.F., ed. 1994. *Race and gender in the American economy: Views from across the spectrum*. Englewood Cliffs, NJ: Prentice Hall.

_____. 1993. Introductory economics textbooks and the treatment of issues relating to women and minorities, 1984 and 1991. *Journal of Economic Education* 24 (Spring): 145-62.

Ferber, M.A. and J.A. Nelson. 1993. Introduction: The social construction of economics and the social construction of gender. In M.A. Ferber and J.A. Nelson, eds. *Beyond economic man: Feminist theory and economics*. Chicago: University of Chicago Press: 1-22.

Gabelnick, F. and C.S. Pearson. 1989. Recognizing the diversity of women's voices by psychological type. In C. S. Pearson, D. L. Shavlik, and J.G. Touchton, eds. *Educating the majority: Women challenge tradition in higher education*. New York: Macmillan: 121-33.

Johnson, D.W., R.T. Johnson, and K.A. Smith. 1991. *Active learning: Cooperation in the college classroom*. Edina, MN: Interaction Book Company.

Kolb, D.A. 1981. Learning styles and disciplinary differences. In A. W. Chickering, and Associates, eds. *The modern American college*. San Francisco: Jossey-Bass: 232-55.

Lage, M.J. and M. Treglia. 1996. The impact of integrating scholarship on women into introductory economics: Evidence from one institution. *Journal of Economic Education* 27 (Winter) 26-36.

Light, R.J. 1990. *The Harvard assessment seminars: Explorations with students and faculty about teaching, learning and student life.* Cambridge: Harvard University Graduate School of Education.

Losee, S., A. Dowell, and T.A. Whalen. 1995. Gender equity through discovering voice. In *Achieving gender equity in the classroom and on the campus: The next steps,* Washington D.C.: American Association of University Women: 161-4.

Lumsden, K.G. and A. Scott. 1987. The economics student revisited: Male-female differences in comprehension. *Journal of Economic Education* 18 (Fall): 365-75.

Madison, S.K. 1995. Creating a more equitable computing environment. In *Achieving gender equity in the classroom and on the campus: The next steps,* 155-60. Washington D.C.: American Association of University Women.

McGill, I. and L. Beaty. 1993. *Action learning: A practitioner's guide.* London: Kogan Page Limited.

McGoldrick, K. 1998. Service-learning in economics: A detailed application. *Journal of Economic Education* 29 (Fall): 365-76.

_____. 1996. The road not taken: An example of feminist pedagogy in economics. Working Paper. University of Richmond.

McTighe, J. 1985. Questioning for quality thinking. Working Paper. Maryland State Department of Education, Department of Instruction.

National Center for Education Statistics. 1995. *Digest of Education Statistics.* Washington, D.C.: US Department of Education.

Sandler, B.R., L.A. Silverberg, and R.M. Hall. 1996. *The chilly classroom climate: A guide to improve the education of women.* Washington, D.C.: National Association for Women in Education.

Shrewsbury, C.M. 1993. What is feminist pedagogy? *Women's Studies Quarterly* 21 (Fall): 8-16.

Siegfried, J. and P.E. Kennedy. 1995. Does pedagogy vary with class size in introductory economics? *American Economic Review Proceedings* 85 (May): 345-51.

_____, R.L. Bartlett, W.L. Hansen, A.C. Kelley, D.N. McCloskey, and T.H. Tietenberg. 1991. The status and prospects of the economics major. *Journal of Economic Education* 22 (Summer): 197-224.

# CHAPTER 4

# STUDENT DECISION MAKING AS ACTIVE LEARNING: EXPERIMENTAL ECONOMICS IN THE CLASSROOM

**Charles Noussair**

**James Walker**

Researchers in many scientific disciplines, such as chemistry, physics and biology, have developed methodologies for conducting controlled laboratory experiments that have become important components of their discipline's processes of scientific research and discovery. In these fields, laboratory methods have long been used by educators as a means of instruction. Classroom exercises, inspired by simple, but scientifically important, experiments allow students to experience directly the operation of fundamental principles.

The last several decades have witnessed the development of laboratory methods as an important research tool in economics.[1] These laboratory methods are now also being applied as an educational tool to supplement undergraduate courses in economics. There are two principal arguments for applying these techniques to instruction. First, they stimulate student interest in economics. Students enjoy the active participation in the exercises, and the exercises bring abstract concepts to life. The second reason for using classroom experiments is that they provide powerful demonstrations of the principles of economics at work, and illustrate the limitations of the stylized models taught in undergraduate courses. Exercises in which fundamental principles are demonstrated help convince students that the abstract models taught in most economics courses are valid. Other exercises provide illustrations of "anomalies" in which standard economic theory needs to be modified to account for observed behavior. The differences between theory and observed behavior are often stimulating topics for classroom discussion.

We describe three exercises we have used in our undergraduate courses: the Voluntary Contributions Mechanism for the Provision of Public Goods (VCM), the Consumption/Investment Tradeoff (CI), and the Supply and Demand with Demand Shift (SD). The VCM exercise illustrates the presence of the free rider problem in public goods provision, but also shows that free riding is not as extensive as game theory predicts. The CI exercise is a simple illustration of the dynamic optimization problems that frequently arise in macroeconomics and illustrates the difficulty people have in optimizing intertemporally. The SD exercise allows students to experience the operation of economic forces that bring market activity to an equilibrium, a demand shock, and the subsequent transition to a new market equilibrium. The exercises are described in some detail. We follow with a general method of setting up a laboratory exercise in economics, and discuss some pitfalls we have encountered and some techniques we have used that increase the effectiveness of these and similar exercises.

## I. THE VOLUNTARY CONTRIBUTIONS MECHANISM

### Purpose

The failure of competitive markets to generate socially optimal outcomes in the presence of public goods and externalities is a cornerstone of most introductory microeconomics courses. The voluntary contribution mechanism (VCM) described in this section is designed to allow students to experience the conflict between private and public interests that exists in the provision of public goods. In the VCM decision exercise, each individual in a group must make an allocation between a private good (where consumption benefits accrue only to the individual) and a public or group good (where consumption benefits accrue to all group members). The exercise is based on a series of research papers (see for example Isaac, Walker and Williams 1994) and is also described in some detail in an article on teaching methodology (Williams and Walker 1993).

In this exercise, students interact in a decision situation in which free riding is individually rational from the perspective of noncooperative game theory. However, if a substantial percentage of students follow such a strategy, the outcome is a significant loss from the standpoint of aggregate group earnings (social welfare). Using this exercise, clearer meanings and precise definitions can be given to theoretical concepts of group valuation of a public good and measures of the degree of market failure. The ability to translate abstract notions of free riding into specific measurements of social welfare losses reinforces the conceptual basis for this theory. Furthermore, the opportunity for students to face a public goods contribution dilemma with real incentives and generate actual data allows the instructor to focus discussions on the important issue of "theory" as a predictive tool, as well as on the evolution of institutions that reduce market failures.

## Structure of the Economy

In the VCM extra-credit exercise, students participate in a series of decision rounds conducted over several weeks during the semester. The exercise is conducted on the NovaNet computer system, utilizing software developed by Arlington Williams. Appendix 4.A presents the portion of the instructions that are used to launch the exercise. Like many computerized exercises, this activity could be conducted without computer assistance. The NovaNet software, however, significantly reduces the time costs for the instructor, facilitates the required accounting, and provides summary graphics to use in classroom discussions.

At the start of each decision round, each participant is endowed with tokens that are to be divided between a "private account" and a "group account." Tokens cannot be carried across rounds. The student is informed that each token placed in the private account earns p cents with certainty and that earnings from the group account are dependent upon the decisions of all group members. Each individual receives earnings from the group account regardless of whether he/she allocates tokens to that account.

For a given round, let $X$ represent the sum of tokens placed in the group account by all individuals in the group. Earnings from the group account are dependent upon the pre-assigned earnings function $G(X)$. For simplicity, each participant earns an equal amount from the group account of $[G(X)]/N$ cents, where $N$ is group size. Prior to the start of each decision round, each individual knows the number of remaining rounds and the group's aggregate token endowment. During each round, participants can view their personal token allocations, earnings, and total tokens placed in the group account for all previous rounds. Figure 4.1 displays an example of the actual screen display each participant sees in a given decision round.

The strategic nature of the VCM decision problem is straightforward. Each participant's decision to allocate a token to the group account costs that individual p cents. This yields a positive marginal gain in group surplus of $[G^N - p]$. The marginal per-capita return from the group account (MPCR) is defined as the ratio of "$" benefits to costs for moving a single token from the individual to the group account, or $[G^N/N]/p$.

**Figure 4.1: VCM Summary Information Table Illustration**
**(*N* = 10, MPCR = .30)**

ROUND 1 CURRENTLY IN PROGRESS

YOUR ENDOWMENT of tokens in each round: 50; Group size: 10
TOTAL GROUP ENDOWMENT of tokens in each round: 500
Each token retained in your PRIVATE ACCOUNT earns: $0.01
Examples of possible earnings from the GROUP ACCOUNT

| Tokens in GROUP ACCOUNT (from the entire group) | Total Group Earnings | Your 10% share of Group Earnings |
|:---:|:---:|:---:|
| 0 | $0.000 | $0.000 |
| 31 | $0.930 | $0.093 |
| 63 | $1.890 | $0.189 |
| 94 | $2.820 | $0.282 |
| 125 | $3.750 | $0.375 |
| 156 | $4.680 | $0.468 |
| 188 | $5.640 | $0.564 |
| 219 | $6.570 | $0.657 |
| 250 | $7.500 | $0.750 |
| 281 | $8.430 | $0.843 |
| 313 | $9.390 | $0.939 |
| 344 | $10.320 | $1.032 |
| 375 | $11.250 | $1.125 |
| 406 | $12.180 | $1.218 |
| 438 | $13.140 | $1.314 |
| 469 | $14.070 | $1.407 |
| 500 | $15.000 | $1.500 |

Help → review instructions
LAB → view the earnings from the group account for any possible value of
   "Tokens in Group Account."

How many tokens do you wish to place in the Group Account?

Displayed in Table 4.1 are the design configurations for the Group Size/MPCR combinations we discuss in the results section below. In these particular configurations, $p = \$.01$ and $G^N$ is a constant greater than $.01$ so that the Pareto Optimum (defined simply as the outcome that maximizes group earnings) is for each individual to place all tokens in the group account. On the other hand, the single-period dominant strategy is for each individual to place zero

**Table 4.1: VCM Valuation Parameters and Group Sizes**

| Group Size | G(X) | G'(X)/N | MPCR | Number of Replications |
|------------|--------|---------|------|------------------------|
| 10 | \$.03X | \$.003 | .30 | 16 |
| 10 | \$.075X | \$.0075 | .75 | 10 |
| 40 | \$.012X | \$.0003 | .03 | 6 |
| 100 | \$.30X | \$.003 | .30 | 3 |

tokens in the group account. Consider the case where $N = 10$ and MPCR $= .30$. Each token allocated to the group account by an individual has an opportunity cost of \$.01, with a gain to that individual of only \$.003. On the other hand, each token returns \$.003 to every individual in the group (regardless of his/her allocation of tokens to the group account). The aggregate earnings function for the group account is \$.03X, where $X$ is the total quantity of tokens placed in the group account. Thus, each token allocated to the group account yields the group \$.03 with a cost to the "contributor" of \$.01.

One problem faced by the instructor is constructing a system of incentives for the exercise. In most of the classroom exercises we have conducted, participant $i$'s dollar earnings were converted into the following "performance index" (P) prior to being converted into extra-credit points:

$$P = \frac{i\text{'s Actual Earnings} - i\text{'s Minimum Possible Earnings}}{i\text{'s Maximum Possible Earnings} - i\text{'s Minimum Possible Earnings}}$$

where $P$ ranges from 0 to 1 for each individual. At the end of the final round, this fraction was computed for each individual (based on earnings in all rounds), multiplied by a desired weight for the exercise, and added to the student's final grade average. In addition to these performance based extra-credit points, we often assigned nonperformance based extra-credit points based on the number of rounds in which a student participates.

The performance index has two important characteristics. First, the resulting reward structure is not a tournament. A reward mechanism based on ranking in a tournament alters the strategic nature of the public goods problem. Specifically, with a tournament, underprovision of the public good would not necessarily imply lower rewards for some individuals. Second, with the performance index defined above, the maximum and minimum possible extra-credit earnings does not depend upon group assignment. Thus, a student's potential to earn the maximum or minimum extra-credit points is not restricted by being in a large versus a small group, or the particular parameters for their group.

## Conducting the VCM Exercise

About mid-semester, before classroom discussions of public goods, market failure, etc., students in our microeconomics classes receive the handout (Appendix 4.A) used to launch the exercise. In summary, the handout informs students: 1) about the basic nature of the group decision-making exercise, 2) that participation is voluntary and offers extra-credit points, 3) about the specific formula used to convert the "cash earnings" reported to them by the computer into extra-credit points, 4) of the days associated with each decision round, and 5) of the specific procedures for accessing the exercise on NovaNET.

The VCM software handles up to 20 decision-making groups running simultaneously. After logging onto the computer for the first time, participants are assigned randomly to a group, after which they work through a set of instructions and then enter their allocation decision for Round 1. Participants are allowed to proceed to the next round only after the "current round" is completed. Our decision rounds usually last 3-5 days. Each time the students log on, they are shown the results of the previous round and then the display for the current round. At this point, they have the option to review the instructions, to review the results from all prior rounds, or to make a decision for the current round. Not all participants make an allocation decision in each round. Therefore, the software allows the instructor to specify a default allocation decision for each participant. Default specifications we have used are placing zero tokens in the group account (because lack of participation can be interpreted as a decision to free ride) and making the default value an explicit decision for each participant.

## Follow-up Discussion

In classroom discussion of the data generated by the VCM exercise, we focus primarily on market failure that is tied to the disparity between individual and social incentives. In this regard, we allow the class to see how alternative groups "performed" with respect to achieving the social optimum. For example, in some cases we have varied the number of decision makers in alternative groups and/or varied the marginal returns from the group account. Using data from groups of different sizes, we can also focus on a standard conjecture found in many textbook discussions of the free rider problem: "As the group size increases, it is more likely that everyone will behave like a free rider, and the public good will not be provided." (Browning and Browning 1989, 586)

Three general findings from our research on VCM are: (1) allocations to the group account are inversely related to marginal per-capita return (MPCR), (2) holding MPCR constant, allocations to the group account are positively related to group size, and (3) increasing group size in conjunction with a decrease in MPCR leads to lower allocations to the group account – a lower level of efficiency in provision of the pure public good. Evidence related to each of these three findings is found in Figure 4.2. Mean levels of allocations as a percentage of optimum across decision rounds are plotted. The top left hand panel displays results from parametric conditions where $N = 10$ and MPCR $= .3$ or MPCR $= .75$. Note the general increase in allocations to the group account for the MPCR $= .75$ condition. The top right hand panel displays results from conditions where MPCR $= .3$ and $N = 10$ or $N = 100$. Contrary to many of the broad generalizations that are found in textbook discussions of public goods, holding MPCR constant, we observe an increase in allocations to the group account (less free riding) with the larger group size. However, we find evidence to support some textbook discussions of free rider phenomena, in which authors explicitly illustrate group size effects with specific arguments related to decreases in the marginal value of the public good in conjunction with increases in group size (crowding effects) and/or illustrations of large group public goods settings with inherently small marginal valuations. The bottom panel displays results from the conditions where $N = 10$, MPCR $= .3$ and $N = 40$, MPCR $= .03$. With an increase in group size, the value of the public good at the margin decreases to group members. In this case, we observe a validation of the proposition that an increase in group size leads to a decrease in the level of public goods provision.

These results allow us to discuss in the classroom the issue of theoretical predictability and possible reasons why the theory does not perfectly predict decisions in this situation. Furthermore, we are able to show that although we do not observe behavior consistent with the strict prediction of "zero" provision of the public good, we do observe high degrees of inefficiency in provision across MPCR and group size conditions, despite the repetition of the decision environment.

## II. OTHER EXAMPLES

### Consumption Investment Tradeoff
A consumption and investment tradeoff exercise (based on the work of Noussair and Olson 1997) is intended to show students the difficulty of solving the dynamic optimization problems studied in modern macroeconomics. The exercise is designed to be run in one session of 60-75 minutes. Subjects are faced with a dynamic optimization problem in the structure of a neo-classical growth model. They choose consumption and investment over a ten period time horizon. They are given an incentive to maximize the total value of consumption over ten periods plus the final value of the capital stock after the ten periods. Consuming too much at any time drives the future capital stock down and thereby decreases future production and consumption. On the other hand, overinvestment in capital at any time decreases utility from current consumption by too much. The task of the student is to find the optimal tradeoff in each period between consumption and investment.

Each period a student can produce new capital and consumption according to the relationship $K_{t+1} + C_{t+1} = 2.45 K_t^2$ where $K$ is capital, $C$ is consumption and $t$

## Figure 4.2: VCM Group Behavior  (Percentage of Tokens Allocated to Group Account)

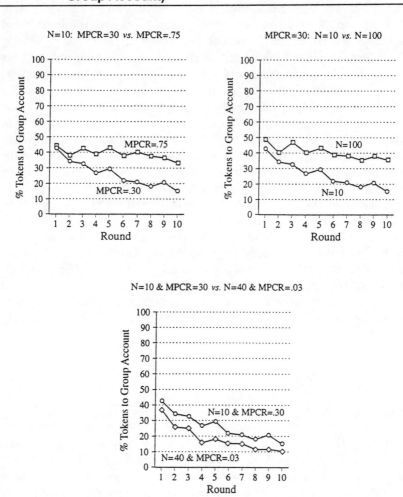

indexes the periods. We use a discrete approximation to this continuous function with existing capital depreciated at 50 percent per period.  Actual possibilities for producing capital and consumption goods each period, taking depreciation into account are given in Table 4.2 that was given to the students. The marginal utility of the consumption good in period $t$, expressed in "tokens," the unit of account for the exercise, is given by $MU(C_t) = 75 - 5\ C_t$. The final marginal buyout value of the capital stock is given by $MBV(K_{11}) = 90 - 5\ K_{11}$, where $K_{11}$ is the amount of capital stock held at the end of period 10. These are presented to students using the information illustrated in Table 4.3. The starting capital stock in period 1 is 7 units. The optimal decision involves equating marginal utilities of consumption and investment in period 10, which implies that the agent wants to consume three units less than the capital stock held after period 10. The optimal decision rule also involves keeping a constant level of capital stock of 6 units throughout the 10 periods and consuming a constant amount of 3 units each period.

The exercise takes one class period or laboratory session and, apart from the information displayed in Tables 4.2 and 4.3, is computerized. Unlike the VCM exercise, participants' payoffs depend only on their own decisions, not on those of any other students or on chance. The instructions used in the exercise are given in Appendix 4.B. Typically, in a 60 minute period, students can go through the instructions and entire decision problem 5-7 times. Many students have great difficulty finding the optimal decision rule, though most easily understand it once it is explained to them afterwards. With practice there is often improvement in their performance. Extra credit points are awarded to the students who earn the most tokens (usually about 10 percent of the students receive extra credit points). The percentage of the maximum possible dollar payoff that subjects in a research setting were able to earn when they received monetary payments proportionally to the tokens they obtained are in Figure 4.3. The data in the figure give the performance of subjects for the third time they attempted to solve the problem.

The follow-up classroom discussion emphasizes that the problem is best solved by recursive backward reasoning, equating marginal utility of consumption and investment in period 10 and keeping a constant level of consumption and capital stock over time. The benefits of smoothing consumption over time are explained. The exercise has also been used with a game theory course as an illustration of the backward reasoning that underlies the concept of subgame perfect equilibrium.

### Supply and Demand with a Demand Shift
The Supply and Demand with a Demand Shift exercise provides a powerful illustration of the tendency of a properly organized market to converge to competitive equilibrium prices and quantities.[2] It is conducted with students in the principles of microeconomics courses at Purdue University, and similar exercises are used at Indiana University, and many other universities throughout the world. Students are divided into buyers and sellers in approximately equal numbers. Students work with demand and supply curves, expressed in terms of a fictitious laboratory currency. The earnings of buyers, in terms of the laboratory currency, are equal to the difference between their willingness to pay minus the price they pay for the units they receive. Sellers' earnings, in terms of the laboratory currency, are equal to the difference between the prices at which they are able to sell units minus their unit costs. One system of incentives awards the buyer with

## Table 4.2: Production Schedule

| A Available (Input) | Possible Output | | | | | | | | | | | | | | |
|---|---|---|---|---|---|---|---|---|---|---|---|---|---|---|---|
| | 1 | | 2 | | 3 | | 4 | | 5 | | 6 | | 7 | | 8 |
| | X | A | X | A | X | A | X | A | X | A | X | A | X | A | X | A |
| 0 | 0 | 0 | | | | | | | | | | | | | | |
| 1 | 2 | 0 | 1 | 1 | 0 | 2 | | | | | | | | | | |
| 2 | 3 | 1 | 2 | 2 | 1 | 3 | 0 | 4 | | | | | | | | |
| 3 | 4 | 1 | 3 | 2 | 2 | 3 | 1 | 4 | 0 | 5 | | | | | | |
| 4 | 5 | 2 | 4 | 3 | 3 | 4 | 2 | 5 | 1 | 6 | 0 | 7 | | | | |
| 5 | 5 | 2 | 4 | 3 | 3 | 4 | 2 | 5 | 1 | 6 | 0 | 7 | | | | |
| 6 | 6 | 3 | 5 | 4 | 4 | 5 | 3 | 6 | 2 | 7 | 1 | 8 | 0 | 9 | | |
| 7 | 6 | 3 | 5 | 4 | 4 | 5 | 3 | 6 | 2 | 7 | 1 | 8 | 0 | 9 | | |
| 8 | 7 | 4 | 6 | 5 | 5 | 6 | 4 | 7 | 3 | 8 | 2 | 9 | 1 | 10 | 0 | 11 |
| 9 | 7 | 4 | 6 | 5 | 5 | 6 | 4 | 7 | 3 | 8 | 2 | 9 | 1 | 10 | 0 | 11 |
| 10 | 8 | 5 | 7 | 6 | 6 | 7 | 5 | 8 | 4 | 9 | 3 | 10 | 2 | 11 | 1 | 12 |
| 11 | 8 | 5 | 7 | 6 | 6 | 7 | 5 | 8 | 4 | 9 | 3 | 10 | 2 | 11 | 1 | 12 |
| 12 | 9 | 5 | 8 | 6 | 7 | 7 | 6 | 8 | 5 | 9 | 4 | 10 | 3 | 11 | 2 | 12 |

## Table 4.3: Token Value Sheets for X and A

| | Token Values for X | | | Token Values for A | | |
|---|---|---|---|---|---|---|
| Unit | X Unit Value | X Total Value | Unit | A Unit Value | A Total Value |
| (1) | 70 | 70 | (1) | 85 | 85 |
| (2) | 65 | 135 | (2) | 80 | 165 |
| (3) | 60 | 195 | (3) | 75 | 240 |
| (4) | 55 | 250 | (4) | 70 | 310 |
| (5) | 50 | 300 | (5) | 65 | 375 |
| (6) | 45 | 345 | (6) | 60 | 435 |
| (7) | 40 | 385 | (7) | 55 | 490 |
| (8) | 35 | 420 | (8) | 50 | 540 |
| (9) | 30 | 450 | (9) | 45 | 585 |
| (10) | 25 | 475 | (10) | 40 | 625 |
| (11) | 20 | 495 | (11) | 35 | 660 |
| (12) | 15 | 510 | (12) | 30 | 690 |
| (13) | 10 | 520 | (13) | 25 | 715 |
| (14) | 5 | 525 | (14) | 20 | 735 |

**Figure 4.3: Percentage of Maximum Tokens Obtained (*n* = 48)**

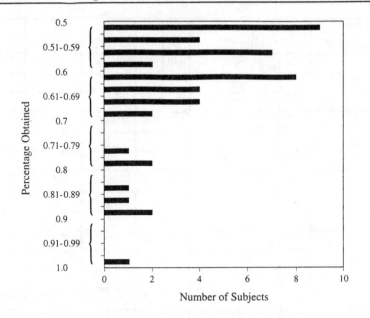

the highest earnings and the seller with the highest earnings a pre-specified number of extra-credit points. Instructions explaining these incentives are given in Appendix 4.C. The forms on which buyers and sellers see their incentives and record their profits are displayed in Tables 4.4a and 4.4b. Each buyer has the demand curve illustrated in Table 4.4a and each seller has the supply curve illustrated in Table 4.4b.

We conduct trade using continuous double auction trading rules. This is a type of market in which buyers can submit price-quantity pairs, called bids, which are offers to buy the specified quantity of units at the indicated per-unit price. Similarly, sellers can submit price-quantity pairs, called asks, which are offers to sell units at the indicated per-unit price. Both buyers and sellers may accept offers made by the other side of the market. When a bid or ask is accepted, a transaction occurs at the offer price. An improvement rule is typically imposed on new offers entering the market, requiring submitted bids (asks) to exceed (be less than) the standing bid (ask).

The exercise is typically run in two class periods of 60-75 minutes each. In the first session subjects are trained in the use of the software and the mechanics of making purchases and sales in a continuous double auction. In the second session the subjects interact in the market setting. There are eight market periods, numbered from zero to seven. Period zero is for practice and earnings in the practice period do not count toward the students' potential extra-credit points. During periods one to three the demand and supply curves are stationary. There is

## Table 4.4a: Record of Purchases and Earnings for Buyers

| Unit Purchased | | Period Number | 0 | 1 | 2 | 3 | 4 | 5 | 6 | 7 |
|---|---|---|---|---|---|---|---|---|---|---|---|
| 1 | row 1 | 1st unit redemption value | 590 | 590 | 590 | 590 | 990 | 990 | 990 | 990 |
| | row 2 | Purchase Price | | | | | | | | |
| | row 3 | Profit (row 1 - row 2) | | | | | | | | |
| 2 | row 4 | 2nd unit redemption value | 490 | 490 | 490 | 490 | 890 | 890 | 890 | 890 |
| | row 5 | Purchase Price | | | | | | | | |
| | row 6 | Profit (row 4 - row 5) | | | | | | | | |
| 3 | row 7 | 3rd unit redemption value | 390 | 390 | 390 | 390 | 790 | 790 | 790 | 790 |
| | row 8 | Purchase Price | | | | | | | | |
| | row 9 | Profit (row 7 - row 8) | | | | | | | | |
| 4 | row 10 | 4th unit redemption value | 290 | 290 | 290 | 290 | 690 | 690 | 690 | 690 |
| | row 11 | Purchase Price | | | | | | | | |
| | row 12 | Profit (row 10 - row 11) | | | | | | | | |
| 5 | row 13 | 5th unit redemption value | 190 | 190 | 190 | 190 | 590 | 590 | 590 | 590 |
| | row 14 | Purchase Price | | | | | | | | |
| | row 15 | Profit (row 13 - row 14) | | | | | | | | |
| 6 | row 16 | 6th unit redemption value | 90 | 90 | 90 | 90 | 490 | 490 | 490 | 490 |
| | row 17 | Purchase Price | | | | | | | | |
| | row 18 | Profit (row 16 - row 17) | | | | | | | | |
| 7 | row 19 | 7th unit redemption value | 0 | 0 | 0 | 0 | 390 | 390 | 390 | 390 |
| | row 20 | Purchase Price | | | | | | | | |
| | row 21 | Profit (row 19 - row 20) | | | | | | | | |
| 8 | row 22 | 8th unit redemption value | 0 | 0 | 0 | 0 | 290 | 290 | 290 | 290 |
| | row 23 | Purchase Price | | | | | | | | |
| | row 24 | Profit (row 22 - row 23) | | | | | | | | |
| 9 | row 25 | 9th unit redemption value | 0 | 0 | 0 | 0 | 190 | 190 | 190 | 190 |
| | row 26 | Purchase Price | | | | | | | | |
| | row 27 | Profit (row 25 - row 26) | | | | | | | | |
| 10 | row 28 | 10th unit redemption value | 0 | 0 | 0 | 0 | 90 | 90 | 90 | 90 |
| | row 29 | Purchase Price | | | | | | | | |
| | row 30 | Profit (row 28 - row 29) | | | | | | | | |
| | row 31 | Total Per Period | | | | | | | | |

## Table 4.4b: Record of Sales and Profits for Sellers

| Unit Sold | | Period Number | 0 | 1 | 2 | 3 | 4 | 5 | 6 | 7 |
|---|---|---|---|---|---|---|---|---|---|---|---|
| 1 | row 1 | Selling price | | | | | | | | |
| | row 2 | Cost of 1st unit | 200 | 200 | 200 | 200 | 200 | 200 | 200 | 200 |
| | row 3 | Profit (row 1 - row 2) | | | | | | | | |
| 2 | row 4 | Selling price | | | | | | | | |
| | row 5 | Cost of 2nd unit | 300 | 300 | 300 | 300 | 300 | 300 | 300 | 300 |
| | row 6 | Profit (row 4 - row 5) | | | | | | | | |
| 3 | row 7 | Selling price | | | | | | | | |
| | row 8 | Cost of 3rd unit | 400 | 400 | 400 | 400 | 400 | 400 | 400 | 400 |
| | row 9 | Profit (row 7 - row 8) | | | | | | | | |
| 4 | row 10 | Selling price | | | | | | | | |
| | row 11 | Cost of 4th unit | 500 | 500 | 500 | 500 | 500 | 500 | 500 | 500 |
| | row 12 | Profit (row 10 - row 11) | | | | | | | | |
| 5 | row 13 | Selling price | | | | | | | | |
| | row 14 | Cost of 5th unit | 600 | 600 | 600 | 600 | 600 | 600 | 600 | 600 |
| | row 15 | Profit (row 13 - row 14) | | | | | | | | |
| 6 | row 16 | Selling price | | | | | | | | |
| | row 17 | Cost of 6th unit | 700 | 700 | 700 | 700 | 700 | 700 | 700 | 700 |
| | row 18 | Profit (row 16 - row 17) | | | | | | | | |
| 7 | row 19 | Selling price | | | | | | | | |
| | row 20 | Cost of 7th unit | 800 | 800 | 800 | 800 | 800 | 800 | 800 | 800 |
| | row 21 | Profit (row 19 - row 20) | | | | | | | | |
| 8 | row 22 | Selling price | | | | | | | | |
| | row 23 | Cost of 8th unit | 900 | 900 | 900 | 900 | 900 | 900 | 900 | 900 |
| | row 24 | Profit (row 22 - row 23) | | | | | | | | |
| 9 | row 25 | Selling price | | | | | | | | |
| | row 26 | Cost of 9th unit | 1000 | 1000 | 1000 | 1000 | 1000 | 1000 | 1000 | 1000 |
| | row 27 | Profit (row 25 - row 26) | | | | | | | | |
| 10 | row 28 | Selling price | | | | | | | | |
| | row 29 | Cost of 10th unit | 1100 | 1100 | 1100 | 1100 | 1100 | 1100 | 1100 | 1100 |
| | row 30 | Profit (row 28 - row 29) | | | | | | | | |
| | row 31 | Total Per Period | | | | | | | | |

a demand shift in period four and the environment is stationary from then on. In the competitive equilibrium, each agent receives identical profit, so the tournament structure of payoffs is not biased in favor of or against any particular agent.

The results from a typical session are given in Figure 4.4. The vertical axis represents prices and the horizontal axis represents clock time. The vertical lines indicate the opening of a new market period. The straight horizontal line represent the midpoints of competitive equilibrium price ranges, which are 390-400 in periods 1-3, and 590-600 in periods 4-7. The data in the table represent the time series of transaction prices in the session. In the practice period, prices fluctuate wildly. After several stationary periods the prices are converging to a level close to the competitive equilibrium price.

In period 4, when the demand shift occurs, there are again large fluctuations of the market price. Because sellers do not have a means of anticipating the price change, buyers are still able to buy at the old prices early in period 4, but by the end of the period, excess demand at the old price forces the price to increase. Beginning in period 5, there is a tendency of re-stabilization at the new market equilibrium.

The subsequent classroom discussion centers on the idea that markets exist in which the market equilibrium can be attained in a very short amount of time. The exercise helps convince the students that the theory of supply and demand is empirically important. In the discussion, students are asked what they thought the equilibrium price was in periods 1-3, and what happened in period 4. Students generally identify the equilibrium prices before and after the demand shift. However, usually only the buyers understand initially that there was a demand shift that caused prices to rise in period 4. Sellers often suggest other explanations of the price increase such as an increase in buyers' cash endowment, rather than an increase in buyers' willingness to pay. The shifting of a demand curve is explained; this illustrates that the price change is less than the amount of the change in willingness to pay. In the exercise, the demand curve shifts upward by 400, as can be observed in Table 4.4a, and the equilibrium price increases by 200.

The exercise also offers a powerful way of illustrating the differences between total and marginal costs and utilities, by requiring profits to be computed individually for each unit an agent buys or sells (using Tables 4.4a and 4.4b and the instructions in Appendix 4.C). The first instinct of many students who are inexperienced in laboratory markets is to buy or sell as large a quantity as possible, but the losses they experience in doing so make them realize the relevance of marginal valuations and costs in formulating strategies.

Several extensions of this exercise have been developed for intermediate microeconomics classes at Purdue University. They include the imposition of an excise tax, the presence of a monopolistic seller, and the simultaneous clearing of input and output markets. Details are available from the authors.

# Figure 4.4: Typical Time Series of Transaction Prices in the SD Exercise

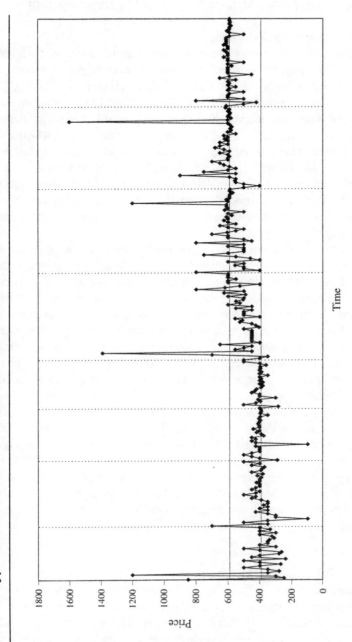

## III. CONSTRUCTING YOUR OWN LABORATORY EXERCISE[3]

### General Design Considerations

When designing a laboratory exercise we attempt to ensure that we meet three criteria. Most exercises we tried that were unsuccessful failed because they did not adequately address one or more of these criteria. The first criterion is simplicity. The experiment should be easily understood by the students, who must be aware of how their actions affect their final payoffs. Simplicity is even more crucial when an exercise must be completed in a class period, which means that limited time is available for explaining the exercise. The introduction to the activity is made through a set of carefully drafted instructions, which are discussed later in this section. All sessions should be precisely planned and scheduled. We usually estimate the duration of the various phases of the exercises based on similar previous classroom exercises or reported times in published research papers.

The second criterion is to make participation in the exercise itself an interesting experience for the students. An enjoyable exercise makes the points illustrated by the exercise more memorable and improves the overall class atmosphere. Exercises can be made more interesting for students by changing the underlying conditions of the economy from time to time, using exercises in which students have incentives to take actions frequently, and by using exercises in which decisions and outcomes are known to evolve over time. For example, in the SD exercise, a demand shift is introduced in period 4. In the VCM exercise, behavior is known to change over time, in that contributions tend to fall as the game is repeated.

The third criterion is to organize the decision situation in a way that makes it easy to focus on (a) the relationship of the decision situation to the theoretical models covered in class, and (b) a small number of key results that students can take away from the subsequent discussion. For example, the VCM exercise emphasizes the conflict between self-interest and the interest of a group. The SD exercise emphasizes the possibility of attaining market equilibria in a short period of time under minimal informational conditions. The CI exercise stresses backward induction and income smoothing in solving dynamic optimization problems.

### Steps in Constructing an Exercise

It is practical to divide the tasks of constructing a laboratory exercise in economics into five subtasks: (1) specify the structure of the laboratory economy (the decision situation), (2) compose the instructions describing the economy and choose the interfaces with which students interact within the economic system, (3) construct a means of recording the data for later analysis and presentation, (4) plan the timing and scheduling of activity for the period in which the exercise takes place, and (5) prepare for a subsequent classroom discussion. We describe each of the subtasks below. We include a few do's and don'ts for each subtask in the following section.

## Specifying the Structure of the Laboratory Economy

The instructor takes what may be a very abstract theory and operationalizes it by constructing a detailed institutional format, with underlying incentives and resources. From a practical point of view, specifying the structure of the economy involves the following steps:

1) Each student is given a set of decision options. For example, in the VCM exercise, each student holds wealth and must distribute it between a private account and a group account. In the SD students are given the ability to either buy or sell units, and sellers are given an inventory of units they can sell.
2) An algorithm is specified to take the decisions of the students and translate them into outcomes. The outcome for an individual agent may (as in the SD and VCM exercises) or may not (as in the CI exercise) depend on the decisions of other agents as well as the agent's own decisions.
3) A reward structure is specified that motivates the students in the ways that the economic theory being illustrated presumes, so that students are not indifferent between good and bad decisions.

Incentives are often created using cash payments in research experiments but we usually use extra credit points in classroom exercises.[4] Awards may be made strictly in the form of a mapping from "cash" awards to extra-credit. Alternatively, if it does not alter the economic incentives in some undesirable fashion, the points can be awarded on a tournament basis to the students who achieve the highest value of the objective function. For example, in the SD exercise, a seller may be awarded extra-credit points proportionally to the firm's profit in the laboratory economy, or a fixed sum of extra-credit points may be awarded to the firm with the highest profit. It is crucial that the expected reward be monotonically increasing in the objective function assumed by the economic theory being illustrated.

## Description of the Economy

A set of experimental instructions is used to describe the environment within which the students interact. The instructions, which are sometimes computerized, represent the principal means by which information about the exercise is transmitted from the instructor to the students. They should be written with great care, because a small error or misplaced emphasis can create a great level of misunderstanding or result in informational conditions different from those the instructor intends. We have provided excerpts from the instructions for the three exercises in the Appendix.

The instructions must explain the particular interfaces used in the exercise and any recordkeeping students must do. Often, as in the three exercises described, the interface and recordkeeping are computerized,[5] but in principle, each of the three exercises can be run without a computer network. See Brock (1991) and Leuthold (1993) for versions of the VCM that do not require a computer network. Bergstrom and Miller (1997) provide many exercises that can be run without computers.

## Recordkeeping

The computer programs used in the exercises described in this chapter store data for use in subsequent classroom discussions, and for access by students during the sessions. However, it is often desirable to have students keep track of some payoff-relevant variables themselves. In addition to providing a way to store the data so that it can easily be used for later classroom discussion and to compute earnings, the recordkeeping helps students see the relationship between their decisions and the amount of the reward they receive. Student recordkeeping thus provides much of the learning that takes place during the exercises. In particular, it should clearly identify any student errors in decision-making that lead to losses. The method of recordkeeping (see Tables 4.4a and 4.4b) in the SD exercise, in which subjects must compute the marginal profit on each unit bought or sold, makes it apparent on which units they are making positive and negative profit.

## Running the Exercise

The timing of a session itself can take on different forms. Some exercises, such as the VCM, are run outside of class time over a period of weeks; the SD exercise is run during two 60-75 minute in-class sessions; and the CI exercise is designed for one 60-75 minute in-class session. Whether an exercise is run during class time or outside of class time, a typical sequence is:

1) Training with any software packages that are used. This phase should focus exclusively on the mechanics of using the software, such as which keys to press to perform particular actions.
2) Instruction and description of the economic system and recordkeeping. Instructions are often read aloud to the class by the instructor or assigned as required reading for the course. For some activities, instruction may precede the training with the software.
3) Quiz on recordkeeping and activity in the economy. In some exercises we find it useful to provide a simple written quiz to verify student comprehension. The instructor should provide the correct answers and clear up any confusion on the part of students. Students should be informed that scores on this quiz will not count toward their grade in the class.

4) Practice iteration(s). In more complex settings it is often important to use one or more practice rounds, where the results are not counted toward the extra-credit earned for the exercise.

5) Actual exercise with real incentives. Usually, as in all of the examples given in this chapter, the economic process is repeated several times.

## Follow-up Classroom Discussion

Design your laboratory economy with an eye to the subsequent classroom discussion. A classroom discussion can be effectively started by asking students to describe the strategies they followed in the exercise and why they chose their particular strategies. After identifying the strategies and reasoning, the relevant theoretical predictions can be revealed. Find and interpret any major discrepancies between theory and data.

We find that running the exercise before going over the relevant theory enhances the experience for students. It allows students to "discover" the theory themselves, and avoids suggesting to them that they follow a particular course of action that the theory specifies. We then find it effective to show students data from related research studies and previous classroom exercises, so that the students realize that their data are not anomalous. This also facilitates using experimental data with the class later in the term, when other topics are discussed.

## IV. DO'S AND DON'TS

This section contains some suggestions that instructors who are inexperienced with laboratory exercises may find helpful.

## Structure of the Economy

- Do make the set of possible decisions simple, so that students can easily evaluate the consequences of all options. A student's role can sometimes be made clearer by assigning a label to the agent indicating her function, such as "buyer" or "seller" in the SD exercise.
- Don't use labels on students' functions and strategies that bias them to make particular decisions. For example, we prefer the terms "group" and "private" account in the VCM exercise to the terms "generous" and "selfish" account, which suggest that one behavior is preferable to another purely because of the attached label.
- Do equalize each student's *expected* payoff so that no student perceives that the exercise is "rigged" against him. For example, in the SD exercise the demand and supply curves were constructed so that each agent receives equal surplus in the competitive equilibrium. In the VCM exercise, within each decision group, the game was symmetric. The CI exercise uses the same parameters for each student.

- Do make sure that *actual* payoffs vary considerably between outcomes resulting from good and from bad decisions in order to motivate students.

## Instructions

- Do provide instructions that follow closely those found in previously published research. These are usually known to be effective with undergraduate student populations, who comprise most subject pools employed in research studies.
- Don't use instructions that suggest specific courses of action. They should merely define possible actions, and the relationship between the students' actions and outcomes of the process.
- Don't use instructions that interpret the economy (such as "think of this as the New York Stock Exchange"); they should focus exclusively on the mechanics of activity in the economy and the recording of appropriate data.
- Do describe all aspects of the exercise. Ask yourself whether the instructions specify all important rules and information conditions. Students' questions can help to pinpoint this type of problem, and students should be encouraged to ask questions before the activity begins.
- Do include examples of the kind of situations that are likely to appear during the exercise. It is very important to include examples of how the students' earnings are calculated.
- Do keep the instructions brief. A clearly focused exercise does not need much explanation.

## Recordkeeping

- Do draw recordkeeping materials from previously published research, in which the data were gathered from undergraduate student populations.
- Do make sure that the students waste no time with recordkeeping. They should not have to record irrelevant information. Prevent extensive calculations by carefully choosing the parameter values used in the exercise.
- Don't allow the recordkeeping to provide misleading feedback to the students. For example, in the CI exercise, recording only the utility from consumption during each period without taking into account the terminal value of the remaining capital stock may mislead students into depleting their entire capital stock.
- Do provide a simple method of cross-checking the records for errors during or after the experiment. We often have the students calculate their earnings by hand and have the computer verify the calculations. This allows the students to receive the feedback provided by calculating their earnings, and also allows the instructor to identify errors and dishonest recordkeeping.
- Do try to have the data recorded in a format that can be easily displayed by a graphics package or a spreadsheet to facilitate classroom discussion.

## Running the Exercise (during class time)

- Do prepare before each session. Arrive early and place all materials required by students at the correct location before the students arrive. Activities that do not require student presence should not use up the limited time in which the students are in class.
- Do use software that has already been tested. If other people may have used the hardware after you last used it, test the software before you use it again.
- Do conduct practice iterations of the process to allow students to understand the exercise before the part of the exercise that counts toward students' earnings. Remember that students learn at different rates.
- Do give a short quiz testing the concepts and procedures given in the instructions, but do not count the quiz toward students' final grades.
- Do carefully estimate the duration of various parts of the session, such as the instructional phase, the practice phase, and the phase that counts toward their earnings, under the assumption that the session runs as planned without glitches. Then allow extra time for the sessions. Unforeseen events such as software, network or other hardware problems, student tardiness, misplacing of materials, or failure of students to understand directions can easily lengthen the time required to complete the exercise.

## Running the Exercise (outside of class time)

In addition to all of the "rules" for running an in-class exercise, keep the following additional rules in mind.

- Do be very clear about what students are and are not allowed to do in collaboration with each other outside of the classroom.
- Do create multiple decision groups, perhaps with different parameters, to minimize the extent to which one student can have another student "make his or her decisions."
- Do convey clearly the consequences of missing a decision round and how default decisions will be made.

## Follow-up discussion

- Do run the exercise before discussing the relevant theory in class. Discussing the theory first tends to lead the students to believe that the exercise is a test in which they are supposed to do what the theory predicts.
- Do emphasize only a small number of key points that students should take away from the exercises.
- Do avoid judgment statements such as "this was a bad decision" or "you should have done the following," in order to avoid embarrassing any student.
- Do provide data from similar research experiments or classroom exercises from previous courses.

## V. FINAL OBSERVATIONS

Introducing laboratory exercises into our undergraduate courses has improved our teaching by facilitating the exposition of economic concepts as well as by providing a refreshing break from the standard classroom lecture format. We recognize that there are substantial fixed costs[6] to be paid in learning a new teaching methodology and, for inexperienced instructors, laboratory exercises may "fail" for a host of reasons. However, as the instructor gains experience with the methodology, the exercises run more and more smoothly and require less and less effort.

Classroom exercises also provide benefits in our research agendas. The exercises create a subject pool of students who are trained in the appropriate software packages, which can be used in subsequent research projects. We find the classroom to be a useful place for testing procedures and programs for use in subsequent research experiments. Finally, the behavior we observe on the part of students adds to our intuition about human behavior in economic settings, and gives us, as experimental economists, research ideas to explore in subsequent projects.

## APPENDIX 4.A: THE VOLUNTARY CONTRIBUTIONS MECHANISM

This appendix contains the part of the instructions used for launching the VCM exercise.

### GROUP INVESTMENT EXERCISE

You will have the opportunity to earn extra-credit points in a decision making exercise referred to as the "Group Investment Exercise." Your participation in this exercise is totally voluntary. It is possible to get an A+ in this class based solely on your examination scores. Extra-credit points can only improve upon the course grade you would earn based solely on your exam scores.

The exercise consists of a series of ten decision-making rounds. In each round you will choose to allocate "tokens" between a "private account" and a "group account". When you log into the exercise for the first time (Round 1) the computer will present detailed instructions describing the exercise. After finishing the instructions you will make your allocation decision for Round 1. You will be able to review the instructions during all subsequent rounds if you wish to do so.

The computerized instructions explain how you can earn money by participating in this exercise. You will **NOT** be paid the money. Rather, you will receive extra-credit points based on: 1) the amount of money you earn over all ten decision rounds, and 2) the number of rounds in which you log on to NovaNET, view the results from the previous round, and enter a decision. The maximum number of extra-credit points that you can earn in this exercise is 3 and the minimum is 0. In general, **the more money you earn the greater the number of extra-credit points that you will receive.** The extra-credit points will be added to your final course average.

The following formula will be used to convert money earnings into extra-credit (EC) points:

EC points = [100 x (Actual Earnings)/(Maximum Possible Earnings)] x .02
              *score recorded in gradebook    weight in gradebook*

The ratio of actual earnings to maximum possible earnings can range from 0 to 1 for each individual. (In the unlikely event that an individual's final earnings are negative, the individual's final earnings will be set equal to zero – it is not possible to lose class points by participating in the exercise.) At the end of the final decision making round, this fraction will be computed for each individual (based on earnings in all rounds) and multiplied by 100. This gives each person a score of 0 to 100 which will be entered in your instructor's gradebook. This score will be multiplied by a weight of .02 to determine the number of extra-credit points received. For example, assume an individual earns 60 percent (100 x .6) of the maximum possible earnings. That person will have 60 x .02 = 1.2 extra-credit points added to their final average for the course.

In addition to the extra-credit points you earn based on your final earnings, you will receive (.1) of an extra-credit point for each round in which you participate by logging onto NovaNET and entering a decision. After the exercise is finished, the number of rounds in which you participated will be recorded in the gradebook with an associated weight of .1. Thus, you can receive 10 x .1 = 1 additional extra-credit point by simply participating in all ten decision rounds.

**Feel free to discuss any aspect of this extra-credit exercise with classmates if you care to do so. However, since extra-credit points are awarded for participation in the market, it is an act of academic dishonesty to have someone else enter your decisions for you.**

You can access the exercise on the NovaNET computer network from any of the Windows-NT-based public computing sites on campus. These sites include Wylie 125, Swain East 045, Lindley 025 and 035, Student Building 221, Ballantine 104, 108, and 118, Business 101, SPEA151, and Main Library 102A.

Access to NovaNET is available from the first level of icons displayed by the Windows-NT Program Manager. (If the previous user left your microcomputer in an application program, you may need to terminate the abandoned program. This can usually be accomplished by clicking on the icon in the upper left corner of the program's display window and then selecting "close".) After you have found the NT Program Manager icon labeled NovaNET double-click it with the left mouse button. This will open the folder containing the NovaNET access software. Double-click the red computer monitor icon labeled NovaNET. After a delay of a few seconds you will be presented with the NovaNET login page asking for your NovaNET group and name. To access the extra-credit exercise you must: 1) log into the NovaNET computer network, and 2) log into the NovaNET application program that runs the market.

To log on to NovaNET type your "NovaNET name" and "NovaNET group" as follows.

NovaNET name: **vcm**          NovaNET group: **iuecon**

After you successfully log on, you will be automatically routed to the title page for the exercise and asked to type your "class file" and your "roster name". Use the following information.

Class file: **jw201**

Roster name: **first 6 letters of your last name** plus the **last 4 numbers in your social security number**.

For example, if R. Raygun has SS#123-45-6789 then this student's roster name is entered as raygun6789. Similarly, O. McDonald with SS#333-24-4321 is entered as mcdona4321. V. Smith with SS#234-56-9876 is entered as smith9876.

After logging in for Round 1, you will be routed to a set of instructions that describe the extra-credit exercise. The first round will probably take less than 15 minutes (feel free to take all the time you find necessary). Entering your decision for subsequent rounds may take less time since you will not have to review the instructions unless you desire to do so. Your allocation decisions are automatically stored in the computer.

The starting times for each of the ten decision rounds are given below.

*[Starting and ending dates for rounds would be given here.]*

**Students who do not enter a decision for Round 1 will be eliminated from participating in all subsequent rounds and thus will earn 0 extra-credit points.** The instructions explain what happens for those students who participate in the first round but do not enter a decision in one or more of the other rounds.

The NovaNET computer uses special keypress names that can be selected by single-clicking with the left mouse button on the graphical "Function Key Bar" that appears to the left of the NovaNET display window. NovaNET keys are also mapped into the PC's function keys. The following NovaNET to PC key mappings are the most important ones to be aware of when using the economics software:

NEXT = Enter or Return, EDIT = F5, HELP = F6, LAB=F7, BACK = F8, DATA = F9, STOP = F10.

To erase a typed response, use the PC Backspace key ( ) or the EDIT = F5 key.

To exit a NovaNET application program, hold down the Shift key and hit F10 (Shift-STOP).

To end a NovaNET session **after properly exiting the application program**, click "File" on the menu bar in the upper-left corner of the NovaNET window and then click "Exit" to end your NovaNET session.

**Take this handout with you when you go to enter your decisions. If you have a problem accessing NovaNET, ask the UCS consultant for assistance. Please report any chronic NovaNET access problems to your instructor.**

## APPENDIX 4.B: CONSUMPTION INVESTMENT TRADEOFF

This appendix contains the complete instructions for the CI exercise.

This is a laboratory exercise in decision making. The instructions are simple and if you follow then carefully you can earn extra credit points for the course. The ........ students who earn the most tokens in the exercise will receive extra credit points. An important rule for this session is that once we begin, no one is allowed to talk or to communicate with anyone else.

1. How does the exercise work?
A. The exercise consists of a series of games
B. Each game will consist of .......... rounds. In each round you will make decisions about how much of two goods, A and X, to produce.
C. At the start of each game you will be given ......... units of good A.
D. You will be asked to make A and X by choosing quantities from the Production Schedule given to you.
E. You will then be awarded a fixed number of tokens based on how much X that you choose. You can see how many tokens you get for each unit of X on the sheet entitled "Token Value for X". You can receive tokens in every round. In each round the tokens you receive are added to your total. You will also receive tokens for the A you have after the final round in the game. You

can see how many tokens you get for A on the sheet entitled "Token Value for A".

F.   You will then be asked to make new A and X from the A you created in the last round. You will be awarded new tokens based on your new X. The new tokens will be added to your previous total.

G.   Notice that if you make too much X and too little A in the early rounds, you may not have enough A remaining to make as much X as you would like in the later rounds.

H.   There will be ...... games played that will count, each of which consist of ....... rounds.

I.   There will be ...... practice games. The practice game will also consist of ....... rounds.

The INPUT SCREEN allows you to input your choice. It also shows you the current game, shows you the choices of A and X you have made, and allows you to see the outcomes of all past games.  It is divided into two parts, the HISTORY window, and the INPUT window. The HISTORY window shows the outcome of the last game and all of the past games by pressing the Page Up and Page Down keys. The INPUT Window allows you to input your choice by moving the cursor to the Input A and Input X position by using the left and right arrow keys. Then type in your choice and press ENTER. After you enter your choices for both A and X, you can complete your choice by pressing the F10 key. You will be asked to confirm it by pressing the Y (for Yes it is the right choice) or by pressing the N (for No that is not the right choice). Pressing the N key will allow you to change your choice.

You have three sheets in front of you: the Production Schedule and two Token Value Sheets, one for X and one for A.

The Production Schedule indicates the amount of X and A which you can make from a given amount of A. This is to be used in all of the games and rounds. The first column indicates the amount of A you currently have. Columns 1-8 show the possible combinations of X and A which you can make. If you currently have 3 units of A you can make a total of 5 units of A and X for the next round. For example, if you have 3 units of A. you can make either:

4 units of X and 1 unit of A, or
3 units of X and 2 units of A, or
2 units of X and 3 units of A, or
1 unit of X and 4 units of A, or
0 units of X and 5 units of A.

The Token Value Sheets: one sheet is for X and the other sheet is for A. The sheet for X is to be used in every round and the sheet for A is to be used only in the last round of each game.

The first column contains the number of units that you made in the round. The last column, entitled Total Value, contains the total number of tokens that you receive from those units. The second column, entitled Unit Value, contains the additional number of tokens that you receive from the last unit you made. For example, in row 5, the number in the unit value column gives the additional number of tokens you receive from making 5 instead of making 4 units. The token value sheet for A contains the number of tokens you will receive for the number of units of A you have in the last round. It is used just like the token value sheet for X.

## APPENDIX 4.C: SUPPLY AND DEMAND WITH DEMAND SHIFT

This appendix contains part of the instructions for the SD exercise

### General Instructions
This is a laboratory exercise in market decision making. You should follow the instructions carefully. We are going to conduct a market in which some of you will be buyers and some of you will be sellers in a sequence of market days or trading periods. You have a sheet entitled Record of Purchases and Earnings which indicates whether you are a buyer or a seller, and describes the value to you of any decisions you might make. The currency used in the market is fictitious. The buyer with the highest earnings and the seller with the highest earnings at the end of the session will each receive 2 extra credit points added to their final course average.

### Specific Instructions to Buyers
During each market period you are free to purchase from any seller or sellers as many units as you might want. For the first unit that you buy during period 0, you receive the amount listed on your Record of Purchases and Earnings Sheet in the column labeled 0  in row (1) market 1st unit Redemption value; if you buy a second unit you receive the additional amount listed in row (4) market second period redemption value, etc.  The profits from each purchase are computed by taking the difference between the redemption value and the purchase price of the unit bought. That is:

YOUR EARNINGS = REDEMPTION VALUE - PURCHASE PRICE

Suppose for example, that you buy two units and that your redemption value for the first unit is 200 and for the second unit is 180. If you pay 150 for the first unit and 160 for your second unit purchased during the market period your earnings are:

earnings from first unit = 200 − 150 = 50
earnings from second unit = 180 − 160 = 20
total earnings = 50 + 20 = 70

The blanks on the sheet will help you record your profits. The purchase price for the first unit you buy during period 0 should be recorded on row (2) in the column labeled 0 at the time of purchase. You should then record the profits on the purchase on row (6). At the end of the period, record the total profits for period 0 in row (31) in the column labeled 0. Subsequent periods should be recorded similarly. The purchase prices and profits for period 1 should be recorded in the column labeled 1, etc.

[Similar Instructions for Sellers Are Omitted Here]

## NOTES

1. For an introduction to the major lines of research in experimental economics, see the textbook by Davis and Holt (1993).

2. The exercise is based on the work of Smith (1962) and uses some materials contained in Plott and Gray (1990).

3. There is a difference between a laboratory economy and a controlled experiment, which can be conducted using a laboratory economy. See Smith (1982) for a detailed discussion. For instructional purposes, we are willing to give up a degree of control over the environment that would be required in an experiment conducted for research purposes. Friedman and Sunder (1994) is a source of methodological advice, and Bergstrom and Miller (1997) offer a number of ready-made exercises.

4. The use of extra-credit points as incentives in classroom exercises is necessitated by the costliness of cash payments, especially for large classes. We cannot ensure that the extra-credit points will motivate all students, but it has been our experience that the incentives are strong enough to keep the interest of most students and induce behavior that allows us to illustrate the ideas we intend. We have allowed up to ten percent of a final semester class grade to depend on results of decisions in classroom exercises over the course of the semester. We have allowed decisions in one 60-75 minute class period to count for up to three percent of a semester class grade. See the discussion in Isaac et al. (1994) for a discussion of the issues related to the use of extra credit.

5. The VCM exercise at Indiana University is run using the NovaNet system. The CI uses a variation of a program developed at the University of Arizona. The SD exercise uses the Multiple Unit Double Auction software (MUDA) developed at the California Institute of Technology.

6. The nature of the fixed costs involved on the part of the instructor include learning how to use software and the time cost of any initial sessions that fail in the sense that no useful data are gathered for either procedural (e.g., poor planning) or technical (e.g., computer malfunction) reasons. It should be noted that another (opportunity) cost of laboratory exercises is any learning of any course material that

would have occurred during the time that students participate in the exercises. We believe that this cost is small for exercises run outside of class time. We also believe that the benefits of appropriately chosen in-class exercises can outweigh the cost in terms of material not covered. We have devoted up to 8 hours a semester (representing 20 percent of the semester's total contact time) to laboratory exercises.

## REFERENCES

Bergstrom, T., and J. Miller. 1997. *Experiments with economic principles*. New York: McGraw Hill.

Brock, J. 1991. A public goods experiment for the classroom. *Economic Inquiry* 29 (April): 395-401.

Browning, E., and J. Browning. 1989. *Microeconomic theory and applications*. Third Edition, Glenview Illinois, Scott-Foresman.

Davis, D., and C. Holt. 1993. *Experimental economics*. Princeton University Press.

Friedman D. and S. Sunder. 1994. *Experimental methods: A primer for economists*. Cambridge University Press.

Isaac, R., J. Walker, and A. Williams. 1994. Group size and the voluntary provision of public goods: Experimental evidence utilizing large groups. *Journal of Public Economics* 54 (May): 1-36.

Leuthold, J. 1993. A free rider experiment for the large class. *Journal of Economic Education* 24 (Spring): 353-63 .

Noussair, C., and M. Olson. 1997. Dynamic decisions in a laboratory setting. *Southern Economic Journal* 63 (April): 978-92.

Plott, C., and P. Gray. 1990. The multiple unit double auction. *Journal of Economic Behavior and Organization* 13 (2): 245-58.

Smith, V. 1962. An experimental study of competitive market behavior. *Journal of Political Economy* 70 (April): 111-37.

Smith, V. 1982. Microeconomic systems as an experimental science. *American Economic Review* 72 (December): 923-55.

Williams, A. and J. Walker. 1993. Computerized laboratory exercises for micro economics education: Three applications motivated by the methodology of experimental economics. *Journal of Economic Education* 24 (Fall): 291-315.

# CHAPTER 5

# INTEGRATING THE PRACTICE OF WRITING INTO ECONOMICS INSTRUCTION

**W. Lee Hansen**

How can the practice of writing be made an integral part of economics instruction in introductory courses, intermediate courses in the major, and graduate courses? To what extent can writing experiences effectively reinforce the process of mastering the content knowledge of economics and internalizing the skills of economic reasoning and analysis? How can writing experiences enhance the proficiencies that students studying economics should be expected to demonstrate at the end of individual courses and by the time they complete their degree work?

These questions are examined in this chapter. The answers offered are based on the author's long experience and interest in making writing an essential element in university instruction and student learning in economics. The success of this approach rests on developing a wide range of challenging writing assignments that give students practice in both writing about economics and learning more about economics. This approach can be even more valuable when writing assignments are nested within a larger framework of what might be called the instruction-learning process.

My interest in writing as a means of learning dates back to my undergraduate experience at UW-Madison. Despite the enrollment bulge of veterans during the late 1940s, faculty required students to do extensive writing, not only in required freshman composition courses but also in most other courses.  Indeed, the average amount of writing required in regular courses then is comparable to that required in what are now called Writing Intensive (WI) courses.  At that time faculty expectations were high, and most students seemed to think that they learned a good deal from their writing experiences.  I profited enormously from being required to write and rewrite papers to meet the high standards of faculty members who read and commented on our papers.  Out of this experience came an appreciation for the craftsmanship involved in transferring one's ideas onto paper.  Believing that my students would benefit at least as much, and because so many of them arrive with weak writing skills, I have always required extensive writing in my courses.

I also participate in the campus Writing Across the Curriculum (WAC) program.  This program, which began in the middle 1980s,  attempts to change faculty thinking about how students learn while it highlights the critical role of writing in the learning process. Participating faculty members, teaching undergraduate courses, give explicit attention to writing in their respective disciplines; writing should not be confined only to composition courses taught in English departments. The rationale behind this program, and comparable programs at other colleges and universities, is that by integrating writing into upper division courses in the major, students will not only improve their writing skills but also enhance their learning of the subject.  At the national level, especially at large research universities and at colleges where teaching loads are high, progress in implementing WAC seems to be slow.  The major challenges facing WAC programs are:  (1) reestablishing the importance of writing as a means of learning; (2) enlisting into these programs those faculty who already emphasize writing in their teaching; and (3) recruiting to the program other faculty members who display some interest in using writing to enhance student learning.  Based on my experience here and anecdotal evidence from other campuses, economists display considerable reluctance both to participate in WAC programs and to give greater priority to writing in their pedagogy.

I support the WAC approach by participating in workshops to help faculty who are scheduled to teach their first WI courses.  In addition, I regularly offer WI economics courses.  Teaching these courses requires little extra effort for me personally because I have always emphasized writing as an integral aspect of learning economics.  For most faculty, however, a considerable up-front investment is required to incorporate writing assignments into their teaching, and there is the ongoing challenge of finding time to read and evaluate student papers. Faculty need not think they must turn themselves into writing experts with an extensive knowledge of grammar and composition.  Rather, the secret lies in finding ways to leverage their efforts so that much of the burden is shifted to students, where it belongs.  The institution is responsible for understanding that faculty, by themselves, can do only so much.  Administrations must commit additional resources to make this approach work. In particular, they must establish writing centers that can offer students the specialized and individualized help most faculty cannot provide. It is also helpful to provide some paid assistance to help read and evaluate student papers, especially for large classes.[1]

The tangible returns from teaching WI courses can be enormously rewarding, notwithstanding the already mentioned costs. Not only can instructors gain much deeper knowledge about what their students are learning, but they are in a better position to improve their effectiveness as instructors. Students learn more economics and learn it better because they must not only explain clearly what they are learning, they must reflect further on what they have learned as they put their ideas into written form.

## I. WRITING IN ECONOMICS INSTRUCTION

The limited information available about writing in economic instruction indicates that undergraduate economics students do relatively little writing in their economics courses. An early 1980s study revealed that economics majors had written an average of about 4.5 papers of 5 pages or more in all their economics courses combined; almost 20 percent wrote no more than a single paper (Siegfried and Raymond 1984). In a 1990 survey, 77 percent of responding economics departments reported that a typical graduating economics major would have written at least 1 major economics paper; in only 22 percent of these same departments would the typical students have written more than 2 papers in all their economics courses (Siegfried et al. 1991). Still more recent information reveals that only 23 percent of instructors require term papers in upper-level courses, with even fewer doing so in principles, theory, and statistics/econometrics courses; shorter papers are even less popular, with only 11 percent of instructors requiring shorter papers (Becker and Watts 1996). An analysis of data used to norm the Test of Understanding College Economics indicates that term papers are required in only 12 percent of the principles courses, and this requirement, surprisingly, does not vary systematically with class size (Siegfried and Kennedy 1995).

The use of essay exams, another means of emphasizing writing, is also limited. The Siegfried-Kennedy study finds that in introductory economics courses, multiple-choice and true-false questions receive a 70 percent weight in determining course grades, as contrasted to a 19 percent weight for short-answer questions, and only 11 percent for essay or long answer questions; again, there is little variation by class size. The limited use of essay exams is consistent with the Becker and Watts study, which shows that only a quarter of the principles and quantitative courses use essay exams. Even more surprising, they report that only 40 percent of the upper-level courses in the major and the theory courses use essay questions.

To learn more about the status of writing in my own department and the writing skills of my students, I initiated several surveys. In an early 1980s survey,

I found that an embarrassingly small fraction of my department colleagues required students to write papers in courses taken by our majors, both because of the time required to evaluate papers and lack of confidence in their ability to help students improve their writing.  This situation has not changed appreciably over the last decade.  Based on surveys in the early 1990s, my freshmen and sophomore students consistently report being required to do relatively little writing in their other university courses.  In more than half of their courses, they wrote no papers.  In those where they did, the median number of papers they wrote came to two, of approximately three pages each.  Moreover, these students did relatively little writing during their senior year of high school;  the median number of papers they report writing for their twelfth-grade English class was four, and those were three to four pages per paper.  Similar surveys of juniors and seniors in intermediate economics courses show they do relatively little writing in their other courses; on average, they had written less than one paper.  In short, students enter the university with weak writing skills and are required to do little to improve these skills after they enroll.

Several changes are occurring.  From time to time, the Department of Economics offers a WI course as part of the WAC program, but offering such courses depends on the willingness of faculty members to teach them.  The all-university communications requirement that has recently been implemented should produce a major change in the amount and quality of student writing.  This requirement mandates a two-semester freshman communication-rhetoric course requirement for all students.  The second-semester course will be offered in a seminar format through departments and taught by regular faculty from those departments in an effort to introduce students to the nature of academic writing.  The requirement also calls for students to take two WI courses in their major, meaning that such courses will have to be created.  In principle, students in these courses will exercise and thus improve their writing skills.

The situation is not much better in doctoral programs.  Faculty in graduate programs have observed that the writing skills of most economics graduate students are at best modest, reflecting in large part students' limited writing experience as undergraduates.  A recent study of graduate economics programs (Hansen 1991, 1078) found that graduate students report having written an average of only three research papers by the beginning of their third year of study, despite completing roughly a dozen courses.  Moreover, less than a third report producing a research paper on their dissertation topic before launching their dissertation research.  Even more disappointing, less than a third of those who reported writing a pre-dissertation research paper had submitted that paper or some other paper for publication.  These patterns may reflect the research environments of departments, where faculty members are preoccupied with their own research, leaving them too busy to encourage paper writing.  These studies may also reflect weaknesses in the research skills of graduate students and their consequent inability to initiate writing research papers.  The cycle continues in part because sizeable numbers of graduate students possess limited writing skills, and thus many graduate faculty members are reluctant to require much writing.[2]

It seems fair to conclude that over the past two decades the writing climate in the economics profession and, similarly, in the University of Wisconsin economics department, has not been conducive to encouraging the development of student writing capabilities. Research demands on faculty have increased, particularly for younger faculty. Thus, faculty find it easier to reduce if not eliminate the assignment of papers and the use of essay-question exams. Additionally, the low quality of student writing skills has in turn discouraged faculty members from requiring students to do much writing. Large classes are another deterrent because substantial time is required to evaluate student papers, even if graduate teaching assistants are available to help in that task. Finally, because many economics faculty members are themselves not confident writers, they are reluctant to inflict what they see as their own weak standards on the papers of their students.

Research in economic education may also have dampened faculty enthusiasm for emphasizing writing as a method of learning in economics. Since 1984, the *Journal of Economic Education* has published only nine articles on writing.[3] For the most part, these articles describe the experiences of particular economists who make a regular practice of requiring student writing in their courses. Unfortunately, no body of research findings has yet emerged on the impact of writing on learning in economics. Research does reveal that inclusion of the essay questions in the Advanced Placement (AP) test in economics adds relatively little information about what students know that is not already captured in the multiple-choice question responses (Walstad and Becker 1994; Kennedy and Walstad 1997).[4] Whereas the authors indicate there may be other reasons for including an essay section in the AP exam, they conclude that the added costs of preparing and grading the essay questions do not justify the small amount of additional information they provide. Some have interpreted this conclusion as verifying a common perception among economics instructors, namely, that objective questions (usually multiple-choice questions) and essay questions measure essentially the same thing.[5]

In my view, multiple-choice and essay questions test different types of knowledge and skills, as do problems sets and term papers. Multiple-choice questions are certainly of great value in determining the relative levels of economic understanding among students in large lecture courses. Essay responses, which are not always feasible in large lecture courses, reveal much more about how individual students are able to analyze issues and express themselves. Papers, whether short or long, are even more valuable in both enhancing student understanding of economics and helping faculty evaluate what and how much students are learning.

The merits of requiring students to do more writing, especially in courses in the major, are discussed below. To help faculty develop writing tasks that contribute to the kind of learning we like to believe happens regularly in our classrooms, the writing assignments I have developed are placed within the context of specific proficiencies we can reasonably expect our students to demonstrate by the time they graduate.

## II. PROFICIENCIES IN THE DISCIPLINE

Faculty interested in using writing to enhance student learning can follow two approaches. One calls for simply inserting into an existing course syllabus a number of writing assignments that are limited to the appropriate material.[6] Students might be asked from time to time to write a short paper on some topic under discussion. But, unless these assignments are carefully developed, their cumulative impact on student learning may be negligible. Often, term papers are assigned, but students are given so little guidance that this exercise may not produce much useful learning. And, because longer research papers are typically submitted in the last week of the class, students learn little about how to improve their writing; nor do they benefit from instructor feedback that could enhance their understanding of the paper's subject.

Another approach takes a more systematic view of the purpose of writing assignments. It incorporates writing assignments that are designed to complement and enhance traditional modes of learning, and additionally, to prepare students to perform more effectively in their subsequent courses. To achieve these ends, students are called upon to produce a series of short papers on well-defined and progressively more complex topics. By receiving quick feedback on both their treatment of the subject matter and the skill they display in presenting the material, students are given opportunities to improve both their economic understanding and their ability to write with confidence and skill about economics. This is the approach I practice and advocate.

My broader objective is to help students develop what I call their proficiencies in economics. Proficiencies refer to the ability to combine subject matter knowledge and a set of complementary skills in ways that go beyond classroom assignments and examinations. The key question is this: after graduating, how can students demonstrate their ability to use the knowledge and skills they acquired while in college? Considerable agreement exists among economists about what we mean by subject matter knowledge in economics, as revealed by the similarities among economics textbooks at every level of instruction. Much less attention is given to skill development. Complementary skills refer to more than what might be called the skills of economists, for example, manipulating graphs, working with calculus, problem-solving, etc. These skills must include students' ability to speak confidently, write effective prose, make enlightening presentations, work together, and provide feedback to each other.[7] Without these skills, students will not be able to demonstrate what they know. The key is for students to use both knowledge and skills so that, once they graduate, they can be valuable employees, assets to the organizations they belong to, and fulfill personal goals as well.

Some years ago, I developed a set of proficiencies that might reasonably be expected of undergraduate economics majors by the time of their graduation. These proficiencies require that students acquire more than content knowledge and skills. The list of proficiencies evolved through consultation with a wide variety of experts, including fellow economists, an array of employers of economics majors, and survey responses from a number of our recently graduated economics majors. Five proficiencies resulted, each embracing progressively higher levels of cognitive skills (Hansen 1986).[8] A short explanation for how these proficiencies might be demonstrated through writing is indicated in each case.[9]

1. *Accessing existing knowledge*: Locate published research in economics and related fields; locate information on particular topics and issues in economics; search out economic data as well as information about the meaning of data and how they are derived.
2. *Displaying command of existing knowledge*: Write a précis of a published journal article; summarize in a two-minute monologue or a 300-word written statement what is known about the current condition of the economy; summarize the principal ideas of an eminent economist; summarize a current controversy in the economics literature; state succinctly the dimensions of a current economic policy issue; explain key economic concepts and describe how they can be used.
3. *Interpreting existing knowledge*: Explain what economic concepts and principles are used in economic analyses published in articles from daily newspapers and weekly news magazines; read and interpret a theoretical analysis, including simple mathematical derivations, reported in an economics journal article; read and interpret a quantitative analysis, including regression results, reported in an economics journal article.
4. *Applying existing knowledge*: Prepare a five-page written analysis of a current economic problem; prepare a two-page decision memorandum for a superior that recommends some action on an economic decision faced by the organization.
5. *Creating new knowledge*: Identify and formulate a question or series of questions about some economic issue that will facilitate investigation of the issue; prepare a five-page proposal for a research project; complete a research study whose results are contained in a polished 20-page paper.[10]

The challenge is to identify writing assignments that contribute to building and strengthening these proficiencies. I developed a grid, which appears later in this paper, listing each proficiency along with the sequence of writing assignments related to the proficiency. My objective is to ensure that the sequence of writing assignments moves from lower to higher-level proficiencies, that each proficiency is reinforced by the writing assignments, and that several overarching assignments simultaneously reinforce several proficiencies.[11] This process is part of the larger challenge of course design, and requires aligning the nature of instruction and student assignments with the objectives of the course.[12]

Reformulating individual courses and degree programs to focus on how they enhance student learning, defined as a set of proficiencies, appears to be an effective way to establish an appropriate teaching-learning process and, in turn, to define the mix of instructional activities within that process. If we want students to be able to demonstrate their proficiencies with distinction, we need to train them to do so. We must also recognize that attaining a set of proficiencies requires more than a lecture-exam approach, with problem sets added for good measure. It demands more active interplay between knowledge and skills, as well as opportunities for students to practice these proficiencies and bring them to bear on economic issues and policies.

In summary, the concept of structuring a course so that students attain a set of proficiencies provides a broader framework for thinking about the teaching-learning process. It helps both instructors and students focus their efforts on increasing learning by developing a coordinated approach to building students' knowledge and skills, with special attention given to writing as a means of learning.

## III. FRESHMAN-SOPHOMORE COURSES

For some years I used a one-semester elementary economics course to test many of my approaches, some of which had been developed earlier in advanced courses in the major. This elementary course covers both microeconomics and macroeconomics and is restricted to freshmen and sophomores. It enrolls between 50 and 100 students per semester, and it meets for four hours per week. Three hours are devoted to lectures, which include questions and some discussion. The fourth hour is a discussion section meeting, which I lead as tightly focused discussions of required reading assignments. For most of the past decade I taught this course as a WI course. This means that students receive some instruction in writing, they do a substantial amount of writing throughout the semester, and the quality of their writing assignments enters into the determination of their course grade. To ensure that students are aware of the writing emphasis and to help them with their writing, I require them to purchase at least one book on writing, such as Elbow (1981), McCloskey (1987), Williams (1994), or a writing handbook.[13] Because of the heavy volume of papers, I am assisted by a graduate student who helps read and evaluate students papers and exams; I also read a share of the papers because I want to know first-hand how my students are performing.

The course has two major objectives: to help students gain practice in thinking about and analyzing current economic issues and policies; and to improve the writing capabilities of the students. The first objective emphasizes (a) knowing about the structure of the U.S. economy, the major issues it faces, and the options for dealing with these issues; (b) understanding the evolution of economic thinking about the role of market economies with special attention to the transition of the former Soviet command economies; (c) internalizing a selected group of economic concepts and tools useful in analyzing current issues and policies; (d) learning how to apply these concepts and tools; and (e) gaining extensive practice in applying these concepts. These objectives reflect a combination of my experience in developing a K-12 curriculum guide for economic education (Hansen et al. 1977), extensive use of an excellent casebook for economics instruction (Fels et al. 1984),[14] and my conceptualization of proficiencies in the economics major (Hansen 1986).

The second major objective emphasizes the importance of (a) clearly written prose, illustrated by the selection of readings available in the course reading packet; (b) close reading of each week's assignments by students; (c) a questioning strategy that students can use in probing the meaning of each reading; (d) a method students can use in distilling the essence of each reading by engaging in structured writing about these readings; and (e) guidelines to help ensure a fruitful discussion of the readings during the discussion sections. These objectives stem from the same three sources mentioned above, and are augmented by my long-standing belief in the importance of writing as a way of achieving deep learning (Hansen 1993a), combined with many years of participating in a Great Books discussion group (Hansen 1978; Hansen and Salemi 1997).

A course that aims to reach these objectives calls for careful planning and coordination. For example, writing assignments must be linked quite directly to the flow of course content, and should involve the exercise of progressively higher proficiencies. The readings and discussion in the section meetings must be geared to course content and the instructional goals of the course. In addition, students need to be observed and evaluated by a consistent standard in all that they do. By teaching both the lecture and the discussion sections myself, it becomes possible for me to maintain tight quality control. Fortunately, I have always been able to select a highly literate and knowledgeable graduate student assistant to help read and evaluate the writing assignments.

With the background and objectives in mind, what kinds of writing assignments have proven successful in helping students learn introductory economics? Two assignments are tied directly to the weekly discussion section assignments. One calls for students to develop their skills at summarizing the assigned reading by preparing, in alternate weeks, either a written summary or a précis, ranging in length from 100 words to a maximum of 300 words (Tables 5.1a and 5.1b). A summary is a free-flowing statement composed on the basis of the student's reading and reflection. A précis is a summary created using the author's own words.[15] Précis writing has a long tradition in the English school system; it consists of progressively eliminating words, phrases, sentence, and paragraphs, until only the

**Table 5.1a: Writing a Précis**

Bring to discussion section next week a 200-word précis of Adam Smith's "Of the natural and market Price of Commodities" (Chapter 7, Book 1), which is included in your course Reading Packet. (See Guidelines on Précis/Summary Writing.)

**Table 5.1b: Writing a Summary**

Bring to discussion section next week a 200-word summary of Adam Smith's "Of the natural and market Price of Commodities" (Chapter 7, Book 1), which is included in your course Reading Packet. (See Guidelines on Précis/Summary Writing.)

essential ideas remain. Both the summary and précis represent challenging writing assignments for college freshmen, but they catch on quickly.[16] Most prefer writing summaries; students seem to want to display their "creativity" rather than going at the task more directly by preparing a précis. I collect the papers, review them quickly, make comments to help students whose writing is weak and to acknowledge those whose writing is strong, and return the papers the following week.

The other assignment asks students to develop questions about each week's readings. Their questions are then used to guide what occurs in the weekly discussion sections (Table 5.2). Students are told to bring to discussion section three questions that arise out of their reading and that they would like to have answered during our discussion. The questions they are asked to prepare are not ordinary questions of the kind they might prepare on their own. Rather, students are instructed on the role of questions in discussion and on the structure of these questions.[17] Essentially, students are asked to prepare one *factual* question, one *interpretive* question, and one *evaluative* question.[18] Factual questions clarify the author's words or facts. Interpretive questions are the most important because they help probe the author's meaning when that meaning may not be fully clear from a quick reading of the selection or some part of it. Evaluative questions focus on such matters as what the material may mean to the reader, or how the reading selection might compare with some other selection. Again, I collect the questions after class, review and comment briefly on them, and return them the following week.

These assignments are designed to help student learn how to display their command of existing knowledge. Most students have no experience with such controlled assignments. Over time, however, they see how these assignments fit into the larger purpose of the course, and their ability to summarize texts and to develop effective questions steadily improves. Even more important, their understanding of economics improves. So also does their appreciation for the positive versus normative aspects of economics, with the distinction between "what is" and "what ought to be." The contrasts between factual, interpretative, and evaluative questions are particularly helpful in reinforcing this distinction.

Another major type of writing assignment has two variants, calling for students to select articles from current newspapers and news magazines and then analyze these articles as "cases" in economic analysis (Fels 1984). The first variant asks students to locate articles that encompass two economic concepts, to write a brief essay elaborating the concepts (which may or may not be stated explicitly in the jargon of economists), and to explain how the concepts help readers understand the news article (Table 5.3).

The second variant calls for students to select articles describing a policy issue that in effect requires a decision by the reader. Students are instructed to follow Fels's (1984) "standard operating procedure" (SOP) in carrying out a case analysis and writing their essay. In essence, this SOP is the well-known scientific method adapted to economics. These case assignments are designed to reinforce the course objectives by equipping students with an array of concepts and principles, demonstrating how they can apply them to current events and policies, and giving them extensive practice in doing so. Because case assignments prove to be difficult for students, I demonstrate the case approach in some of my lecture presentations, first with descriptive concept cases and subsequently with policy cases. These

## Table 5.2: Formulating Discussion Questions

Bring to discussion section next week at least three questions---one factual, one interpretative, and one evaluative---for use in discussing Adam Smith's "Of the natural and market Price of Commodities" (Chapter 7, Book 1), which is included in your reading packet. (See Guidelines on Discussion Question Writing.)

## Table 5. 3: Identifying Economic Concepts

Select a recent newspaper article that deals with some economic issue and contains at least two economic concepts, either explicit or implied, that can help readers understand the article. On a photocopy of the article underline the portion pertaining to each concept and identify the concept in the adjacent margin. Then, on a single-spaced typewritten page explain these concepts and describe how they are being used. Think of yourself illuminating for a friend what these concepts mean and how they are used. This assignment is due two weeks from today. Be sure to staple a photocopy of the article to your paper. (See Guidelines on Concept Identification.)

demonstrations help students learn what kinds of news articles "work," and how to carry out their analyses. I also advise them on how to select good articles. In the process, they become better informed about newspapers and news-business magazines, and also about the many current economic problems and issues reported in these publications.    While students' first attempts to deal with the cases are weak, their work steadily improves; that is, they learn how to locate and select better articles and to analyze them with care. Typically, students are required to write one concept case (Table 5.3) and two to four policy cases (Table 5.4) during the semester.

In an effort to help students better understand what is expected in their case writing assignments, I use a special form to provide them with systematic feedback (Table 5.5).   I do not provide comments on every item in the Evaluation Sheet; often, an overall comment is all that is required. In other cases, specific comments offer guidance in particular areas. In addition, I often reproduce and distribute to the class copies of outstanding student responses, again, to help students see more clearly what is expected of them.  On occasion, I ask students to bring in an extra copy of their assignment, to be reviewed by another student, sometimes in class and at other times outside of class. The Evaluation Sheet helps students review the writing assignments of other students.  To make this a useful learning experience, I ask students to meet with each other for up to five minutes to discuss what they learned from reading each other's papers.  These discussions, while intense, are clearly beneficial; students regularly indicate the value of these exchanges on the course evaluation.

### Table 5.4: Analyzing a Policy Case

Select a recent newspaper article that deals with some policy issue and then apply Fels's "standard operating procedure" (SOP) in coming to a decision about what should be done.  The procedure you should follow calls for:

1. Defining the problem;
2. Specifying (a) the goals or objectives, (b) the policy options, and (c) the relevant economic concepts and principles;
3. Analyzing the consequences of each policy option, drawing on the relevant concepts and principles;
4. Using the results of (3) to evaluate the options according to each goal in turn; and
5. Deciding which option is best in light of not only the evaluations (4)  but also the importance of the different goals (2a).

Complete this assignment using no more than three single-spaced typewritten pages; be sure to attach a photocopy of the article to your paper.  Your paper is due two weeks from today. (See Fels's SOP in your Reading Packet.)

**Table 5.5: Evaluating Writing Assignments**

Name of Student Author _____

Adherence to Instructions in Reading Packet _____

Richness of the Article_____

Identification of Concepts _____

Adequacy of Analysis _____

Effectiveness of Presentation, (e.g., organization, grammar, punctuation, spelling, etc.) _____

General Comments _____

Grade on Content _____

Grade on Presentation _____

Still another assignment is an in-class essay based on a question that tests the ability of students to synthesize how they have learned to think about economic issues by drawing on a major reading from the last part of the course. By writing these essays, students not only interpret existing knowledge but also create new understandings and knowledge for themselves. These gains come from a combination of reading a probing and extended essay, engaging an in-depth discussion of the reading centered about the three-question format described earlier, and constructing an effective response to an encompassing interpretive question about the essay.

I distinguish between an in-class essay and an essay exam as follows. Examinations are usually time-pressured because students must answer a substantial number of short-answer and essay questions that are designed to sample their knowledge on a variety of topics covered over the previous 4-6 weeks. The in-class essay focuses on a topic they have studied and discussed extensively in class during the prior week. The in-class essay is designed to demonstrate how well they can synthesize their understanding of the material, express themselves within an explicit word limit, and do so when given a bit of time to reflect on what they are trying to write. An in-class essay is akin to the experience of having to draft a report for an employer or committee. I want students to learn how to write under what might be more reasonable constraints than those imposed by examinations.

I also believe it is important to encourage students to think deeply about the role of markets. An excellent reading on this topic is the classic book *Equality and Efficiency: The Big Tradeoff* by Arthur Okun (1975). For this in-class essay assignment, students are given a question that cuts across two or more of the four chapters in this book and requires them to really think, rather than to regurgitate what they have learned (Table 5.6).[19] During the several class meetings preceding the essay-writing exercise, the Okun book is discussed in detail. In addition, students are instructed on how to prepare to write their essays, the importance of collecting their wits and making a quick outline of their ideas before beginning to write, and the need for care in presenting their ideas clearly and effectively.[20] Students are told their essays should not exceed 500 words; to help guide them, they are given special sheets of lined paper on which to write their essays. Many essays are thoughtful and well written. The best essays reveal that students read and reflected on the readings. They provide specific detail to illustrate their argument, offer insights that have application beyond what is discussed in the reading, and connect their ideas smoothly and effectively. Simply reproducing the author's views is not sufficient. Students must also react intelligently to the reading selection. The grade on this in-class essay, which is evaluated both for content and presentation, counts for approximately one-third of the final examination grade.

Unlike other writing assignments, these papers are not returned to students, for three reasons: the grading cannot be completed before the end of formal classes, there is no time to provide even a helpful summary comment on each paper, and such comments would probably be ignored when students pick up their papers (at the end of the final exam). An additional reason is to prevent the questions (there are only a few good ones that can be used) from finding their way into the readily available exam files in the department, the dormitories, fraternities and sororities, and campus tutoring services. Although my failure to return these papers may seem at odds with the philosophy expressed here, I do offer students an opportunity to find out their grade on this part of the exam.[21] Here is one of those difficult compromises we all have to make. I further rationalize my decision by the extensive feedback they have already received on their writing.

One other writing assignment rounds out the list and helps students interpret and understand their knowledge of the course. Two days before the six-week, mid-term, and final examinations, each student must prepare and turn in two essay or short-answer questions suitable for inclusion in the upcoming exam (Table 5.7). Specifically, these questions should test students' analytical thinking. After students turn in these questions, I edit them, augment them to fill in any glaring omissions, and then duplicate copies for students to use in studying for the

### Table 5.6: Composing an In-Class Essay

Based on your reading of the Okun book, what is the relationship between Okun's concept of the "leaky bucket" and the goals of income equality and equality of opportunity? How would you characterize the relationship?

*or*

Drawing on all of your knowledge about the Okun book, how does Okun suggest we should evaluate the tradeoff between efficiency and equality in thinking about how to reduce poverty?

## Table 5.7: Preparing Exam Questions/Answers

Prepare two short-answer or essay questions for the upcoming exam, and write out your answers to each question. Do not submit factual questions, true-false questions, or multiple-choice questions. Instead, the questions should test people's analytical powers rather than simple recall of facts and figures, historical events, etc. You can gain some sense for the effectiveness of your questions by trying to answer them in writing.

---

examination; I also record whether these questions are turned in and rank the effectiveness of each student's questions in my record book. In making the assignment, I tell students that approximately half the exam questions will come from the list, although not all of the questions will be expressed in exactly the same words. This assignment is an excellent way to encourage student preparation for the examination. An added benefit is that I rarely receive any complaints about my examinations; students not only know how difficult it is to construct good short-answer and essay-exam questions, but they know that each of them had a potential role in creating the questions in the exam.

At the beginning of the term, students always ask how their writing assignments will be graded. I begin by explaining that they can expect quick feedback on their papers, with papers returned the week after submission, along with comments on both substance and presentation. They are also told that their papers will receive separate marks for substance and for presentation, with the overall grade on the assignment being an average of the two separate grades. The reason for two grades is quite simple; I want students to be aware that their writing skills are typically weaker than their ability to grasp the subject matter.[22] There is usually some grousing about this weighting scheme. My reply is that unless students can present their ideas clearly, the people reading and grading their papers will have difficulty knowing how well they understand the economics they are presumably learning.[23] Students generally accept this approach. A few are critical of the process when I return their first one or two assignments, perhaps because they have never been told that their writing is deficient in some way. Their objections fade as they come to realize that presentation and content are integrally related and as they discover that the comments on their papers are designed to help them improve their writing.

## IV. JUNIOR-SENIOR COURSES IN THE MAJOR[24]

For many years I regularly taught a labor economics course designed for economics majors; it was structured as a WI course, emphasizing the five proficiencies expected of economics majors, as described earlier. I assumed that through their earlier courses, in economics or other departments, students had acquired some level of the first two proficiencies: accessing existing knowledge, and displaying command of existing knowledge. Students had less experience developing higher-level cognitive skills. Thus, I gave more attention to enhancing the third and fourth proficiencies: interpreting existing knowledge, and applying existing knowledge. On several occasions, I concentrated heavily on the fifth proficiency, creating new knowledge, including the formulation of questions and analytical approaches needed to answer those questions.

As in my elementary economics courses, I assigned précis writing and question framing, along the lines indicated in Tables 5.1 and 5.2. These assignments proved to be both new and useful to my students. I also regularly asked students to prepare questions for inclusion in the exams (Table 5.7). This practice is more beneficial in smaller classes, where I rely exclusively on essay and short-answer examination questions.

To help students think about quality writing and to induce them to read beyond the textbook and other assigned readings, I ask them to begin collecting well-written articles by economists, preferably on topics closely related to the subject matter of the course (Table 5.8). I wanted students to look for examples of good writing and to learn from analyzing these examples, thus reinforcing the first three proficiencies. I advised students on the prime sources of exemplary writing about economics, *The Economist*, the *Wall Street Journal*, *The New York Times*, and *Business Week*. I also directed them to the work of such writers in economics as Paul Krugman, Milton Friedman, Peter Passell, Leonard Silk, and Lester Thurow. In addition, I provided some formal instruction in writing, making use of a book on improving writing skills (e.g., Elbow 1981; Lanham 1979; McCloskey 1987; Williams 1990), critiques of student papers from previous semesters, and other published materials. During the semester each student located perhaps a half-dozen examples and learned a good deal from the search and evaluation process. After

## Table 5.8: Identifying Excellent Writing in Economics

During the course of the semester you should keep an eye out for well-written articles about economics, particularly about the subjects covered in this course. After finding such items, you should write a brief, one-page critique of each article and submit a photocopy of the article and your critique to me. This assignment will help hone your critical abilities and force you to read more widely. By the 12th week of the term, I want copies of what you consider to be two good pieces of economics writing, accompanied by a one-page analysis of each as to why the writing is good. I urge you to pick something out of a recent newspaper or magazine; see the syllabus for suggested sources. One of your selections can be part of some larger work; but, if you follow this approach, confine yourself to a section of prose no longer than 10 pages.

students turn in their examples and interpretative essays on each example, I read and returned their submissions, offering several summary comments on their essays and my qualitative assessment of their submissions.

Much of economics, and certainly my approach to it,  focuses on developing students' proficiencies in applying existing knowledge to real world, current issues and problems.  This means I regularly construct new writing assignments that pick up on these issues and problems.  Here I describe a few of the assignments that successfully emphasize both substantive knowledge of labor economics and how to present that knowledge effectively.

In reviewing these assignment descriptions, readers should realize that the key to effective writing assignments is to ensure that they utilize the knowledge and skills students have already acquired; are specific as to purpose, audience, and required details; and are defined in terms of length and due date.  When assignments meet this test, students can focus on the substance of the assignment without having to guess what the instructor is "looking for."

In one assignment, I assume that students have mastered the lecture and reading materials on the minimum wage (Table 5.9).  The assignment asks them to go beyond that knowledge and indicate how the effects of a change in the minimum wage might be evaluated or assessed.  This is a demanding assignment that forces them to think about how to evaluate empirically the impact of a government program.

## Table 5.9: Analyzing the Minimum Wage

Because you have learned more about the minimum wage issue than (by my rough estimates) 99.9999 percent of the adult population, 99.8 percent of all undergraduates, and 95.0 percent of all college economics majors, you find yourself employed by a major economics research organization that wants you to prepare a quantitatively-oriented paper or report evaluating the likely effects of the currently debated increase in the minimum wage. The focus should be on comparing the situation over the past several years with the situation in the several years after next year's expected increase in the minimum wage. Your instructions are to prepare a double-spaced report, not to exceed four pages (you may attach illustrative tables or data as appendices on no more than three additional sheets of paper), that outlines your plans. Turn in three copies, two for me and one for another reader. Papers will be due in class on Wednesday of the 6th week of the term.  I suggest that you begin early so that you don't have to write your paper under pressure the night before it is due. Also, talk with other people to test your ideas.  Read whatever seems to be on the subject and useful to you.  At the same time, try to figure out what people would want to know about the effects of raising the minimum wage. Think even harder about how you would discover or estimate what these effects might be.

Another assignment asks students to exercise all five proficiencies, particularly the one calling for the creation of new knowledge. I wanted students to go beyond what is already known, in this case what is known about the meaning of the "misery index." Students are asked to tap their creative juices to help resolve a problem so apparent during the late 1980s when the misery index fell, indicating improved economic conditions, while at the same time real economic well-being declined (Table 5.10). The challenge for students is to define economic well-being, seek out a measure of it, and integrate that measure with the other two misery index measures of inflation and unemployment. Of course, there is no single correct response. Indeed, finding some way to blend these several measures is very difficult, and few students do a first-rate job on this assignment. When the papers are returned, we have a lively discussion of the assignment and how various students tackled it.

Still another assignment requires students to synthesize what they are learning and in the process enhance their proficiencies of interpretation, application, and creation. Specifically, they must incorporate the substance of a controversial research paper into their textbook presentation of that subject (Table 5.11). The particular paper argues that women's preferences for particular jobs and working conditions, rather than employer wage discrimination, account for most of the

## Table 5.10: Creating a Quantitative Analysis

While Arthur Okun's "misery index" is well known for capturing the combined effects of unemployment and price increases, it says little about changes in the real level of economic well-being. Based on the attached tables B-46 and B-47 from the *Economic Report of the President*, it is quite apparent that gains in employment have been substantial over most of the entire postwar period but that increases in real well-being slackened since the early 1970s. The reasons for this change are not at all clear.

Your task is to prepare a two-page, single-spaced, memo, addressed to labor economists and perhaps macroeconomists as well, responding to the following question: How would you modify the misery index, which is a combination of the unemployment rate and the consumer price index, so that it also takes account of changes in real economic well-being? In preparing your response, make clear what you mean by "real economic well-being." Insert the appropriate information in a worksheet and calculate a new misery index. Be sure to describe exactly how you calculated your new index: readers should be able to replicate your work.

You may find it helpful to consult additional tables in the *Economic Report*, notably B-27, B-30, B-32, B-44, and B-45. (Copies of the tables are on reserve.) Your papers are to be turned in two weeks from today.

### Table 5.11: Understanding Wage Discrimination

Your assignment is to write either a new section in the Ehrenberg-Smith (E-S) textbook or a separate essay, based on the "The XYZ Corporation," an article that appeared in *The Public Interest* journal some years ago, and which is in the reading packet. The new section in the E-S book is to be written for insertion somewhere between pages 544 and 560. Your task is to write a section that deals with the situation discussed in the XYZ piece, showing how that situation fits with the other explanations of discrimination presented by E-S. Be sure to describe exactly where you would insert your section and indicate what the title of the section would be. Alternatively, you can write a separate essay to describe how the situation discussed in the XYZ piece fits into the literature that seeks to explain wage discrimination against women.

Your response should not exceed four double-spaced pages. You should assume that readers of your essay do not know the contents of the XYZ piece, thus making it incumbent on you to give them some indication of what the piece has to say. Your main task is not to summarize the XYZ situation. Rather, you are to interpret it and apply your knowledge so that readers can better understand the explanations of discrimination against women workers traditionally discussed in the textbooks, as in the E-S text we are using. Three copies of this paper will be due in class two weeks from today.

male-female difference in earnings. Discussing this assignment when the papers are returned requires tact because most students, particularly female students, accept the employer wage-discrimination view.

Another assignment calls for students to display their creativity and ingenuity in using the knowledge already acquired in the course, and to conduct research on a particular topic. Each student is asked to prepare a labor market analysis for an occupation (Table 5.12) of the kind they or their fellow students hope to enter after graduation. This assignment works well because students have an opportunity to indicate their preference for the occupational labor market they will investigate; if too many students request the same occupation, I give them their second request. One semester, I allowed students to work in pairs to help resolve this problem. What distinguishes this assignment from the others is that it requires research skills. Most students like this assignment because of its obvious value to them; recently a returning student said this assignment directly influenced his career choice.

Several years ago, I decided to do something quite different in an advanced undergraduate course in labor economics, namely, emphasize the proficiency of creating new knowledge through a research project. I developed a list of researchable topics that could not be answered by library research; the topics all required independent creative effort. Among them were the following: What is the

## Table 5.12: Completing a Labor Market Analysis

Your assignment is to prepare an occupational labor market analysis whose purpose is to inform interested people like yourself about the conditions that prevail in that line of work. This analysis should include a brief description of the nature of the occupation, the training and skills normally required for entry, barriers to entry, numbers and compensation of those in the occupation, the evolution of this labor market over the past decade or so, and the future outlook for this occupation in the near term (next couple of years) and the long term (next decade or so). To the extent that you can identify special problems with this labor market, please do so.

You will be assigned a particular occupation to analyze. I will try to select an occupation you listed in your preferences today. But, to avoid having many people working on the same occupation, some of you will be assigned other occupations. You can pick up your specific occupational assignment, along with selected sources of information, beginning at 11:30 am Thursday. You are encouraged to discuss this project with other students in the class for source material and ideas.

Your paper is to be completed and submitted at class time on Monday during the 5th week of the term. Turn in three copies of the paper; one will be for me to retain; another will be returned with my comments; and the third will be read and evaluated by another student. Your paper should not exceed ten double-spaced pages, and is to be followed by an additional page citing your information sources. You may include up to five additional pages of tables, figures, etc. to help illuminate your text; these materials can be photocopies from the original sources, but you must provide exact information on the sources of this information. The text of your paper should tell the story you want to convey, with explicit references to each table, figure, or other material you append to the paper.

likely impact of the current recession (this was January 1991) on employment and unemployment in Wisconsin? If the Gulf War requires reimposition of a military draft, analyze the possible effects on pay structure and war costs resulting from the necessity of integrating new draftees with volunteers. What is the current magnitude of the "union wage effect" (the percentage difference between the wages of unionized and nonunionized workers)? Because the class enrolled 50 students, I used a team approach. Thus, rather than attempting to supervise fifty individual research papers, the use of five-person teams of students cut the number of projects to ten. This step greatly reduced the time needed to supervise these research projects. In addition, students benefitted from the process of collaboration and the interplay among team participants. Considerable care is required in pursuing this approach, which is described more fully elsewhere (Hansen 1993b). Everyone enjoyed participating in this venture, despite some inevitable problems. I recommend this approach to faculty who feel comfortable breaking away from traditional modes of instruction and learning.

One class period near the end of the semester is always devoted to an in-class writing assignment that gives students an opportunity to demonstrate their proficiencies. In short, I want to find out how well students can respond to an issue, one we have read about and discussed at some length in class, in a less pressured situation than an examination, which puts a premium on speed of recall and quickness in composing answers. In this assignment students are given the full class period to compose a 600-word essay on some major topic of interest in the course, usually centered on a recent reading assignment and class discussion (Table 5.13). The topic is phrased in the form of a question so as to help students focus their essays. The question is not revealed before the class meets, but students have a good idea of the possibilities because we typically spend the previous two class periods analyzing and discussing the subject. Thus, students have the necessary background information to use in constructing their responses to what is a quite open-ended question.

For all but this last assignment, I make sure that students have ample opportunity to read and comment on the papers written by their fellow students. I begin early in the semester by having students bring extra copies of their writing assignments, which are distributed to pairs of students. Students are asked to read each other's papers and then given about five minutes to exchange comments on their respective papers. In another variation, students are asked to provide written comments on the papers of other students, using a standard appraisal form, depending on the assignment, to guide them in developing their comments. To help students understand the importance of this activity, I explain that the academic

## Table 5.13: Writing an In-Class Analysis

Write an essay of approximately 600 words that describes what modifications might be required in the recently proposed voluntary national service program (assume the program goes into effect next year) in light of the changing demography of the youth population. You should assume your audience has read the same book on national service you have read and hence does not need to have the concept or the program's details explained. Your presentation should reflect what you are learning in this course: Economics 450, Wages and the Labor Market.

Before beginning, you may want to outline your ideas so that you will have a better conception of how to write your essay and what to include in it. Write your essay on the three lined sheets given to you to help you limit the length of your response (three pages with eight words per line and 25 lines per page yields 600 words).

papers faculty members write are regularly reviewed by other academics to determine if they are worthy of publication, and that faculty regularly seek comments and suggestions by circulating drafts of their papers to colleagues.

Students are given several opportunities to comment on the papers of other students in what might be called a peer review process. The guidelines and appraisal form prepared to facilitate student comments on each other's papers appear in Tables 5.14 and 5.15. After students have commented on other students' papers twice, I ask them to give me a copy of their paper, to which they have stapled the written comments of their fellow student. I do not grade their submissions but do review them and present a summary at the beginning of the next class period about what I observe in the comments. Several benefits result from this practice. Students learn that there are many different ways to approach a single topic, both in substance and mode of presentation. Moreover, students not only become more critical readers but also learn that writing critiques is not an easy task. Students realize that they can benefit enormously from talking with fellow students before and after writing their papers about both the substance and presentation of their ideas. Finally, students become much better acquainted with

## Table 5.14: Evaluating Student Papers

Give thought beforehand to how you want to evaluate the paper based on the criteria listed below. As you read the paper, write down in the margins whatever comments or questions occur to you about its substance, problems of presentation, etc. After you complete an initial reading of the paper, go back over it and think about your responses to each of the criteria listed below. Note your comments under each criteria. If you are able, indicate what weight (e.g., 20 percent) you would give to each criteria.

*Responsiveness and Understanding.* Is the paper responsive to the question it addresses? Does it reveal a clear understanding of the topic? Does it reflect a high level of thinking? Does it reflect careful research? Does it demonstrate originality?

*Communicating the Results.* Is the paper thoughtfully organized? Does it make its major points in some logical way? Does it present pertinent information and illustrations? Does it address effectively its presumed audience?

*Writing Style and Mechanics.* Are the paragraphs coherent and fully developed? Are the individual sentences constructed so that they contribute effectively to the author's purpose? Are the words used appropriately, with exactness, and clear sense of their meaning? Is the paper free or nearly free of mechanical errors (spelling, grammar, sentence fragments, and punctuation)?

*Your Overall Evaluation.* How do you rate the overall effectiveness of this paper?

*Note Specific Matters Requiring Attention.*

## Table 5.15: Appraising Student Papers

Title of Paper _____

Author's Name _____

Reviewer's Name _____

Comments

Is the problem clearly stated? _____

Does the paper address its audience? _____

Does the paper reflect in-depth analysis? _____

Is the paper thoughtfully organized? _____

Is the grammar correct? Is the sentence structure correct?_____

Are the style and tone appropriate? _____

Other comments

What did you learn from this paper? _____

What questions do you have for the author? _____

What, if anything, has the author overlooked? _____

What is the paper's greatest weakness?_____

What is the paper's greatest strength?_____

What is your overall evaluation of the paper? _____

---

each other and as a result are more likely to discuss the course material with each other both before and after class. Even a couple of minutes of additional discussion can reinforce the learning process. In a sense the peer review assignment gives students a chance to draw on their proficiencies while they assess how fellow students can demonstrate these same proficiencies. The effect reinforces my focus on proficiencies as an organizing device for the course.

In grading student papers, I used both forms. Early in the semester I rely on the appraisal form (Table 5.15); later I shift to the evaluation form (Table 5.14) because of its greater emphasis on the quality of student writing.

On the matter of grading, I take a somewhat different approach in both the elementary and intermediate courses. I give the précis and question assignments scores of 2 for excellent, 1 for okay, and 0 for unsatisfactory. The first concept case and first policy case are not counted in the final grade, but I do give students some indication of their performance, using a 3, 2, 1, 0 scale, rather than conventional grades (A, AB, B, etc.). I follow this approach so that students will realize very early in the semester the importance of trying to improve the quality of their work. Thereafter, two conventional grades are assigned to each paper, one for content and one for presentation. When students turn in weak papers, I withhold their grades until a revised paper is turned in that incorporates my comments; students cannot improve their grade but I do note in my records if they submit a revised paper. At the end of the semester, I convert the numeric scores into letter grades, weight the various grades for the different elements of the course, as described in the syllabus, and arrive at a final course grade.[25]

Obtaining feedback from students on the writing component of a course can be both rewarding and painful. Believing that it is better to know what students think, I supplement the standard course evaluation form with several questions about the writing intensive emphasis. The questions I typically ask include the following: (1) Did you find the writing assignments useful? Please explain; (2) Were my comments on your papers helpful? Not helpful? Please explain. (3) What did you learn from reading and commenting on the papers of other students? Do you recommend continuing this practice? (4) Should there have been more writing assignments? Fewer? Different kinds of writing assignments? Explain. (5) What reactions did you have to the assigned book on writing more effectively (e.g., Elbow 1981; Lanham 1979; McCloskey 1987; Williams 1992; or the writing handbook)? (6) Do you have any other suggestions for improving the writing component of the course?

Students' responses are always useful in refashioning some assignments and fine-tuning others. Frequently, some assignments that I thought were brilliant turn out to have been too difficult for students to handle. Repeated assignments, for example, policy cases, are often not appreciated by students because "they didn't require us to do anything different." Other students indicate their gratitude for being required to write and for the helpful comments made on their papers. More important than any of these comments is the elusive sense that students gain substantially from the explicit interplay between course content and writing about that content, and from the focus of these assignments on an explicit set of proficiencies the course seeks to develop.

## V. GRADUATE EDUCATION

Writing to learn played a major role in my graduate education. While working for an M.A. at the University of Wisconsin-Madison and subsequently for a Ph.D. at The Johns Hopkins University, research papers were regularly required in virtually every course, from the beginning theory/and statistics courses to the most advanced seminars. At Johns Hopkins, the Political Economy Department's Journal Club gave students excellent experience in critiquing recently published papers they selected from the major economics journals. Indeed, flaws were typically uncovered, and writing up the criticisms later often led to a published note. As a result, graduate students gained substantial research experience, from time to time were able to start building their publication record, and sometimes discovered a dissertation topic as well.

Because graduate education is dedicated to building the research capabilities of students, because writing is so critical to that process, and because less writing seems to be demanded in recent years, more emphasis on writing is clearly required. Providing this emphasis poses several challenges. One is convincing both faculty members and graduate students that more writing must be done. The next is figuring out how to integrate writing into individual courses and into graduate programs. The third is finding the best way to integrate more writing in the first-year courses that focus strongly on mastering the intricacies of economic theory, the needed mathematics, and the econometric skills now expected of new economics doctorates.[26]

Just as proficiencies can be specified for the undergraduate major, they can be specified for graduate study, as they were in the American Economic Association's study by the Commission on Graduate Education in Economics (Krueger et al. 1991; Hansen 1991). In graduate study, the key proficiency to be developed is the ability to formulate, carry out, and produce research studies. The Ph.D. dissertation provides the culminating experience. The challenge of most graduate courses is to help students prepare for that experience. Traditionally, the focus of graduate study is on content knowledge. In economics, such knowledge can be grouped into six categories: economic theory, econometrics, economic institutions and policy, economic literature, economic applications and policy issues, and empirical economics. Equally important, though, are what might be called "complementary skills" that can be divided into seven categories: critical judgment, analytics, applications, mathematics, computation, communication, and creativity.[27] These categories of knowledge and skills are honed through core and field courses, minor requirements, preliminary examinations, research papers, and ultimately the dissertation. Yet, evidence from the extensive surveys of economics faculty, graduate students, recent Ph.D.s, and employers of new Ph.D.s indicates that the two skills receiving the least attention are communication, which includes writing, and creativity (Hansen 1991). Most graduate students believe it is too late to develop strong communication skills. And, although many faculty would argue that creativity cannot be taught, it certainly can be nurtured.

An ideal vehicle for simultaneously developing the skills of communication and creativity, and enhancing research skills, is through preparation of what I call "idea papers." The purpose of these papers, which are limited to one single-spaced page, is to unleash the creative potential of students at the very start of the semester when they are still barely acquainted with the subject matter of the course. In these papers, students are expected to identify questions, issues, or puzzles they would like to understand, suggest how they would go about gaining this understanding, and in effect develop a brief but well-written research proposal (Table 5.16). Students are told that these papers can help them identify topics for the research papers they will write in the course.

To write good idea papers, students must begin to sample the course readings immediately, particularly the readings assigned early in the semester that provide an overview of the substantive material to be studied later. Equally important, they need guidance on how best to expand and deepen their learning capacities, skills

## Table 5.16: Composing Idea Papers

Bring to next week's class meeting two single-spaced, approximately 500-word "idea papers." Each paper should focus on a question, highlight an issue, deal with some policy proposal, etc., that arises out of your initial reading assignments and your reflections on what you are learning. Each paper should also indicate what steps might be taken to investigate your question, issue, or proposal. In effect, you can think of your idea papers as brief proposals for research projects.

that most undergraduate courses fail to emphasize. They also need help in developing their ability to frame creative yet manageable research questions. Several readings offer helpful guidance: Platt (1963); Mills (1959); Patton (1980); Roberts and Sergesketter (1993). The two chapters by Platt on "The Art of Creation" (ch. 7), and "The Motivation of Creation" (ch. 8) are excellent in conveying what is involved in intellectual work. Mills's Appendix "On Intellectual Craftsmanship" offers valuable suggestions for generating and pursuing potential research topics. Patton describes how he wrote an assigned research paper during a seven-day period, as part of a doctoral program requirement. The Roberts and Sergesketter book describes useful ways of increasing both personal and professional efficiency in the knowledge field. All of these readings emphasize the importance of developing thinking skills and stimulating one's own creativity.

For each of the first three weeks of a graduate seminar, students are required to write and turn in two 500-word idea papers per week, for a total of six papers. Each week students circulate copies of their two papers to all other seminar participants, briefly summarize one of their papers in class, listen to oral comments on their proposals from fellow students, receive brief written comments from a designated commentator, and benefit from both the class reaction and the inevitable informal discussion that occurs after the class session ends. I provide brief comments on their first two papers to ensure that students are on track. The papers improve each week as students learn how to pose researchable questions, narrow the focus of their questions, and appreciate the importance of writing clear, economical prose. One of the six papers each student writes usually offers a useful starting point for an individual research project. Graduate students always comment favorably on the practice of writing idea papers, both in the course evaluation survey and in their informal comments to me. Indeed, many remark that it is the high point of the seminar because it allows them to begin thinking for themselves.

Traditionally, graduate students in seminars are required to write research papers or produce a well-developed research proposal. Rather than giving students free rein, I impose a structure on how they select their research topics, organize their research activity, turn in timely drafts, produce the final paper, and respond to my comments on their papers. To help them get started, I distribute a standard proposal format long used by the Department of Labor to select recipients of doctoral dissertation research grants; unfortunately, this program is now defunct. Yet, the proposal format is helpful because most students have neither seen nor written a research proposal. Spelling out the ground rules for producing students papers and proposals, presenting them, and critiquing them is also critical to the success of the seminar. A copy of the schedule is attached (Table 5.17).

Students experience their greatest difficulty figuring out how to present their results. Again, most students have never had to meet the demanding standards we associate with graduate-level research papers. Having worked with doctoral students and listened to their job market presentations, it is clear that many students have no sense for how to present their ideas, either in writing or in an oral

## Table 5.17: Preparing Research Papers/Proposals

You are to prepare two, two-page idea papers for each of our meetings during the second, third, and fourth meetings of the semester. The purpose is to prime the "idea pump," in the belief that one of these idea papers will prove to be the subject of your research paper. By the end of the fifth week, each seminar member is to have selected a research topic, clearing it with me during a personal meeting during my office hours. To assess your progress, keep you on track, and offer helpful suggestions, I want to see a preliminary draft of eight pages, by the end of the seventh week. Copies of this draft should also be given to the two students who are designated as your readers. Each reader is responsible for providing written comments on that draft by the beginning of the ninth week.

Students will give oral presentations beginning during the thirteenth week. Authors are to deliver two copies of their paper to me and one to each of their two readers at least two days before their scheduled presentation. After the author's brief ten-minute presentation, one reader will present a five-minute oral comment on the paper; before the presentation, the reader will distribute to other seminar members, including the author, a one-page summary of these comments. On the day following the presentation, the other reader will provide to the author and the other reader detailed written comments on the paper and its presentation. Copies of these written comments are also provided to me.

Authors have one week to make whatever revisions seem appropriate, after which they turn in two copies of their paper for grading. They will also submit a two- to three-page statement describing the changes they made in their paper since presenting it and the rationale for these changes. I will comment on the paper, grade it, and return one copy of the paper within a week of its receipt.

Seminar papers and proposals will be evaluated on the basis of the early draft, final draft, oral presentation, oral and written comments of the readers, and improvements in the paper made in response to the oral and written comments of the readers, as well as reactions from other seminar participants.

presentation. Some years ago I devised a set of questions, along with the underlying purpose for each question, to guide their preparation (Table 5.18). Basically, I suggest they try to respond to questions that members of their audience are likely to raise as they read a draft paper or hear it presented. If researchers can answer these questions, they should feel reasonably confident that they have done as much as they can to cover likely points of weakness. While these questions may not fit every presentation, they will help to ensure that listeners, as

## Table 5.18: Organizing Research Papers/Proposals

Students often experience difficulty organizing a research paper or proposal. In my own work, I find it useful to force myself to answer a well-structured set of questions. Here they are. I hope they will be helpful.

1.  What, in 25 words or less, is the question you are trying to answer?
    *Purpose*: Framing a question helps sharpen your focus.
2.  Why is this question important, and to whom? What is the puzzle you want to unravel? Are you merely curious? Do you hope to affect policy, resolve a dispute, illustrate a new approach?
    *Purpose*: Tell the reader about your intentions.
3.  What approach do you plan to follow in trying to answer your question? Is the approach entirely new? A variant on an existing approach? A unique combination of several existing approaches?
    *Purpose*: Provide a framework for conceptualizing the topic and spelling out the research plan.
4.  What methodology will be applied in carrying out your research? What data will you use and how will it be gathered or obtained? What other kinds of information will be utilized?
    *Purpose*: Explain how you will produce your evidence and how it will answer the question guiding your inquiry.
5.  What difficulties are you likely to encounter in applying your approach or methodology to the data and other information you gather?
    *Purpose*: Be up front about difficulties so that you recognize potential problems and possible shortcomings in your work.
6.  What is the answer to your question? How can you summarize your results? How can you explain or account for your results in some intuitive fashion? How must your results be qualified? What are the implications of your results?
    *Purpose*: Tell the reader what you have learned and what it means.
7.  What are the next steps in needed research that will further our understanding of the question under examination?
    *Purpose*: Inform those who will be reading or listening to your report what insights you gained that can guide subsequent researchers.

well as those who can only read the paper, are able both to follow the presentation and understand the results it presents.

## VI. LINKING ASSIGNMENTS TO PROFICIENCIES

The earlier discussion of proficiencies in the major mentioned a grid used to show how the various writing assignments enhance each proficiency. Now that the full range of writing assignments has been elaborated, this grid is presented to show the links among those assignments and the five proficiencies (Table 5.19). A single X indicates that a writing assignment is important in developing a particular proficiency, while a double X indicates it is very important. Some assignments, as already described, contribute to the development of several proficiencies.

Several striking features emerge. First, most writing assignments emphasize Interpreting Existing Knowledge (proficiency 3), followed by the Displaying Existing Knowledge (proficiency 2), Applying Existing Knowledge (proficiency 4) and Accessing Existing Knowledge (proficiency 1). The smallest number emphasize Creating New Knowledge (proficiency 5). Second, four of the eighteen assignments are oriented toward a single proficiency, three assignments contribute to the development of all five proficiencies, and five assignments contribute to four proficiencies. Third, the sequencing of the writing assignments moves from the simpler to the more complex and difficult, as evidenced by the general downward drift to the right of the double XX's.

**Table 5.19: Grid Ranking Importance of Writing Assignments to Development of Proficiencies (X indicates important; XX indicates very important)**

| Table No. | Writing Assignment | Proficiencies | | | | |
| --- | --- | --- | --- | --- | --- | --- |
| | | Accessing Existing Knowledge | Displaying Existing Knowledge | Interpreting Existing Knowledge | Applying Existing Knowledge | Creating New Knowledge |
| 1a. | Writing a Précis | | XX | | | |
| 1b. | Writing a Summary | | XX | | | |
| 2. | Formulating Discussion Questions | | X | XX | | |
| 3. | Identifying Economic Concepts | X | XX | | | |

**Table 5.19: Grid Ranking Importance of Writing Assignments to Development of Proficiencies (X indicates important; XX indicates very important) (Continued)**

| Table No. | Writing Assignment | Proficiencies | | | | |
|---|---|---|---|---|---|---|
| | | Accessing Existing Knowledge | Displaying Existing Knowledge | Interpreting Existing Knowledge | Applying Existing Knowledge | Creating New Knowledge |
| 4. | Analyzing a Policy Case | X | X | XX | X | |
| 5. | Evaluating Writing Assignments | | X | XX | | |
| 6. | Composing an In-Class Essay | | X | XX | X | |
| 7. | Preparing Exam Questions/Answers | | XX | X | | |
| 8. | Identifying Excellent Writing | X | X | XX | | |
| 9. | Analyzing the Minimum Wage | X | X | X | XX | |
| 10. | Creating a Quantitative Analysis | X | | X | X | XX |
| 11. | Understanding Wage Discrimination | | X | XX | XX | X |
| 12. | Completing a Labor Market Analysis | X | X | XX | X | X |
| 13. | Writing an In-Class Analysis | | | X | XX | |
| 14. | Evaluating Student Papers | | | XX | | |
| 15. | Appraising Student Papers | | | XX | | |
| 16. | Composing Idea Papers | X | X | XX | X | XX |
| 17. | Preparing Research Papers/Proposals | X | | X | X | XX |
| 18. | Organizing Research Papers/Proposals | X | X | X | X | XX |

## VII. INSTRUCTION IN WRITING

Colleagues often ask me what I can teach students about writing and whether I have any special expertise in such teaching. Although I admit to no special training, I do emphasize my keen interest in good writing. Here are the basics I try to convey.

I concentrate on helping students think through what they want to say, aided by Tables 5.14 and 5.15. The most important point is to state clearly the objective of their paper or the question it is addressing. Equally important is the paper's organization, which should begin with an introduction, be followed by supporting material, and end with a conclusion. I also emphasize the importance of revising their papers before turning them in to me. When I receive what is obviously a first draft, I return it unread for revision. Style is another concern in revision. The best basic advice on stylistic revision comes from Lanham's *Revising Prose* (1979) which offers a few simple and effective guidelines. More advanced guidance on style is provided by Williams in *Style: Toward Clarity and Grace* (1997).

I offer little or no formal, general instruction on how to write, organize, revise, and cope with writing problems as might occur in a composition course. Instead, my "instruction" is always related to what we are doing in the course, whether it be commenting on an upcoming assignment, observing the strengths of written material we are discussing to illustrate some economic principle or issue, or commenting on particular writing problems gleaned from the papers I return to students. For example, when making a new assignment, I sometimes work with the class as a group to help them construct a topic sentence or even paragraph showing how to set out a useful approach to the assignment. Using the handouts of newspaper articles that relate to the specific economic issues we are discussing, I ask students to comment on the skills authors display in presenting these issues and on the prose they use to do so; I point out subtle features they may have missed. Reading aloud and sometimes reproducing copies of particularly strong papers helps provide models for students to emulate. More specific help in analyzing the particular strengths or weaknesses of student papers can be provided effectively (and also inexpensively) with the help of overhead transparencies. In short, I try to impress upon my students that improving their capacity to write effective prose is integral to mastering the economics content of the course and being able to demonstrate the proficiencies we expect of our graduates.

Because time and my own limitations prevent me from offering adequate help to students who need extensive help with their writing, I refer these students to our Campus Writing Center. The Center's trained faculty and staff are much better equipped to first diagnose the specific weaknesses of students and then help them overcome these weaknesses through individual conferences and through workshops that deal with particular writing problems. If a program of writing intensive courses is to succeed, it must be backed by a well-staffed writing center. Such centers can also help faculty members develop effective ways of integrating writing into their subject matter courses and offer guidance in constructing effective writing assignments.

## VIII. MANAGING THE COSTS

The most common objection by economists to incorporating more writing into economics courses is the familiar tradeoff problem, namely, that giving more attention to writing means giving less attention to content knowledge. At a more practical level, individual faculty are concerned about the time costs of evaluating student papers, even though they may appreciate the smaller class size that is characteristic of writing intensive courses. Departments, of course, are concerned about the resource costs of teaching small enrollment WI courses and finding faculty who are willing to do this kind of teaching.

There is no question that evaluating student papers requires time. In some cases, paid graduate student assistance is available or can be made available to help read undergraduate student papers. In others cases, faculty must choose between reading the papers themselves or not requiring them.

The secret of economizing on time spent reading papers lies in making certain that students turn in quality papers, both in terms of content and presentation. Four steps can improve the quality of student papers. First, give students clear, manageable assignments, and discuss these assignments with students before they begin writing their papers. Doing so eliminates the uncertainty students face in trying to guess "what the professor is looking for." Second, provide students with a checklist to guide them in making certain that their papers meet some minimum standard before being turned in; you want to avoid getting first drafts. This calls for emphasizing revising their drafts before turning in their finished papers, and indicating that poor papers will be returned for further revision. Third, create incentives that ensure high-quality performance. My system of grading papers (50 percent on content and 50 percent on presentation) grabs the attention of students. Fourth, create another set of incentives to complement those already mentioned. By involving students in reading, evaluating, and discussing their papers with fellow students, students can learn much about what makes for effective writing and good economics. This approach takes some pressure off the instructor, and at the same time it stimulates students to do their best by capitalizing effectively on students' fears of being embarrassed in front of their fellow classmates.[28]

Faculty also need to realize that writing assignments perform a unique function. Writing assignments should be used not to check on whether students' content knowledge is right or wrong. Rather, they are designed to help the students clarify and deepen their own thinking and understanding. Enlisting students in the process of evaluating each other's papers is an excellent way to accomplish this. When student writers find that other students cannot understand their papers, they begin to recognize the virtues of reorganizing, rewriting, and polishing their papers. They learn that writing is a craft that can be enhanced with careful and hard work.

Faculty must also learn the secrets of keeping to a minimum the time they spend evaluating papers, all the while ensuring that writing assignments are productive in stimulating student learning. The key is leveraging their time. For example, many hours can be spent commenting in great detail on student papers, but many faculty members do not realize that students rarely pay much attention to the numerous corrections and comments appearing on their papers. The only exception is when students are required to revise their papers as a condition of completing the writing assignment. To overcome this problem, it is important to give writers some indication of their writing problems in evaluating the first writing assignment. This point can be reinforced by requiring students to revise these papers, with instructions to detail separately what revisions they made and why they made them. Faculty also need to emphasize that students must be responsible for improving both the quality of their papers' content and presentation. (As already noted, students with serious writing problems should be directed to the campus writing center.) In evaluating the second and third papers, faculty must convey through summary comments and grades their expectations of high level of performance. In addition, students need to be reminded constantly of the importance of deadlines and the severe penalties that can and will be assessed for late papers.

Sometimes faculty assume too much of the burden and require too little responsibility from their student writers. The limits of faculty responsibility can be illustrated by Henry Kissinger's approach, recounted in a *New York Times* article some years ago. A young man who had worked for Kissinger in the White House met him several years later at a party. He approached Kissinger in awe, remarking how Kissinger helped him develop his skill in writing memos and reports. He told how his carefully prepared drafts inevitably came back with the notation: "A good start. K." After submitting a new draft, it too came back again, with the notation: "Needs more work. K." or "Improving. Keep at it. K." And so on. Finally, more detailed comments would arrive, and eventually after another version, the much-sought comment arrived: "Good job. K." Kissinger listened carefully and then slowly responded: "I'm glad you thought I was so helpful. My practice is never to look closely at anything until the 4th or 5th draft comes to me." There is much to be said for insisting that students with modest writing skills be held to high standards and that students with excellent writing skills be continually encouraged to meet and exceed those standards.

## IX. CONCLUSIONS

This chapter offers my rationale for giving writing a more prominent role in the teaching and learning of economics, provides numerous examples of effective writing assignments for students at different levels, describes how to enhance the effectiveness of these writing assignments, and reveals how these assignments can contribute to the larger objectives of my teaching, namely helping students develop the proficiencies that can reasonably be expected of new graduates who majored in economics. This approach does require more work on the part of the instructor. I find, however, that incorporating writing into my teaching is stimulating because I learn more about what my students are learning, students develop valuable writing and learning skills in addition to learning the content knowledge, and the interaction between learning economics and writing about economics adds to the excitement of both teaching and learning.

At the same time, I have difficulty objectively assessing the usefulness of this proficiencies approach and the writing assignments in enhancing student learning of economics in my teaching. The most I can offer is some limited information gleaned from students through their responses to a detailed course-instructor evaluation form they complete each semester. Typically, my course and instruction receive strong evaluations, notwithstanding the additional demands placed on students by my writing-intensive focus. In my one-semester course, students report, not surprisingly, that the assignments centering on economic content are most helpful in improving their ability to use their knowledge.[29] They also report that learning how to write an analysis of economic concepts in news articles is as helpful as learning how to identify these concepts and how to interpret these news articles. They value learning how to formulate different types of questions, participating in small group discussion, receiving written comments on their papers, and being pushed to think critically in both the writing assignments and class discussion. The feedback obtained through student evaluations has been useful in sharpening the focus of my writing assignments and fine-tuning the mix of instruction and learning activities in the course as a whole.

Although this qualitative evidence may not satisfy many of my colleagues, I continue to believe that writing is the most powerful learning tool available to us, that we should make better use of this tool in our teaching, and that both we as faculty members and students will learn more as a result.

## X. DO'S AND DON'TS

- Do take the first step, by incorporating writing into your teaching.
- Do think about how your writing assignments fit into the overall goals of the course, what you want each of these assignments to accomplish, and how to design these assignments.
- Do try proven assignments of the kind presented in this chapter or that your colleagues have found successful. Do not try to reinvent what already exists.

- Do show how much fun writing well can be.  Write your syllabus so that it is interesting to read and conveys your excitement about economics and writing. Make certain your assignments are well-written and stimulate the interest of your students.
- Do emphasize why you incorporate writing into your course: writing helps students learn economics, being able to write well is useful in and of itself, and writing more is often the surest way of improving one's writing skills.
- Do make sure that your writing assignments utilize the knowledge and skills students possess, are specific about purpose, audience, and other pertinent details, and are explicit as to length and due date.
- Do require students to purchase at least one book on writing and show them over the semester how they can use the book to improve their writing.
- Do read and evaluate student papers promptly, making sure that short papers (less than 5-6 pages) are returned within a week at the most.
- Do always give some positive feedback; find some redeeming feature in even bad papers.  Do not hesitate to point out key weaknesses, but do so in a gentle and constructive way.
- Do refer students to the campus writing center when they are clearly in need of help that is beyond your ability to provide.
- Do weigh writing heavily in your grading, and give students information on the quality of both content and presentation.
- Do show students examples of good and not-so-good student writing so that everyone can have a better idea of what to shoot for.  Asking students for permission to use their papers, or at least informing them that you plan to do that, is much appreciated by students, even when their papers are bad. However, it is important not to disclose the names of student authors of these bad papers.
- Do get students involved in writing critiques of papers by other students.  This relieves some of the pressures on the instructor; it also benefits students as they discover their own strengths and weakness by interacting with each other.
- Do share your experience with your colleagues and department, in the hope of not only encouraging others to join you but also getting some recognition for your efforts.
- Do obtain feedback from your students on how the writing assignments contributed to their learning; the best method is through the end-of-the-semester course/instruction student evaluation questionnaire.
- Don't start too fast.  If you have never required writing assignments in your class, start out using a few of the easier assignments and allow yourself to learn from experience.  The next time you can introduce additional assignments if you wish.  Do not schedule yourself for "burnout" by starting too ambitiously.
- Don't think you have to comment on every grammatical or spelling error, even though part of the writing grade should encompass grammar and spelling.  If

you notice numerous errors, comment to that effect and encourage students to identify their own errors.

- Don't overwhelm students with criticism or praise. The first is discouraging and the second produces a false sense of confidence. For bad writers, try to suggest some limited approaches to improvement. For good writers, suggest how they can become even better writers, but also acknowledge their strengths.
- Don't let the size of the class preclude writing assignments. In larger classes you can assign fewer, shorter, or team-written papers; you can enlist students to do more reading of each other's papers; or you can try to seek funding for a reader to assist you, not substitute for you, in evaluating student papers.
- Don't expect perfection the first time you attempt to incorporate writing into your economics teaching. You will gradually learn how to do it, and you will find that it enriches your teaching and enhances the learning of your students.

## NOTES

\*   The comments and criticisms of Suzanne Becker, Nancy Brower, Bradley Hughes, Jenny Minier, Peggy Nightingale, and Corri Taylor have added immeasurably to the quality of this paper. I appreciate the support and encouragement of Bradley Hughes of the Department of English, who heads the campus Writing Across the Curriculum program. I also appreciate the earlier support of English Department Professor Joyce Steward who established the campus Writing Laboratory and encouraged faculty members like me to incorporate more writing into their instruction. Finally, thanks go to the many students who showed me how to help them better understand economics by requiring them to write about what they were learning.

1.   For a useful guide to Writing Across the Curriculum programs, see Bean (1996).

2.   Partly for these reasons, but also in an effort to move students through the Ph.D. program more rapidly and ensure they are better prepared for the job market, the University of Wisconsin-Madison Economics Department several years ago began requiring graduate students to complete a major field research paper by the end of their second year in the graduate program. In lieu of students taking and passing the field preliminary examination, some fields now require students to revise their papers to make them suitable for submission to an economics journal; at this point faculty may suggest or require submission of the paper.

3.   Personal communication from the editor of the *Journal of Economic Education*.

4.   Walstad and Becker (1996) conclude that the "one-third contribution of the essay to the composite score adds minimal information about the student for determining the AP grade beyond what is already contained in the multiple-choice score." (p. 195)

5.   The justification for relying so heavily on multiple-choice questions rests on assertions that such questions are able to test effectively not only factual knowledge but also simple and complex applications of economic concepts (Welsh and Saunders 1990).

6.   The problem sets so often assigned in economics courses are not what I would describe as writing assignments.

7.   A comprehensive list of skills needs to be developed. As an example, the author,

in conjunction with students in a graduate seminar, attempted to develop an inventory of skills needed to complement the content knowledge acquired largely through course work by master's degree students in industrial relations/human resources (Hansen et al. 1996).

8.  These proficiencies presume that students learn the same content knowledge and skills that are currently taught; they are not meant to substitute for content knowledge.

9.  Developing this proficiencies approach received a major stimulus from my exposure to what is called "problem-based learning." It came as a result of being invited to spend some time in 1984 and again in 1986 at the University of Maastricht in The Netherlands. Its newly created Department of Economics, preparing to enroll its first class of undergraduate students, was using a problem-based approach to instruction. This approach was pioneered by the McMaster University (Canada) medical school and is now used extensively in Canada, Australia, and the United States. Students meet and learn in small discussion groups of 10. They are provided with a faculty-developed course book that contains a long series of problems---interpretative questions---the student group works through during the semester. At their regular weekly meetings, they devise not only the strategies for answering these questions but also the answers themselves. At the end of each academic year students are tested on what they know and what they can do with their knowledge. The focus of this approach is to help students perform at ever higher levels each year.

10. For an interesting parallel development of proficiencies, see Davenport et al. (1996).

11. Wyrick (1994, 1995) has published two books built around the proficiencies described by Hansen (1986).

12. Several other organizing approaches have been brought to my attention by Brad Hughes. Bloom's taxonomy of cognitive objectives offers a useful starting point in giving systematic emphasis to student thinking skills; however, the challenge is to build economics writing assignments around this taxonomy. Two other models are helpful, including Bean, Drenk, and Lee (1982) and Kinery and Strenski (1985). In addition, I recently stumbled upon Jones (1995). This is an intriguing attempt to define and measure the essential writing skills of college graduates; the study also notes disparities in the views of faculty, employers, and policy makers as to the importance of different writing skills.

13. For other recent, useful books on writing, see Rhodes (1995) and the less reverent Lamott (1994).

14. The 1984 Fels book is now, sadly, out of print. This book proved to be particularly useful in large introductory courses where working through the cases gives teaching assistants a well-defined task for their discussion section meetings. In addition, the enhanced analytical skills of students developed with this approach helped extend the reach of the course to other more complex economic issues.

15. A series of Guidelines available in the course reading packet instruct students on how to approach particular types of writing assignments, such as these.

16. The précis and discussion question assignments focus on prose selections from a representative group of the best writers and thinkers in economics, including Adam Smith, Karl Marx, John Maynard Keynes, Joseph Schumpeter, Friederich von Hayek, Milton Friedman, Robert Heilbroner, plus Arthur Okun (1975), whose writing is also considered in Table 5.6.

17. Another Guideline elaborates this particular assignment.

18. For more details on the nature and use of questions in discussion, see Hansen

(1978) and Hansen and Salemi (1997).

19. This assignment has worked effectively in large lecture sections of the economics principles course, most recently in Fall 1995 with more than 700 students and 10 teaching assistants to help grade student essays.

20. The current vogue among composition instructors is to discourage in-class essays. They argue that time pressures militate against good writing, that no opportunities are offered for revision, etc. I disagree, believing they are an effective assignment. They represent the kind of academic writing regularly required in the essay exams students write in courses in their major, and they are similar to the memos and reports many college-educated workers must regularly write in their professional jobs.

21. Students are advised they can leave postcards or envelopes requesting information on their final example grade, including that on the in-class essay. On occasion, students have stopped by my office to inquire about their essays, and I have am happy to discuss their papers with them. In fact, relatively few students request their grades and even fewer stop by to ask about these essays.

22. Unfortunately, many students arrive with inflated notions about their writing skills, and in the absence of a required composition course (beginning in 1996-97 a new writing requirement was instituted), students had no formal way of improving their writing skills.

23. I realize that this holistic approach to grading has one obvious disadvantage, namely, that some good writers may be able to camouflage their inadequate knowledge of the subject matter with their beguiling prose. I accept this risk, though I believe it is minimal. Above all, I want to impress on students the importance of explicit attention to their writing and presentation skills.

24. For a recent description of the economics major, see Siegfried et al. (1991).

25. The weight given to writing assignments is substantial: 25 percent for the writing assignments, one-third of the final exam grade which amounts to another 8 percent, 5 percent based on generating exam questions, for a total of almost 40 percent of their overall grade. Of course, the writing of their summaries, précis, and questions for discussion section meetings also contribute to their performance in the course.

26. These developments, which necessarily give greater emphasis to solving problem sets and homework assignments than dealing with technical matters, reduce the opportunities for meaningful writing assignments; as a consequence students are less well prepared than they might be to tackle writing their doctoral dissertations.

27. While these categories may appear to be rather similar, see Hansen (1991) for more detailed information.

28. For my experience in the labor economics course, see Hansen (1993b).

29. For students' comments on my labor economics course, see Hansen (1993a).

## REFERENCES

Bean, J.C. 1996. *Engaging ideas: The professor's guide to integrating writing, critical thinking, and active learning in the classroom*, San Francisco, CA: Jossey-Bass.

_____, D. Drenk, and F. D. Lees. 1982. Microtheme strategies for developing cognitive skills. In C. W. Griffin (ed.). *Teaching Writing in All Disciplines*. San Francisco, CA: Jossey-Bass: 27-38.

Becker, W. E., and M. Watts. 1996. Chalk and talk: A national survey on teaching undergraduate economics. *American Economic Review* 86 (May): 448-53.

Davenport, T. H., S. L. Jarvenpaa, and M. C. Beers. 1996. Improving knowledge work processes. *Sloan Management Review* 37 (Summer): 53-66.

Elbow, P. 1981. *Writing with power: Techniques for mastering the writing process.* New York: Oxford University Press.

Fels, R. and S. Buckles. 1981. *Casebook of economic problems and policies: Practice in thinking.* 5th ed. St. Paul, MN: West Publishing Co.

Hansen, W. L. 1978. Improving classroom discussion in economics courses. In P. Saunders, A. R. Welsh, and W. L. Hansen, eds., *Resource manual for teacher training programs.* New York: Joint Council on Economic Education.

_____. 1986. What knowledge is most worth knowing – for economics majors? *American Economic Review* 76 (May): 149-52.

_____. 1991. The education and training of economics doctorates: Major findings of the executive secretary of the American Economic Association's commission on graduate education in economics. *Journal of Economic Literature* 29 (September): 1054-94.

_____. 1993a. Teaching a 'writing intensive' course in economics. *Journal of Economic Education* 24 (Summer): 213-18.

_____. 1993b. Bringing TQI into the college classroom. *Higher Education* 25 (April): 259-79.

_____. 1996. Needed skills for human resource professionals. *Labor Law Journal (Proceedings of 1996 Spring Meeting of the Industrial Relations Research Association)*: 524-34.

_____ and M. K. Salemi. 1997. Improving classroom discussion in economics courses. In P. Saunders and W. B. Walstad. *Teaching Undergraduate Economics: A Handbook for Instructors.* New York: McGraw-Hill.

_____, P. Saunders, G. L. Bach, and J. D. Calderwood. 1977. *Basic concepts in economics: A framework for teaching economics in the nation's schools.* New York: Joint Council on Economic Education.

Jones, E. A., with S. Hoffman et al. 1995. *National assessment of college student learning: Identifying college graduates' essential skills in writing, speech and listening, and critical thinking.* National Center for Education Statistics. Office of Educational Research and Improvement. Washington, DC: U.S. Department of Education.

Kennedy, P., and W. B. Walstad. 1998. Combining multiple-choice and constructed-response test scores: An economist's view. *Applied Measurement in Education:* forthcoming.

Kiniry, M., and E. Strenski. 1985. Sequencing expository writing: A recursive approach. *College Composition and Communication* 36 (May): 191-202.

Krueger, A. O., et al. 1991. Report of the commission on graduate education in economics. *Journal of Economic Literature* 29 (September): 1035-53.

Lamott, A. 1994. *Bird by bird: Some instructions on writing and life.* New York: Doubleday.

Lanham, R. A. 1979. *Revising prose.* New York: Charles Scribner's.

McCloskey, D. N. 1987. *The writing of economics.* New York: Macmillan.

Mills, C. W. 1959. On intellectual craftsmanship. In *The sociological imagination.* New York: Oxford University Press.

Okun, A. 1975. *Equality and efficiency: The big tradeoff.* Washington, DC: Brookings.

Patton, C. V. 1975. A seven day research project. *Policy Analysis* 1 (Winter): 731-53.

Platt, J. R. 1962. The art of creation (Chapter 7), and The motivation of creation (Chapter 8). In *The excitement of science*. New York: Houghton Mifflin.

Rhodes, R. 1995. *How to write: Advice and reflections*. New York: William Morrow and Co.

Roberts, H. V., and B. F. Sergesketter. 1993. Quality, personal quality, and personal quality checklists; and How to get started on your own personal quality checklist. In *Quality is personal: A foundation for total quality management*. New York: The Free Press.

Siegfried, J. J., and P. E. Kennedy. 1995. Does pedagogy vary with class size in introductory courses? *American Economic Review* 85 (May): 347-51.

_____ and J. E. Raymond. 1984. A profile of senior economics majors in the United States. *American Economic Review* 74 (May): 19-25.

_____, R. L. Bartlett, W. L. Hansen, A. C. Kelley, D. N. McCloskey, and T. H. Tietenberg. 1991. The economics major in American higher education. *Journal of Economic Education* 22 (Summer): 197-224.

Walstad, W. B., and W. E. Becker. 1994. Achievement differences on multiple-choice and essay tests in economics. *American Economic Review* 84 (May): 193-6.

Welsh, A. L., and P. Saunders. 1990. Essay questions and tests. In P. Saunders and W. B. Walstad,eds., *The principles of economics course: A handbook for instructors*. New York: McGraw-Hill.

Williams, J. M. 1990. *Style: Toward clarity and grace*. 5th ed. New York: Addison-Wesley.

Wyrick, T. L. 1994. *The economists's handbook: A research and writing guide*. Minneapolis/St. Paul: West Publishing Co.

_____. 1995. *The writer's guide to college economics*. Minneapolis/St. Paul: West Publishing Co.

CHAPTER **6**

# USING THE INTERNET AND COMPUTER TECHNOLOGY TO TEACH ECONOMICS

## Kim Sosin

Economics teachers have not embraced the practice of using computers in courses other than econometrics and statistics, according to a recent survey by Becker and Watts (1996). However, many economics faculty members have the equipment and software necessary to use computers in teaching (Sosin 1997). In a survey of economics departments, 56 percent reported that all faculty members have adequate computers in their offices, 75 percent of departments reported that over three-fourths of faculty members have computers in offices, and 45 percent report adequate student access. The reasons for the disparity between technology use and availability are not clear. Recent conferences of major economics associations have had well-attended sessions on using the Internet and computers.[1] Conversations at these sessions suggest that some faculty members are truly excited with what they regard as a new way to engage students in learning and are developing their courses accordingly, whereas others worry that technology is a time-consuming way to add glitz and entertainment rather than substance to teaching. Many are intrigued by the possibilities but perhaps have doubts about their ability to develop a course or project that effectively uses technology to enhance learning. This chapter is written primarily for these cautiously optimistic teachers.

Experts also have disparate viewpoints about the instructional benefits of technology. The chapter begins by discussing some of these viewpoints and the research on using technology in teaching. Where is this technology headed and is it a "good thing?" What are the strengths of technology-enhanced teaching and what are the dangers? What does the research show about the effect on students' learning? An examination of some of the ways that one technology – the Internet/web network – is being incorporated into teaching both inside and out of the classroom is presented. Two specific web projects are developed in detail, the first for the teacher who has basic knowledge of the web and the second for the teacher who is skilled and ready to provide documents on the web. Finally, the "do's" and "don'ts" of using this technology effectively in teaching are discussed, emphasizing what teachers should do and what they should avoid.

## I.   USING TECHNOLOGY IN TEACHING: VIEWPOINTS AND RESEARCH

It is customary to observe that technology will create sweeping transformations in the delivery of education. But what form will this transformation take? How extensive will it be; for example, are traditional universities endangered organizations? Where are computer and networking technology headed? Are there economies of scale to teaching with technology that could eventually put some institutions and teachers out of business? Will technology help teachers be more effective and efficient at their jobs? And, of primary importance to educators, how and to what extent might their roles change?

At one end of the spectrum of viewpoints is James Burke, the British television host of "Connections," the acclaimed program on the evolution of technology: "the next fifty years are going to make everything that went before it look like 'See Spot Run.' "[2] He believes that in ten years newspapers, books, and television sets will be replaced by the web (or its successors) and the machines that connect us to networks will be wireless, portable flat-screen pages that are voice-responsive. At the other extreme are dissenters such as computer scientist Clifford Stoll, who asks if computers are a way to avoid learning, which is "hard work," rather than a new way to learn (Stoll 1995; O'Neil 1996). Stoll is concerned that the use of computers in education jeopardizes the position of teachers as the central source of information, reduces students' attention spans, and inhibits development of their writing abilities. Likewise, Talbott (1995, 347) views the dangers of technologically networked society: "It is not that society and culture are managing to assimilate technology. Rather, technology is swallowing culture."

Discussing efforts in Colorado to bring more computer technology into teaching, Eric Feder of the Colorado Department of Education is quoted on this modern Rip Van Winkle story (described in Griggs 1995). If someone fell asleep in the 1880s and woke up today in a doctor's office, he would have no idea where he was. If he woke up on mass transportation such as high-speed train or airplane, he would be terrified. But if he woke up in a classroom, he would feel quite at home. Can the same be said of the "modern" economics classroom? And more to the point, is that one-hundred year old classroom a fine antique that can still perform beautifully or could it benefit from a technological facelift? The answers to the two parts of this question are arguably both "yes."

A fundamental question must be answered as economics teachers develop experience with technology and Internet teaching: how effectively do students using new technologies learn? Few studies are available because the use of this technology is too new to have generated a critical mass of evaluations. Also, because the economics teachers who currently use computer technology extensively in their teaching are those most enthusiastic and experienced with it, generalizations about its effectiveness for all teachers must be interpreted cautiously or studies must account for selection bias.

Studies on using the Internet in economics classes show enhanced learning, which the authors attribute primarily to improved instructor-student communications (Agarwal and Day 1997; Leuthold 1998; Manning 1996). Agarwal and Day use standardized test scores and final grades to compare control and test classes, concluding that the Internet has a positive influence on learning, attitude towards economics, and student perception of instructor effectiveness. Leuthold reports that 65 percent of the students in introductory economics agreed or strongly agreed that being able to utilize the web helped them understand the concepts, 86 percent felt the web increased or somewhat increased their learning and 66 percent reported increased motivation. In her classes, attendance was as high or higher than in a traditional class.[3] In an earlier survey of the literature on using computers in economics classes, Grimes and Ray (1993) conclude that computerized tutorials and simulations are shown to enhance student learning and perhaps to improve attitudes towards economics.

The results from other disciplines that have used technology-enhanced learning (including multimedia, Internet, web, conferencing) provide a wider perspective. According to a survey by Conrad (1997), the overall evidence is mixed, with some studies showing no significant difference in learning and others showing significant increase. These studies rarely find a decline in learning. Some research also suggests that using educational technology has spillover benefits beyond learning economics. Levin and Thurston (1996) report positive "audience effects" when students publish papers on the web. Apparently students make a greater effort to produce polished work if the paper will be web-published. Finally, because students enjoy the technology component of courses, their improved attitudes towards learning and the subject matter may make the effort worthwhile even if the economics learning outcomes are the about the same rather than significantly enhanced.

Will future students be accustomed to and expect web, Internet, and computer mediated/assisted lessons as components of their learning when they get to college? If computers and the web are the way society deals with information in the future, it is almost certainly the way students will expect to find and learn information in school. After they experience computer-based learning in their K-12 education, will colleges seem out of date, both technologically and culturally, if they do otherwise?

## II. USING THE WORLD WIDE WEB TO TEACH ECONOMICS

The web can be used in a variety of ways in teaching. This section discusses the types of web sites that have been developed for educational use and some of the myriad ways webs have been and can be used for teaching. Other Internet features, such as e-mail and listservs, will not be included here except as they relate to the web. Additional information about e-mail uses of the Internet can be found in Manning (1996) and listserv uses in Hannah (1996).

The level of access to and knowledge about the web by a faculty member makes a substantial difference in the way the web can be used to teach classes. Web assignments can be made if the teacher has basic knowledge of how to use a browser and a search engine. Ability to download and decode files, which can be quickly learned from the web, is also needed. If the teacher has some skill with HyperText Markup Language (HTML) and has access to a web server, the possibilities for taking advantage of the web are much more extensive because documents can be created and placed on the web, i.e., the teacher is not limited to accessing others' work. Many programs (such as Microsoft Word 97) are now available to create hypertext documents with no knowledge of the details of HTML code.

### Basic Web Knowledge
The basic knowledge required for use of the web by teachers and students follows:

*Server vs. client:* A computer that is set up to provide Internet/web documents is the "server," the computer on the receiving end interpreting the document is the "client." As users of the web, teachers and students must know how to work on client machines that run *browser* software (e.g., Netscape, Internet Explorer) to interact with the servers of web documents.

*URL:* A *uniform resource locator* (URL) is the form of address that identifies any resource on the web. This address appears in the "location" box along the top of the browser. It is not necessary to understand an address to use it (but a few points might satisfy the interested reader). The address has two parts: a protocol name and a document address e.g., < *http://host/path* > or more generally < *protocol://hostaddress/filelocation&name* > .

The *protocol* position informs the browser how to connect to (or what kind of) site; *http* refers to a web site document most likely written in HTML. Other common protocols are *ftp*, which indicates a file transfer protocol site that has material that is set up to be moved (downloaded) through the net, and *gopher,* which specifies a gopher site, another way to present information and links.

The *hostaddress* section gives the Internet address of the machine that holds the document, and *filelocation&name* is the path and filename of the particular document. The host address goes from specific address to broad reading from right to left. The specific server computer address appears first, additional information about the server follows (not really where it is, but who controls it), and the letters after the last "dot" are the broadest category of the address (.*edu*, .*gov*, .*com*, .*mil*, .*org*, .*net*, or country code).

*Using browser software:* The ability to use a web browser, such as Netscape or Internet Explorer, is required. Because browsers are much easier to use than to explain, little need be said but some mouse clicking is required. Note that the **back** button means go back to the last address, often handy if a list of links are on one page and you are working through the link list one site at a time. The URLs visited in the current web session are listed in the **Go** or **History** menu items; clicking here will also navigate back to sites visited earlier in the same session. An easy way to navigate to any address is to type it into the location box, beginning with *http://* and hit **Enter**. Web documents can be printed from **File/Print** and text highlighted with the mouse can be copied and pasted into other documents. And don't forget to bookmark worthwhile sites for future reference by clicking on **Bookmarks/Add** while the web page is on your screen.[4]

*Saving files:* One of the most frequent uses of the web is to download programs, data, and graphics files. Files from any kind of site—web, gopher, or ftp—can be saved to a local disk. Because an FTP site is set up to deliver files, clicking on a file that is coded in the form *ftp://host/path* will automatically bring up the **Save As** dialog box. The file name and type should not be changed: these are usually programs (.*exe*) or compressed (.*zip*) files that must be run or decompressed before they are used. A normal HTML (*http://host/path*) web document can be saved also. This is worth learning because it is often the easiest way to get economics data: information is placed on your screen and you save it to disk. With the document on the screen, click on **File/Save As** and note the two long boxes along the bottom. These give the user the option to change the **filename** and the format (in some cases) via **Save as type**. If the file is saved as type HTML, all web document coding will be included in the file. This is useful if the file is to be read in a browser or if you are interested in learning the HTML coding. However, it is counterproductive if you want to read the file or import it to other software. If saved as type "plain text," the coding will not be included and the material will be placed in a text file to be used in a text editor (e.g., Notepad), a word processor, or imported into a spreadsheet. If the **Save as type** is changed to plain text, the filename should be changed to the extension *.txt* so other software will interpret the format correctly.

*Searching for Information:* The easiest approach to finding information on the web is to use on-line search engines. Excite, Infoseek, Lycos, and Yahoo are a few of the many now available. A number of these are found at search megasites such as < http://www.search.com >. Each search site has rules for conducting advanced searches using the Boolean logic concepts of "and," "or," and "not." These are necessary to narrow the search results to your interests; otherwise many word searches will turn up hundreds of sites and end in frustration.

## Educational Uses Requiring Basic Web Knowledge

Economists using the web are fortunate to have a thorough and up-to-date web resource publication. Bill Goffe's "Resources for Economists on the Internet" is an on-line publication at < http://econwpa.wustl.edu/EconFAQ/EconFAQ. html > that is thoroughly indexed to extensive economic information available on the web. It can be searched by keywords, and it is hot-linked to the final web sites.[5]

Here are some educational uses of the web that do not require knowledge of HTML or access to a web server.

*Acquire up-to-date economic information:* The web is a wonderful storehouse of electronic text archives and databases; an obvious educational use of the web is to acquire up-to-date economic information. Sources of primary data on the web are valuable for students and faculty who are working on statistical or other applied projects. Such sites as FRED < http://www.stls.frb.org/fred/ > provided by the St. Louis Federal Reserve Bank, LABSTAT < http://stats.bls.gov/blshome.html > from the Department of Labor, and the two sites for the international dataset Penn World Tables, < http://cansim.epas.utoronto.ca:5680/pwt/ > and < http://www.nber.org >, have statistical series that economics students can collect before it is published in hard copy. Instructors also use these sites to assign applied or statistical projects and to get the latest information for class discussions or presentations. Likewise, news sources on the web provide a way to target the categories of news desired (e.g., business and financial) and to receive articles from several news sources on the chosen categories. Some other valuable web sites for economics information and data are in Table 6.1.

*Specialty sites for economics faculty or students:* Some sites exist to provide information to assist economics teaching and educators. The *EcEdWeb* < http://ecedweb.unomaha.edu/ > has resources for both K-12 and college economics teaching. The *Web Teaching Ideas* page on *EcEdWeb* presents a host of ideas and additional links for using the Internet in economics classes. Examples include an interactive self-quiz with animated demonstrations reviewing demand and supply, and several "WebQuests" involving on-line investigations of the deficit, the Federal Reserve System, and other issues.

Ray Fair has created an ingenious web site that permits simulation of economic outcomes using his well known macroeconomics model at < http://fairmodel.econ.yale.edu/ >. During the 1996 Presidential campaign, for example, this site featured an election prediction based on assumptions about the state of the economy. Students can see how macroeconometric models might be used to evaluate outcomes based on different economic assumptions, and then investigate some of those outcomes themselves.

**Table 6.1: Selected Web Resources for Economics Information and Data**

| Web Resource | Web Address |
| --- | --- |
| Goffe's Resources for Economists on the Internet | http://econwpa.wustl.edu/EconFAQ/EconFAQ.html |
| Federal Reserve Bank, St. Louis FRED | http://www.stls.frb.org/fred/ |
| Department of Labor LABSTAT | http://stats.bls.gov/blshome.html |
| Penn World Tables | http://cansim.epas.utoronto.ca:5680/pwt/ |
| EcEdWeb | http://ecedweb.unomaha.edu/ |
| U.S. Department of Commerce | http://www.doc.gov/ |
| Federal Reserve Bank, Minneapolis WOODROW | http://woodrow.mpls.frb.fed.us/econed/ |
| Fair's Econometric Model | http://fairmodel.econ.yale.edu/ |
| NBER Macroeconomic Historical Database | http://www.nber.org/ |
| Berkeley On-line Federal Budget Simulation | http://garnet.berkeley.edu:3333/budget/budget.html |
| Financial Economics Server Univ. of TX | http://www.finweb.edu/ |
| Hoover's profiles of over 1000 companies | http://www.hoovers.com/ |
| CIA Factbook (use link to publications) | http://www.odci.gov/cia/ |
| Dun and Bradstreet | http://www.dnb.com/ |
| Standard and Poor's News Service | http://www.quote.com/ |
| Security APL Stock Information | http://www.secapl.com/ |
| Economics America | http://www.economicsamerica.org |

These and other useful links are maintained at <http://ecedweb.unomaha.edu/econinfo.htm>

The *oo_Micro* site by J. Daniels offers an interactive and animated site for intermediate microeconomics teaching. If your browser can handle Java, watch the curves shift as the concepts are presented at <http://medusa.be.udel.edu/ WWW_Sites/oo_Micro.html>. Students can change the parameters of the equations and curves to explore the mathematical relationships that are a part of microeconomics.

On-line journals, web sites for most leading economics journals, and working papers on the web provide extensive sources of searchable economic papers on all subjects. The *Journal of Economic Education* was the first of the leading journals to make printed articles available as pdf files in the Adobe Acrobat format. A few of the many available web sites in this category are shown in Table 6.2.

*Expand and enhance discussion of issues:* Students can hear from and sometimes interact with economics experts via the web. Several sites have "ask the experts" features, which involve students sending e-mail to experts initiated from a web page. See, for example, the *New Jersey Networking Infrastructure in Education* economy and business page at the site <http://njnie.dl.stevens-tech.edu/>. Along these same lines, economists analyze current economics news from Dow Jones News and key them to textbooks by Varian and Stiglitz at the Dow Jones and W.W. Norton web site, <http://www.wwnorton.com/ wsj/welcome.htm>. Instructors can easily have their students draw on and critique these analyses to enhance class discussions of current events. Also the President and most Congressional representatives have on-line sites, which can be accessed at <http://www.whitehouse.gov>, <http://www.senate.gov>, and <http://www.house.gov>.

### Table 6.2: Selected Web Resources for Economics Papers and Pre-Prints

| Web Resource | Web Address |
| --- | --- |
| Journal of Economic Education | http://www.indiana.edu/~econed/index.html |
| National Center, Research in Economic Education | http://www.cba.unl.edu/additional/econed/ |
| International Association for Feminist Economists | http://www.bucknell.edu/~jshackel/iaffe/ |
| Economic Growth Resources | http://www.nuff.ox.ac.uk/Economics/Growth/ |
| Hal Varian's Economics WWW Server | http://www.sims.berkeley.edu/~hal/ |
| Econ-WP: Economics Working Papers Archive | http://econwpa.wustl.edu/ |
| National Bureau of Economic Research | http://www.nber.org/ |
| NetEc: BibEc and WoPec Working Papers | http://netec.mcc.ac.uk/ |
| IDEAS: Access to Economics Working Papers | http://ideas.uqam.ca/ |

*Web-only textbooks and on-line asynchronous Internet/web courses:* Authors and technology specialists are working on on-line textbooks and other published material. Although not many of these courses are ready, according to a recent survey, 23 percent of departments plan one or more Internet courses in two years compared to 8.9 percent providing at least one course today (Sosin 1997).

*Class home pages of other economics teachers:*  Faculty members can benefit from ideas gleaned from the class homepages of other teachers.  For example, new teachers or those teaching new courses can look over a variety of syllabi on the web to see what others are teaching.  Some class homepages also provide useful information and links for the students in the class—often on pages accessible by students from anywhere in the world.  The course web sites in Table 6.3 are only a few of those available. (In some cases, you will have to follow the links to the instructor's name or to class or course pages.)

## A Detailed Project Requiring Basic Web Knowledge: Investment and Economic Growth

The wealth of economics data on the web creates a myriad of possibilities for student projects.  Many of the stylized facts of economic relationships presented in class discussions of economic theory can readily be reinforced using real data from web sites.  The project described in detail in this section is an example of this approach.

What is the relationship between the investment share of the output of a country and its per-capita output growth?  This is an important topic that comes up in several economics courses, but first appears in the principles course when production possibility curves are used to illustrate allocation between investment and consumption in a full employment economy.  In any discussion of economic growth and economic development, understanding the relationship between investment and output growth is important.

## Table 6.3: Examples of Economists' Web Sites

| Web Site Address | Instructor |
|---|---|
| Http://medusa.be.udel.edu/WWW_Sites/oo_Micro.html | Joe Daniels |
| http://www.indiana.edu/~statist/e270.htm | William Becker |
| Http://william-king.www.drexel.edu/ | Roger McCain |
| Http://www.mtsu.edu/~rlhannah/ | Richard Hannah |
| Http://www.colorado.edu/cewww/econ2020/ | Jules Kaplan |
| Http://www.cba.uiuc.edu/college/econ/econ102/ | Jane Leuthold |
| Http://mmcbride.sba.muohio.edu/ | Mark McBride |
| Http://wuecon.wustl.edu/~bob/ | Bob Parks |

The project described here goes beyond teaching students the investment-growth relationship. It also teaches them to learn to use the web to gather information, reinforces their ability to compute and interpret percent changes and to understand real vs. nominal values and per-capita data, and challenges them to think about the causes of economic growth. The "hands on" nature of the project and subsequent group work and class discussions create active learning for students who learn and remember best by engaging with the information and applying real data to theories.

The project can be limited to these goals, or additional web information for each country in the project can be used to develop an understanding of the countries' resources, economic organization, and level of development. Students should also learn that investment share is not the only determinant of economic growth. The relationship between investment share and economic growth is robust statistically across countries; however, dramatic counterexamples can be shown for some time periods.

The countries and time period suggested in Table 6.4 provide real data that illustrate the relationship. Ten countries are shown; however, it would be enough to choose five countries, making sure to get some from the top and bottom of the range of investment shares. Countries in addition these could be added, perhaps including some counterexamples to further expand class discussion of factors involved in economic growth.[6]

## Table 6.4: Investment Share and Economic Growth in Selected Countries

| Country (Code) | Investment Share (Percent) 1980 | Percent Change, Real GDP per Capita, 1980-90 |
|---|---|---|
| Singapore (SNG) | 37.8 | 65.6 |
| Norway (NOR) | 35.0 | 22.9 |
| Malaysia (MYS) | 27.4 | 34.5 |
| Japan (JPN) | 34.1 | 42.2 |
| Cyprus (CYP) | 30.3 | 58.2 |
| Rep. Of Korea (KOR) | 28.0 | 115.5 |
| United States (USA) | 20.3 | 18.0 |
| Argentina (ARG) | 19.6 | -27.6 |
| Guatemala (GTM) | 9.2 | -17.4 |
| El Salvador (SLV) | 7.3 | -9.5 |
| Ghana (GHA) | 4.0 | -7.8 |

Source: Penn World Tables 5.5, < http://cansim.epas.utoronto.ca:5680/pwt/ >

The student participation in this project can be organized in various ways. Each student can put together the information for all countries, chart the information, then write about or discuss the relationship found and the reason investment is important for economic growth. An approach that students enjoy is working in teams, with each team assigned one country to analyze from additional economic information on the web. At a minimum, the students will want to use the CIA factbook web site at < http://www.odci.gov/cia/ > (follow the links to publications and select the latest factbook) that has a section on the economies of each country.[7] They can also learn to use web "search engines" by starting at < http://www.search.com/ >, a site that lists several web search sites, and searching for more economic information about the assigned country. In the team approach, each team presents its findings to the class, using web links and presentation software if possible. Then the class uses data from each team, graphs it, and discusses the reasons for the relationship between investment and economic growth. Other growth factors, such as a country's resource base and economic policies, are also included in the discussion.

The web site for this project is CHASS at < http://cansim.epas.utoronto.ca: 5680/pwt/ >, which has the data set PWT (Penn World Tables) on-line (Summers and Heston 1991). This data set includes 29 variables (also called "topics" and "subjects") of annual macroeconomic data for 152 countries beginning in 1950.[8] The opening web page has links to the country codes to show the codes needed to specify the countries desired, and data codes to show codes needed to get specific variables. The process of getting the data is actually easier to do than to explain, but a brief explanation follows. The students should be guided to gather and interpret the information themselves.

Look at the country and data (or topic) lists (click on the links) to find the codes and definitions, for example, the code for the Republic of Korea is KOR, the code for the investment share is I, and for the level of real GDP per capita is RGDPL. Going back to the opening page (click the browser **back** button) and use the link called "Retrieve/Plot PWT Series by Label." Clicking on this phrase provides a simple form into which to type KOR/I and the dates desired, for example, 1980 to 1990 (or 1990 in both boxes to get 1990 only). Multiple data formats are also available; "plain" works well. Finally, click on "Submit Query" and wait for the data to be compiled and appear on the screen. The easiest way for students to complete the data gathering phase of the project is to simply use **File/Print** from the browser. If the data is to be further processed by computer, download the file with **File/Save As**, as described earlier.

The procedure can be followed to acquire each country or variable; however, the web page authors have provided a method of retrieving multiple countries and data. By using KOR/(I, RGDPL) both variables are retrieved for Korea for the dates specified. By using (USA,KOR)/(I,RGDPL), the variables are retrieved for both Korea and the United States. The data needed for this project (investment share and RGDPL for 1980, RGDPL for 1990 for all countries) can be retrieved by single step for each year. To retrieve all ten countries in one spreadsheet, the code (SGP,NOR,MYS,JPN,CYP,KOR,MEX, USA,ARG,GTM,SLV,GHA)/(I,RGDPL) is used for 1980 and again for 1990. Students will compute percent changes in RGDPL between the two years and compare these to the countries' investment shares in 1980.

More advanced classes can learn from using expanded versions of this project. For example, students could construct averages of the investment share and growth over several time periods, which is more reliable than using two years. The role of other variables in growth of real GDP per capita, such as population growth, government shares of output, inflation rates, and indices of the openness of the economy are instructive additions. These data are also available in the Penn World Tables. For example, the addition of Mexico could be used to illustrate some of these points. Investment share was above average (21.4 percent) in 1980 but fell to below average (15.0 percent) by 1990, while population growth exceeded output growth resulting in a negative per-capita growth over the ten years. An extension for statistics or econometrics classes is to collect additional data and estimate relationships among growth, investment shares, and other variables mentioned.

## Educational Uses Requiring Web Skill and Server Access

If a teacher has access to a web server and some knowledge of how to create a web page, several additional uses of the web in teaching are possible. Some knowledge of HTML is usually necessary to achieve exactly the results desired, though web pages can be created within some word processors (e.g., Microsoft Word 97) and presentation software (e.g., Microsoft Powerpoint 97) or with specialized web authoring software. The primary advantages of using the web in courses are to:

- *Provide a course web site:* Some teachers have found it very useful to provide a web page for each course taught. In the next section, additional information about the potential uses of a course web site and a detailed description of how to develop one is presented.
- *Set up a discussion or "chat" group:* A web page can include a chat gateway or roundtable software to access to create group discussions for students. Economics experts or members of the community can be included to discuss issues with students.
- *Publish students' papers and reports:* Students' papers can be published on the web to share with the class, or the world.
- *Teach an asynchronous web-only course:* A few full Internet/web asynchronous courses are being offered, and according to the survey more are under development (Sosin 1997). An advantage of web-only courses

over video-broadcast, distance learning classes is that the student controls the place and time of day he or she accesses the class.

## A Detailed Project Requiring Some Web Skill: A Course Web Site

The creation and fine-tuning of an HTML document does **not** require a server. The document can be created on any computer with browser software available to examine the results. The server is needed later, when the completed file is to be "published" on the web. This project assumes that you have access to a web server or to a person who can place your completed files on a server.

A course web site can be used to accomplish several goals:

- Add material to supplement the textbook and create links to additional sources of information, perhaps with pictures, maps, audio, video and bibliographic information. Class assignments, notes, sample tests, and outlines can be created with a word processor and saved as HTML files.
- Provide on the web Powerpoint slides or multimedia presentations based on material covered in the classroom. This solves a common problem caused by multimedia presentations in economics classes: students find it difficult to take adequate notes, particularly on the graphs.
- Set up practice tests, self-tutorials, and actual tests. These tests can be automatically computer-scored with results returned to the student, to you, or to both.
- Coordinate large sections or multiple sections by providing one source of information.
- Include a link to your e-mail or put a text "input" section on the page for questions from students. Links to other experts' e-mail could also be provided, with their permission.

In this project, a few basics of HTML are presented to demonstrate how to create a simple top level page (or homepage) for a principles class. Then weekly class outlines or assignments can be written in a word processor (or directly in HTML) and linked to the top level page. Additional details on developing the class home page can be found in Leuthold (1998).

The first part of this project uses a text editor (e.g., Notepad in the Windows Accessories Group) and a browser. The second part uses a word processor that will save a file in HTML code.[9] The descriptions below assume that Microsoft Word is being used because it offers this feature for several versions of the program. For those who create class materials with Microsoft Powerpoint, the instructions are the same as for Microsoft Word. For versions earlier than Word 97 and Powerpoint 97, additional steps are necessary to install the HTML enhancement.[10]

*Example of HTML for a Class Web Site:*  An example of a class web page
is shown in Figure 6.1, which shows the web page beside its corresponding
HTML code. One of the easiest ways to learn HTML is to compare web results
to code.

This might look complex, but it is not difficult to create. First, using a text
editor (e.g., Notepad), type the code as shown (don't use bold text, which is
used here for display purposes). Don't worry about spacing or line breaks in the
text file because HTML ignores spacing and line breaks. Only the code matters
for rendering the document on a web screen. The code need not be capitalized,
but it makes the HTML document easier to read. Quotation marks are
necessary where shown. After typing the file, save it as a text file named
econclas.htm (or econclas.html). In what follows, the filename econclas.htm is
assumed. Remember to note the disk drive letter and subdirectory into which
the file is saved, for example, *C:\TEMP* or *C:\WEBDOCS*.

Keep the text editor open and run Netscape or another browser program. In
the browser, use **File/Open File** and type in the full address of the file, for
example C:/TEMP/econclas.htm.[11] The web page will have **[Principles of
Economics]** on the title bar at the top of the browser and should display Figure
6.1. If further editing is necessary, use the text editor to make changes, save
the file again, and in the browser click on **reload**.

The first line, <HTML>, tells the browser software to interpret the
document according to HTML standards. The < > signs and their contents
are HTML code called "tags." Tags are interpreted by the browser to render
the document on the screen. Many HTML tags are referred to as "containers"
because the code within an initial < > applies to what follows until reaching
an end point with the same code letters following a forward slash, </ >. The
code is applied to the material "contained" between the tags, for example, the
line beginning <H1> calls for a level one (large) heading to extend over the
text until </H1> turns it off.

The HEAD section does not appear in the web browser screen; the BODY
section does appear. The code <HEAD><TITLE>**Principles of
Economics**</TITLE> </HEAD> is the HEAD section and the text between
the TITLE tag containers appears at the top on the browser title bar.. The
<BODY> tag includes the background color information for the body, i.e.,
BGCOLOR="white." Within the BODY of the document, the code <H1> ...
</H1> "contains" a large on-screen header and the smaller on-screen headers
are enclosed in <H2> ... </H2> to <H6> ... </H6>. Try one of these
smaller tags by using the text editor to replace <H1> and </H1> with
<H6> and </H6> and save the document again. Then, in the browser, click
on **Reload** to see how the title is affected. A few tags do not have to be
containers; for example, <P>, the "paragraph" tag, denotes a new paragraph
after a double space and <BR>, the "break" tag, creates a single spaced new
line.[12]

**Figure 6.1: Sample Course Web Page and Corresponding HTML Document**

| Sample Course Web Page | HTML Document |
|---|---|
| | `<HTML>` |
| | `<HEAD><TITLE>Principles of Economics</TITLE></HEAD>` |
| | `<BODY BGCOLOR="white">` |
| # Professor X's Principles of Economics | `<H1>Professor X's Principles of Economics</H1>` |
| ## Syllabus | `<H2>Syllabus</H2>` |
| Here is the course syllabus for Economics 100: | `Here is the course syllabus for Economics 100:  <P>` |
| • Econ100 Syllabus | `<img src="button.gif"><A HREF="econ100.htm">Econ100 Syllabus</A>` |
| | `<P>` |
| ## Class Outline | `<H2>Class Outline</H2>` |
| • Week One Outline | `<A HREF="weekone.htm">Week One Outline</A> <BR>` |
| • Week Two Outline | `<A HREF="weektwo.htm">Week Two Outline</A>` |
| | `<P>` |
| ## Other class web sites: | `<H2>Other class web sites:</H2>` |
| | `<img src="button.gif">` |
| • Links to Economic Information | `<A HREF="http://ecedweb.unomaha.edu/econinfo.htm">Links to Economic Information</A>` |
| | `<P>` |
| Send me e-mail | `<A HREF="mailto:name@address">Send me e-mail!</A>` |
| | `</BODY>` |
| | `</HTML>` |

The code for showing a graphics image is < img src = "filename.ext" > (quotation marks required) where img src means "image source." The graphics format should be either a .gif or a .jpg format graphics file. Unless you happen to have a file named button.gif in the same subdirectory as econclas.htm, the graphic you see on the screen is the "broken graphic" indicator. Button images and other graphics files can be found at web sites that provide free graphics to download. A graphic on the browser screen can be saved to local disk by clicking on it with the right mouse button and selecting **Save Image As**. However, graphics on web pages are copyrighted unless specifically offered for free use, so a graphic acquired this way should not be published on your web page without permission.

The final tag needed for this project creates links in your document to other documents or to e-mail. This is the function of the lines that begin with < A HREF= ... > and end with < /A >. The first < A HREF=... > in Figure 6.1 creates a link (Hypertext Reference) to another HTML document econ100.htm in the same subdirectory as this document (econclas.htm). These tags are containers < A HREF=... > ... < /A > with URL information entirely inside the initial < A > tag. For example, "econ100.htm" is the fictional syllabus address link for this tag.

The next < A HREF=... > tag links to a file on another server, requiring the full address. The phrase "Links to Economic Information" between the < A > ... < /A > tags, is the visible "hotspot" line on the browser screen. The web page readers can click on these words to inform their browser to set up the connection. The last tag sets up an e-mail link. Students can communicate with you from the web page if your e-mail address is substituted for *name@address*.

If you wish to know more about HTML, many books and several on-line HTML web sites are available; some of the latter are linked to the National Association of Economic Educators site at < http://ecedweb.unomaha.edu/ NAEE/nethelp.htm >.

*Using a word processor to create a web page:* In Microsoft Word, create or open an existing course syllabus. Headings can be any desired size or typeface; however, Times Roman 12 is the font that will be translated without special coding in the HTML document. The browser software of your web page visitors is unlikely to recognize unusual typefaces. Word will also imbed equations, pictures, tables, or drawings. These will be rendered as graphic links in the HTML file. Symbols created with the equation editor will be accurately transcribed as image files. However, some symbol fonts in the text and formatting, such as paragraph indents, will not be rendered precisely.

With the syllabus on your Word screen, select **File/Save As**, and in the drop-down box labeled **Type of file** select **HTML document .htm**. Give the filename *econ100.htm* and save in the same subdirectory with econclas.htm.

Now in your browser open econclas.htm once more. Click on "Econ 100 Syllabus" and admire your work![13]

In Microsoft Powerpoint, the **File** menu has a selection for saving in *.htm* format. Save a "slide show" as weekone.htm (for example) in the same subdirectory as econclas.htm. Powerpoint presentations are saved in multiple HTML files, each representing one of the slides. They can be browsed as graphics or as text, as the student chooses. This is an excellent way to allow students to examine your Powerpoint diagrams and outlines at any time.

Use Microsoft Word or Powerpoint to create handouts, assignments, self-study questions, quizzes, or any other kind of information. Each new document you place on the website requires another line < A HREF = "filename.htm" > Link Name < /A > < BR > in econclas.htm to create the link to the document. Also remember to place the files in the same subdirectory on the web server computer.[14]

## III. HOW TO GET THE MOST FROM TECHNOLOGY IN TEACHING: A DO LIST

- Do take advantage of specialization of labor. Get help from your campus computer specialists when possible.
- Do proofread carefully on the browser screen. Be sure your web material is readable and without errors. Some tweaking of the HTML output of word processors might be necessary.
- Do test all external links regularly. Other sites occasionally disappear or change addresses.
- Do make your technology projects an integral part of the course. Although it is worthwhile to students to learn to use computers, remember that you are teaching economics.
- Do update the technology portion of the course frequently. A web-enhanced course can be updated while the course is in progress and should be updated each time the course is offered. The economics information and data on the web are updated frequently.
- Do use technology to appeal to a diversity of learning styles. Use self-paced materials, practice exams, simulations, and other projects with student involvement to create "active learning." Use computer and Internet/web assignments that connect real data to the theory. Use projects that connect theory to the students' own lives, for example, researching the economics of a career choice or the return to education.
- Do teach students how to search the Internet for information. The search engine is a basic tool for finding information, but will lead to frustration if

students don't know how to narrow their searches to find specific information.

- Do use technology to reduce barriers of time and space. Provide materials that take advantage of the fact that the faculty member and student can be separated by both time and space for the web portion of a course. Asynchronous teaching and learning is particularly attractive to working and adult students, disabled students, and perhaps shy students who prefer to learn at a distance or to participate in chat groups.

- Do use technology to lower marginal costs of additional students or additional course sections. The initial fixed costs for adding technology to a course are likely to be high. However, the marginal costs for updating computer and web presentations are usually not high. The number of students and classes who can use the material, particularly web sites, is very large.

- Do use e-mail to increase student-faculty and student-student communication. Manning (1996) found that computer-mediated communication between teacher and students increases rather than decreases traditional communications. An e-mail tag to the teacher from the web pages encourages students to ask questions as they work through the materials.

- Do use online chat groups to enhance interaction among students.

- Do coordinate several sections of a class or large sections by using the web to provide course information.

- Do share web materials world-wide. For example, faculty members geographically separated can develop a course, with each specializing, and then share teaching materials for students on the web.

- Do include comments on web proficiency when you write recommendations for internships, jobs, or graduate school.

- Do ask students to evaluate the technology portion of the course. In their opinions, did it contribute to their learning and attitudes about economics?


## IV. WHAT TO AVOID IN USING TECHNOLOGY IN TEACHING: A DON'T LIST

- Don't overwhelm students with information. Provide focus in your assignments, particularly the initial assignment. Diminishing or negative returns set in when the amount of information begins to overwhelm students' ability to see the overall picture, the key relationships, and the relevance of the information.

- Don't take significant time from the economics curriculum. Make technology an integral part of the course without subtracting from the economics material.
- Don't assume students can evaluate information. Teach students to ask these questions of on-line information: Who is offering the information? What are his or her qualifications? Is this information consistent with what other experts say? Does this web page reflect a particular point of view? If so, what are other viewpoints? What can I learn from this information and on which points must I reserve judgment? To give an economics example, an economist who is sanguine about the government deficit is not likely to create a web page saying so; however, someone extremely concerned is more likely to provide that point of view on the web. Send students to sources beyond the web for a balanced view of an issue.
- Don't ignore students reactions to using technology. Students can become addicted to the Internet to the detriment of all of their other activities. Eddy and Spaulding (1996) list other problems such as psychological stress from too many e-mail messages, loss of personal contact with people, and misuse of the Internet. They also note problems of hostility, shyness, or disrespect highly computer-oriented students might display if face-to-face contact is attempted by the teacher.
- Don't rely on equipment without a backup plan. If a class depends on a web presentation, it might be placed on a local or floppy disk and shown from there in case the network fails.
- Don't ignore the costs to yourself. The opportunity costs to yourself of using various levels of technology in teaching, such as lower research output, should be considered in your pedagogical decisions.

## V. FINAL OBSERVATIONS

The early research finds that positive contributions to learning and attitude result from using some forms of technology – e-mail, world wide web, computer mediated instruction, for example – in teaching. Communications are improved and a diversity of learning styles and preferences and time and distance preferences can be accommodated. The important consideration is that the technology be carefully planned to serve the educational goal of learning economics.

## NOTES

1. For example, the Allied Social Sciences Association (American Economic Association) meetings in 1996 and 1997 had Internet sessions (in two time slots in

1997) led by Bob Parks, Bill Goffe, and George Greenwade. The 1997 Midwest Economics Association and the Missouri Valley Economics Association meetings each had sessions on Internet and computers in teaching economics.

2. Keynote speech in Omaha on October 25, 1996. Reported in the *Omaha World Herald* by Doug Thomas on October 26, 1996, p. 61, "Speaker Touts Reach of Web."

3. Much of the evidence on using technology is at the K-12 rather than the college level. Dwyer (1996) includes a list of articles that evaluate learning in the K-12 schools, concluding that technology, when it is an integral part of comprehensive plan for instructional improvement, improves students' mastery of basic skill, test scores, writing, and engagement in school. Other K-12 evidence is mixed between "improved learning" and "no significant difference," though many studies do conclude that learning is improved. An interesting web site, McRel (1997) is devoted to reporting on Internet-enhanced teaching and providing links to additional research, mostly K-12 based.

4. The bookmark file can be edited and bookmarks deleted by clicking on **Bookmarks/Go to bookmarks**. To delete a bookmark, select it on this screen and select **Edit/Delete.**

5. All web sites mentioned in this chapter can be reached by starting at *EcEdWeb* at < http://ecedweb.unomaha.edu/ >. Go to the *EconInfo* page for links to information and data or to the *College Teaching* page for links to course web sites and teaching information.

6. Some countries that are exceptions to the expected relationship between the investment share and economic growth: Thailand and Mauritius have high growth with lower investment shares than typically found; Mexico, New Zealand, South Africa, Liberia, and Zambia, and Guyana have high investment shares but not high growth rates.

7. A. Edward Day suggested that the CIA site can be used by students to discuss and compare developed and less developed countries, in an e-mail message to the list *TCH-ECON* on Oct. 10, 1994.

8. This data set is updated periodically. If the number of the data set is higher than PWT5.6, the data has been revised and might be slightly different than the numbers provided here. An alternate site for these data is < http://www.nber.org >.

9. This project can also be done entirely in a word processor; the objective of using the text editor for the initial page is to introduce some basic HTML.

10. Microsoft Word 6.0 for Windows, Word 95, Powerpoint 95, and MAC Word require an add-on program, Word Internet Assistant, available free from the Microsoft web site. Go to < http://www.microsoft.com/ >, follow the links to the "free downloads" section, and look for "web authoring software." Follow the instructions to download the Word Internet Assistant (or Powerpoint Internet Assistant) file for your version of the software, keeping track of the subdirectory where it is being saved. (The **save** dialog box will show the open subdirectory on your drive.) The downloaded file is a program that must be run to install in Word. From Program Manager or the Start menu, type *run C:/path/filename.exe,* substituting the correct path and filename. The install wizard will guide you through the setup process. Although these steps might take from thirty to forty-five minutes, depending on your Internet access speed, the time saved by this method of creating HTML is substantial.

11. It is a good habit to refer to a filename exactly as saved. In some cases, upper- and lowercase letters are not equivalent in an address.

12. You can also use the paragraph formatting options in Word to control headings. A paragraph formatted with the paragraph style "Heading 1" will become <H1> ... </H1>, for example.

13. Documents do not have to be in the same subdirectory. Interested readers should check HTML manuals to learn how to designate different directories.


# REFERENCES

Agarwal, R. and A. E. Day. 1997. The impact of the Internet on economic education. Presentation at the 1997 Allied Social Sciences Association annual meeting. January 5, 1997: 1-24.

Becker, W. and M. Watts. 1996. Chalk and talk: A national survey on teaching undergraduate economics. *American Economic Review* 86 (May): 448-53.

Conrad, C. 1997. Computers and pedagogy: Lessons from other disciplines. Presentation at the 1997 Allied Social Sciences Association annual meeting. January 5, 1997: 1-12. (Available in Adobe Acrobat format at http://gsmith.pomona.edu/pedagogy.pdf.)

Dwyer, D. 1996. We're in this together. *Educational Leadership* 54 (November): 24-6.

Eddy, J. P. and D. Spaulding. 1996. Internet, computers, distance education and people failure: Research on technology. *Education* 116 (Spring): 391-2.

Griggs, R. 1995. Technology in the classroom. *Colorado Business* 22 (December): 17-21.

Grimes, P. W. and M. A. Ray. 1993. Economics: Microcomputers in the college classroom – a review of the academic literature. *Social Science Computer Review* 11 (Winter): 452-63.

Hannah, R. 1996. Internet sources for business educators. *Journal of Education for Business* 71(March): 209-13.

Leuthold, J. 1998. Building a homepage for your economics class. *Journal of Economic Education* 29 (Summer): 247-61.

Levin, J. A. and C. Thurston. 1996. Research summary: Educational electronic networks. *Educational Leadership* 54 (November): 46-50.

Manning, L. 1996. Economics on the internet: Electronic mail in the classroom. *Journal of Economic Education* 27 (Summer): 201-4.

McREL (Mid-continent Regional Educational Laboratory). 1997. The impact of technology. Web page compilation of research links found at <http://www.mcrel.org/connect/impact.html>.

O'Neil, J. 1996. On surfing—and steering—the net: Conversations with Crawford Kilian and Clifford Stoll. *Educational Leadership* 54 (November): 12-18.

Sell, R. G. 1996. Using technology and distance instruction to improve postsecondary education. [online] <http://www.uni.edu/teachctr/technol2.htm> p. 1-21.

Sosin, K. 1997. Impact of the web on economics pedagogy. Paper presented at the Allied Social Sciences Association Meeting. (January 5). (Available in Adobe Acrobat format at <http://ecedweb.unomaha.edu/ksosin/webteach.pdf>)

Stoll, C. 1995. *Silicon snake oil: Second thoughts on the information highway*. New York : Doubleday.

Summers, R. and A. Heston. 1991. The Penn World Table (Mark 5): An expanded set of international comparisons, 1950-1988. *Quarterly Journal of Economics* 106 (May): 327-68.

Talbott, S. L. 1995. *The future does not compute: Transcending the machines in our midst*. Sebastopol, CA: O'Reilly and Associates, Inc.

CHAPTER **7**

# USING MONTE CARLO STUDIES FOR TEACHING ECONOMETRICS

**Peter Kennedy**

What do we want our students to know upon completion of an undergraduate econometrics course? Most instructors would agree that we want them to be able to analyze data with an econometrics software package, and we want them to have some understanding of the theory of econometrics. I argue that what currently is done fails miserably in regard to the second of these goals and propose an alternative approach.

Instructors do not realize that students do not understand the basic logic of statistics as reflected in the concept of a sampling distribution and consequently are inherently uncomfortable with econometrics. Because instructors do not realize this deficiency, they press on with technical material, which students deal with by becoming adept at mathematical manipulation without understanding what is actually going on. At the end of the course, students continue to be uncomfortable with econometrics. This can be remedied if instructors begin by emphasizing the concept of a sampling distribution and thereafter force students to generate explanations of how Monte Carlo studies would be structured to examine the econometric issues dealt with at each stage of the course. Examples are given in Appendix 7.A. (By Monte Carlo study I mean a specific variant of a generic technique known as resampling; to smooth exposition, discussion of resampling and its related literature is presented in Appendix 7.B.)

## I. WHAT'S WRONG

Upon completion of introductory statistics courses, the vast majority of students do not understand the basic logic of classical statistics as captured in the concept of repeated samples and a sampling distribution. They know how to do mechanical things such as compute a sample variance, run a regression, and test an hypothesis, but they do not have a feel for the "big picture." They have learned a bunch of techniques, but to them they are just that, a bunch of techniques, and they know they can pass the course by remembering how these techniques work. They view statistics as a branch of mathematics because it uses mathematical formulas, so they look at statistics through a mathematical lens. What they are missing is the statistical lens through which to view this world, allowing this world to make sense. The concept of a sampling distribution is this statistical lens. My own experience discovering this lens was a revelation, akin to the experience I had when I put on my first pair of eyeglasses – suddenly everything was sharp and clear.

Those of us who teach statistics should be aware of this phenomenon. We frequently encounter students with A grades in their introductory statistics courses who clearly have no understanding of statistics beyond an ability to mechanically apply standard statistical procedures. We often see graduate students with an impressive ability to derive statistical formulas but a remarkable inability to explain how to evaluate those formulas via a Monte Carlo study. Occasionally technically competent students admit that although they can do the mathematics, they are not really comfortable with statistics. These shortcomings of students may be a result of the way we teach this material.

How has this state of affairs come about? It is not because the introductory statistics books ignore sampling distributions – they all have plenty of good material on this concept and give it appropriate emphasis. And it is not because instructors ignore this dimension of the introductory textbooks – all instructors will swear that they teach this concept thoroughly. But students are utility maximizers. They know that their exams are going to require an ability to interpret regressions, calculate $t$ statistics, and perform hypothesis tests, not an ability to explain the concept of a sampling distribution. They can not imagine, and instructors and textbooks do not provide, examples of exam questions that in any meaningful way probe student understanding of this concept.

As a result, most students, even good students, go on from introductory statistics to econometrics without an adequate understanding of the fundamentals of statistics. The better instructors realize that students have mostly forgotten their introductory statistics material, or never learned it properly in the first place, and proceed on the basis that this introductory material needs to be reviewed. Unfortunately, this review suffers from the same problem noted earlier – there is little motivation for students to buckle down and properly learn the concept of a sampling distribution and the role it plays in econometrics because instructors' expositions of this concept, however clear, are not accompanied by appropriate example exam questions. Such questions provide motivation and, more importantly, force students to work out answers. Although we lecturers like to think otherwise, brilliant expositions seldom cause students fully to understand – such understanding comes through working out problems based on the concept to be learned. An old adage bears repeating: I hear and I learn; I see and I realize; I do and I understand.

Econometrics textbooks do not help much. They are in too big a hurry to produce the theorems, proofs, and formulas that define theoretical econometrics. Some review introductory statistics but do so without much emphasis on sampling distributions and seldom provide meaningful questions that force student understanding of the sampling distribution concept. Two things are needed. First, instructors need to produce for students a good exposition of what is a sampling distribution and what role it plays in econometrics. Second, a means must be found to construct problems that cause students to learn this concept properly. In the next section, I offer my own exposition of sampling distributions and suggest that the needed problems can be constructed by asking students to explain how to conduct Monte Carlo studies.

## II. SAMPLING DISTRIBUTIONS: AN EXPOSITION

In my experience, students fail to grasp the meaning and import of a sampling distribution if it is described in general terms. A successful exposition must be couched in terms of a specific example such as the following.

Suppose that you have 45 observations on variables $x$ and $y$. You know that $y$ has been produced from $x$ by using the formula $y = \beta x + \varepsilon$ where $\varepsilon$ is an error with mean zero and variance $\sigma^2$. Note that there is no intercept in this linear relationship, so there is only one unknown parameter, $\beta$, the slope of $x$. This means that $y_1$, the first observation on $y$, was created by multiplying $x_1$, the first observation on $x$, by the unknown number $\beta$ and then adding $\varepsilon_1$, the first error, obtained by randomly grabbing an error from a bowl of errors with mean zero and variance $\sigma^2$. The other 44 observations on $y$ were created in similar fashion.

You are interested in estimating the unknown parameter $\beta$. Professor A suggests using the formula $\beta^* = \Sigma y/\Sigma x$ and professor B suggests using the formula $\beta^{**} = \Sigma xy/\Sigma x^2$, where the subscripts have been omitted for convenience. Both of these suggestions just involve putting the data into an algebraic formula to produce a single number that is proposed as the estimate of $\beta$. Suppose this is done using your data, producing $\beta^* = 2.34$ and $\beta^{**} = 2.73$. Which of these two estimates should you choose?

Take a closer look at these two formulas to see if a rationale can be produced for choosing one in preference to the other. Since $y = \beta x + \varepsilon$ you can substitute this into professor A's formula to get

$$\beta^* = \Sigma \, (\beta x + \varepsilon)/\Sigma x = \beta + \Sigma \varepsilon / \Sigma x$$

and you can substitute it into professor B's formula to get

$$\beta^{**} = \Sigma \, (\beta x + \varepsilon)/\Sigma x^2 = \beta + \Sigma \varepsilon / \Sigma x^2.$$

From this it is apparent that both these formulas are such that they are equal to $\beta$ plus an expression that involves the unknown $\varepsilon$ values. Because the $\varepsilon$ values are positive about half the time and negative about half the time, it looks as though in both cases this expression involving the errors is probably going to be fairly close to zero, suggesting that both of these formulas are reasonable – they each appear to be creating a suitable estimate of $\beta$.

Consider professor A's estimate $\beta^* = \beta + \Sigma \varepsilon / \Sigma x = 2.34$. How close $\beta^* = 2.34$ is to $\beta$ clearly depends on the particular set of 45 error terms that were drawn out of the bowl of errors to produce the $y$ observations. If in obtaining the data, mostly large positive errors were drawn, $\beta^*$ would substantially overestimate $\beta$. If mostly large negative errors were drawn, $\beta^*$ would substantially underestimate $\beta$. If a more typical set of errors were drawn, $\beta^*$ would produce an estimate fairly close to $\beta$. The point here is that the set of 45 unknown error terms drawn determines the estimate produced by the $\beta^*$ formula and so there is no way of knowing how close the particular estimate 2.34 is to the true $\beta$ value.

Now suppose for a moment that you know the true value of $\beta$. Visualize grabbing 45 error terms, calculating $y$ using $\beta$ and the $x$ values, computing $\beta^*$, and recording the result. Mentally do this 2,000 times, each time grabbing 45 new error terms. This produces 2,000 hypothetical $\beta^*$ values, each produced by mimicking exactly the process thought to be generating the actual $y$ data. These 2,000 $\beta^*$ values can be used to construct a histogram of possible $\beta^*$ values. This histogram should show that very high values of $\beta^*$ will be relatively rare because such a $\beta^*$ value would require an unusual draw of 45 error terms. Similarly, very low values of $\beta^*$ will also be rare. Values of $\beta^*$ closer to the true $\beta$ value will be more common because they would result from more typical draws of 45 errors. This histogram estimates a distribution of possible $\beta^*$ values, providing a picture of the relative probabilities of obtaining different $\beta^*$ values. This distribution is called the sampling distribution of $\beta^*$. Professor B's formula $\beta^{**}$ will also have a sampling distribution, but because it is a different formula its sampling distribution should look slightly different. (I exposit the algebra above for the two estimators side-by-side on the overhead/blackboard, finishing with a sampling distribution picture for each, both drawn as normal-looking distributions centered over the true value of $\beta$ but with the variance of $\beta^*$ noticeably larger than the variance of $\beta^{**}$.)

The logic of all this delivers the following punch line: **Using $\beta^*$ to produce an estimate of $\beta$ can be conceptualized as the econometrician shutting his or her**

**eyes and obtaining an estimate of $\beta$ by reaching blindly into the sampling distribution of $\beta^*$ to obtain a single number.**

An immediate implication of this is that our choice between $\beta^*$ and $\beta^{**}$ comes down to the following: **Would I prefer to produce my estimate of $\beta$ by reaching blindly into the sampling distribution of $\beta^*$ or by reaching blindly into the sampling distribution of $\beta^{**}$?**

At this stage, the instructor can confess that most of econometricians' fancy algebraic derivations are just efforts to investigate what the sampling distributions of suggested estimators or test statistics look like and that much of the essence of econometrics can be summarized by addressing four basic questions related to the sampling distribution concept:

1. What would make one sampling distribution better than another in this regard? This motivates a discussion of bias, variance, and mean square error.

2. How does one find out what a sampling distribution looks like? This underlines the importance of knowing how to calculate expected values and variances, either algebraically, perhaps relying on asymptotics, or via Monte Carlo procedures.

3. What is a Monte Carlo study? This permits exposition of Monte Carlo studies as using the computer to perform the mental experiment of generating thousands of $\beta^*$ values for cases in which the algebra is "too difficult."

4. Do sampling distributions play any other role in econometrics? This allows hypothesis testing to be exposited in terms of the sampling distributions of test statistics.

## III. WHAT DO THESE SAMPLING DISTRIBUTIONS LOOK LIKE?

It is useful to pursue this example to illustrate these basic questions associated with the sampling distribution concept. The example can be exploited/extended in several ways.

1. Begin by explaining that an estimator is unbiased if its sampling distribution is centered over the true value of the parameter being estimated. Note that as we will see later, these two estimators are unbiased so their sampling distributions are both drawn (as I suggested earlier) centered over $\beta$. Now ask students which of these two sampling distributions they would prefer to shut their eyes and draw from to produce their estimate of $\beta$. They should quickly agree that they would prefer the sampling distribution of $\beta^{**}$, allowing you to announce the minimum variance (efficiency) criterion.

2. Next, illustrate the possibility of a biased estimator. Do this by changing the data-generating process so that there is now a nonzero intercept: $y = \alpha + \beta x + \varepsilon$. The algebra on $\beta^{**}$ now produces

$$\beta^{**} = \alpha \sum x / \sum x^2 + \beta + \sum x\varepsilon / \sum x^2$$

so that it appears as though $\beta^{**}$ will be biased by an amount $\alpha \Sigma x / \Sigma x^2$. An important point to stress here is that the sampling distribution properties of an estimator depend crucially on the data-generating process – an estimator with an attractive sampling distribution for one data-generating process may have a very unattractive sampling distribution for another data-generating process.

3. Econometricians work hard to find ways of modifying popular estimators so that they will have attractive sampling distributions in new data-generating situations. In this case consider the estimator

$$\beta^{***} = \sum (x - \bar{x})(y - \bar{y}) / \sum (x - \bar{x})^2 = \beta + \sum (x - \bar{x})(\varepsilon - \bar{\varepsilon}) / \sum (x - \bar{x})^2$$

which removes the bias. If we were to use bias as our criterion of choice, we would choose $\beta^{***}$ in preference to $\beta^{**}$.

4. Next, draw the sampling distributions of $\beta^{**}$ and of $\beta^{***}$ for this case of a nonzero intercept. Draw the sampling distribution of $\beta^{***}$ as centered over $\beta$ and the sampling distribution of $\beta^{**}$ as biased slightly but with a much smaller variance than the variance of $\beta^{***}$. At this point, just state that it turns out that $\beta^{**}$ has a smaller variance, a result you will explore later. Now if you have drawn your diagram judiciously, the students should quickly agree that despite $\beta^{**}$ being biased they would prefer to obtain their estimate of $\beta$ by reaching blindly into the sampling distribution of $\beta^{**}$, rather than the sampling distribution of $\beta^{***}$. Conclude that maybe unbiasedness is not as important as we thought.

5. Now redraw the sampling distribution of $\beta^{**}$ so that its variance is just a bit smaller than that of $\beta^{***}$, so that it is not clear which of $\beta^{**}$ and $\beta^{***}$ is preferred. Note that what is needed is some formal way of trading off bias and variance. Introduce mean square error, MSE, as a tradeoff taking the form MSE = bias$^2$ + variance, a result equivalent to minimizing the expected square of the difference between the estimate and what it is estimating. You might wish to show this algebraically at this point, if that is your style.

6. Now that you have introduced the three main criteria defining an attractive sampling distribution for an estimator, move on to how in simple cases such as this example we can use algebra to deduce these properties. (I will continue the example using $\beta^{**}$ and $\beta^{***}$, but you may wish to return to comparing $\beta^{*}$ and

$\beta$**.) You can show formally that $\beta$** is biased and $\beta$*** unbiased. Then you can derive

$$\text{Var}(\beta^{**}) = \sigma^2/\sum x^2 \text{ and } \text{Var}(\beta^{***}) = \sigma^2/\sum(x-\bar{x})^2$$

which is clearly bigger. Then you can note that $\beta$*** will have a smaller MSE than

$$\beta^{**} \text{ if } \left[\alpha\sum x/\sum x^2\right]^2 + \sigma^2/\sum x^2 \text{ is greater than } \sigma^2/\sum(x-\bar{x})^2.$$

This is an example of a major problem associated with using MSE as a criterion: Which estimator has the smaller MSE depends on the unknown true values of the parameters, in this case $\alpha$ and $\sigma^2$.

7. By now, students should be receptive to a means of finding the characteristics of the sampling distribution without having to do algebra. Announce that Monte Carlo studies are designed to do just that, by using a computer to simulate the repeated draws of error terms that affect the estimates produced by competing formulas estimating $\beta$. Show explicitly how a Monte Carlo study would be performed in the context of this example:

a.  Choose 45 values for $x$, either by using the $x$ values from an actual empirical study or by using the computer to generate 45 values in some way.
b.  Choose values for the unknown parameters, say $\alpha = 1$, $\beta = 2$ and $\sigma^2 = 4$.
c.  Get the computer to draw 45 error terms ($\varepsilon$) randomly from a distribution with mean zero and variance 4.
d.  Calculate 45 $y$ values as $1 + 2x + \varepsilon$.
e.  Calculate $\beta$** and $\beta$*** and save them.
f.  Return to step c and repeat this procedure until you have, say, 2,000 $\beta$** and $\beta$*** values.
g.  Use the 2,000 $\beta$** values and 2,000 $\beta$*** values to draw a histogram showing the features of the sampling distributions of $\beta$** and $\beta$***. Then announce that this is seldom done because usually the sampling distribution is characterized by only three measures, its mean, its variance, and its MSE. The mean is estimated by the average of the 2,000 estimates, the variance is estimated by the sample variance of the 2,000 estimates, and the MSE is estimated by subtracting the true value of $\beta$, in this case 2, from each estimate, squaring these numbers and then averaging these 2,000 squared numbers.

## IV. EXPLAINING MONTE CARLO STUDIES: DO'S AND DON'TS

A careful exposition of sampling distributions and a clear discussion of their connection to econometricians' focus on deriving expected values, variances, and test statistics should be a welcome addition to the beginning of an econometrics course, but it is only that – a beginning. Some way must be found to hammer home this lesson so that the perspective it provides for later study is not forgotten. I suggest the use of explain-how-to-do-a-Monte-Carlo-study problems. By forcing students to structure a Monte Carlo study to examine an econometric question, they are forced to spell out very clearly their understanding of this question. Some advice in this regard follows, based on many years of experience teaching using this approach.

- Do not ask students actually to do a Monte Carlo study. Although students are supposed to be computer literate, they are not able to quickly learn how to program. Be content with having them write down a detailed step-by-step set of instructions for a hypothetical research assistant.
- Do prepare for the question: Won't our choice of parameter values affect the results of the Monte Carlo study? There are three possible answers. First, the kinds of problems addressed by undergraduates are such that the results about variances and about test statistics usually do not depend on the true parameter values. Admit that if bias exists its magnitude is affected by the true parameter values and so in these situations MSE also is affected. Second, if there is reason to believe that the results are affected, then the study should be repeated for a variety of parameter values to see in what way the results are affected. Third, for a particular study, we can choose the true parameter values equal to the parameter estimates from the data at hand, so that the results of the Monte Carlo study are specific to parameter values that are likely close to the true parameter values for that study.
- Do make students describe a Monte Carlo study for every major topic in the course. The detail required in the expected answers can diminish markedly over time because certain things (such as formulas for estimating bias, variance, and mean square error) become unquestionably known by all, so such tasks should not be time-consuming. As noted later, they could be no more than exercises designed to ensure that the students understand how the data-generating process operates.
- Do evaluate students' instructions carefully. Small mistakes can reflect major misunderstandings. Be particularly on guard for vagueness in these instructions; this is students' favorite way of attempting to conceal lack of understanding. For example, they may not specify their parameter values because they are not sure if they should use values satisfying the null hypothesis, or they may omit describing how to get the first error needed to generate a sequence of first-order autocorrelated errors. They may not know how to do it or whether it is important.
- Do spend lots of time on this. Most students have a remarkably difficult time grasping the logic of what is going on. At first their attention is monopolized by the mechanical steps of a Monte Carlo study, at the expense of

understanding the overall logic of what the particular study they are explaining is trying to accomplish. Consequently the first Monte Carlo problems should be very easy in terms of the econometric question they address because students will be preoccupied with questions such as: What is the computer capable of doing? How should fixed-in-repeated-samples observations be selected? How do we decide what parameter values to use? What sample size should be used? What variance of the error should be chosen? How can an error with this variance be created? What formulas should be used to estimate the mean and variance of the sampling distribution? Exactly which steps need to be repeated? How many repeated samples should be taken?

- Do reverse the problem – provide students with an outline of a Monte Carlo study and ask them a question about what results would be expected, as illustrated in the first three examples in Appendix 7.A. This approach makes students think about relevant concepts as it provides examples of the set of instructions students should later be able to produce on their own. The next stage is to ask them to describe how to conduct a study to address a specific issue in the context of a specific problem. It is important that the question spell out many of the details of the study, such as is done in examples E, F, G and I in Appendix 7.A. (The problems gathered in example H of Appendix 7.A illustrate a variety of issues that can form the basis of a Monte Carlo study problem but as written are unsuitable for students because most students require a very specific context.)

- Do ask students how to simulate the data-generating process. The fact that the properties of an estimator's or a test statistic's sampling distribution depend on the process generating the data is not quickly appreciated. If you ask students to explain how to generate data to perform a Monte Carlo study for every major econometric topic you cover in the course, you will be unpleasantly surprised by the problems they have, but they will benefit immensely by understanding the role of the data-generating mechanism. If they cannot explain how to generate raw data for a heteroskedastic error model, for a two-equation simultaneous equation system, or for a qualitative choice model, can you be confident that they understand what any of the equations you have been putting on the blackboard really mean?

- Do call on a student to suggest the first step, then go around the room asking each student in turn to supply the next step, or correct an incorrect step suggested by an earlier student. In-class development of a step-by-step set of Monte Carlo instructions can be an effective means of generating classroom participation.

- Do consider introducing students to bootstrapping as an advanced topic, after traditional Monte Carlo studies have been mastered. (Bootstrapping is a special type of Monte Carlo study that is becoming quite common in econometrics.) Further comment on this is provided in Appendix 7.B.

- Do allow better students who wish to perform a Monte Carlo study the opportunity, perhaps as a term paper. The popular econometrics packages have programming capabilities. Be cautious if using a statistical package designed to perform resampling experiments, such as Resampling Stats. Although these packages are an extremely useful means of showing students the logic of repeated samples, they mix a variety of resampling techniques without drawing students' attention to the fact that some of these different techniques do not correspond to the rationale that underlies econometric analysis. For example, for some problems, they employ Monte Carlo, for others, they use bootstrapping, and for still others they exploit a randomization methodology. Furthermore, they do not provide packaged econometric techniques, so investigation of the properties of econometric methods is awkward. See Appendix 7.B for further discussion.

## V. OPPORTUNITY COST

As should be evident from the discussion above, my proposal requires that instructors spend considerable time on sampling distributions and Monte Carlo studies, something they do not now do. What should be given up to accommodate this new feature?

This is a matter for each individual instructor to decide. I believe that the benefit of my innovation is so large that no instructor could possibly claim that the least-valued subset of their course has more benefit. Indeed, my innovation should enhance student understanding of all dimensions of a course, creating benefits beyond those attached solely to learning about sampling distributions and Monte Carlo studies. Advanced estimation or testing techniques do not mean much to students if they do not understand the fundamental principles that lie behind them; such advanced material is quickly forgotten once the course is completed.

In my own courses, I have given up most mathematical derivations. Do we really want our students at the end of their course to be able to do technical things like derive the OLS estimator and prove that it is BLUE, show that the expected value of $s^2$ is $\sigma^2$, or show mathematically that MSE is the sum of bias squared and variance? I think not. These things in any event have little meaning if the concept of a sampling distribution is not thoroughly understood.

## VI. CONCLUSION

By the end of my econometrics course, I want my students to understand the basic principles of classical statistics well enough to allow them to sit down with a textbook and figure out the rationale of any new statistical procedure that they are likely to encounter in their postundergraduate lives. In keeping with this, all my exams are open-book. Is my approach easier for the student? In my experience, the answer to this is yes and no. For those who quickly learn the Monte Carlo view of the statistical world, the entire econometrics course becomes easier because these students understand what is going on. But for all students this approach is intellectually very challenging because it forces them to think hard to understand an abstract concept. Simon and Bruce (1991, 29) make the same point in the context of their resampling approach to learning basic statistics, claiming that it "requires only hard, clear thinking. You cannot beg off by saying 'I have no brain for math!'" Some students do not rise to this challenge; they are more comfortable learning by rote a bunch of techniques and mathematical proofs and so find my approach more difficult.

I like to think that my approach works well for those who obtain jobs in which statistical analysis plays some role, but unfortunately such students tend to disappear permanently from one's life. Feedback from students who have gone on to graduate studies has been illuminating, however. One such student confessed that all he really needed to know about econometrics he learned in my course. Another told me that during the first half of his graduate econometrics course he was far behind the rest of the class because he had to learn from scratch a lot of formulas and algebraic derivations that other students had encountered in their more-traditional undergraduate econometrics courses. But he found that after the first month or so he had become comfortable with the math and suddenly leapfrogged far ahead of the rest of the class because, he said, he understood what was going on but they understood only the mathematics. Can an instructor ask for a better endorsement?

## Appendix 7.A: Monte Carlo Problem Examples

This appendix provides some examples of how questions based on Monte Carlo studies can be structured. Additional examples can be found in Kennedy (1998). Examples A, B, and C reverse the sequence of the usual problem. Rather than asking students to describe a Monte Carlo study, these questions provide descriptions of Monte Carlo studies and then ask students to explain what results are expected. This makes them suitable as introductory Monte Carlo problems because they ease students into this unfamiliar territory by providing illustrations of how Monte Carlo studies are structured. Example D is similar in that it provides the results of a Monte Carlo study and asks students to work with them. Examples E, F and G illustrate typical Monte Carlo problems, in which the question provides considerable detail regarding the setup of the study. Example H suggests a variety of topics that can be investigated by Monte Carlo studies, but offers the student no specific context. I recommend that before being given to students these examples be converted into problems with specific context, such as is illustrated in example I. Some examples of typical mistakes students make when structuring Monte Carlo studies are given after the examples.

A. Suppose you have programmed a computer to do the following:

1. Draw randomly 25 values from a standard normal distribution.
2. Multiply each of these values by 3 and add 2.
3. Take their average and call it A1.
4. Repeat this procedure to obtain 500 averages A1 through A500.
5. Compute the average of these 500 A values. Call it Abar.
6. Compute the variance of these 500 A values. Call it Avar.
   a. What number do you think Abar should be close to? Explain your logic.
   b. What number do you think Avar should be close to? Explain your logic.

B. Suppose you have programmed a computer to do the following:

1. Draw randomly a hundred values from a standard normal distribution.
2. Multiply each of these values by 5 and add 1.
3. Average the resulting hundred values.
4. Call the average A1 and save it.
5. Repeat the procedure above to produce 2,000 averages A1 through A2,000.
6. Order these 2,000 values from the smallest to the largest.
   a. What is your best guess of the 1,900th ordered value? Explain your logic.
   b. What is your best guess of how many of these values are negative? Explain your logic.

C. Suppose you have programmed a computer to do the following:

1. Draw 20 $x$ values from a distribution uniform between 2 and 8.
2. Draw 20 $z$ values from a normal distribution with mean 12 and variance 2.
3. Draw 20 $\varepsilon$ values from a standard normal distribution.
4. Create 20 $y$ values using the formula $y = 2 + 3x + 4z + 5\varepsilon$.
5. Regress $y$ on $x$ and $z$, obtaining the estimate $b_z$ of the coefficient of $z$ and the estimate $seb_z$ of its standard error.
6. Subtract 4 from $b_z$, divide this by $seb_z$ and call it $w1$.
7. Repeat the process described above beginning with step 3 until 5,000 $w$ values have been created, $w1$ through $w5,000$.
8. Order the 5,000 $w$ values from smallest to largest.
9. Average the 4,750th and 4,751st values.
   What is your best guess of this average? Explain your reasoning.

D. Suppose you have conducted a Monte Carlo study to investigate, for sample size 25, the bias of an estimator $\beta^*$ of the slope coefficient in the relationship $y = 2 + 3x + \varepsilon$ where you drew 400 repeated samples of errors ($\varepsilon$) from a normal distribution with mean zero and variance 9.0. Your study estimates the bias of $\beta^*$ as 0.04 and the variance of $\beta^*$ as .01. You are not sure if 0.04 is small enough to be considered zero.

Test the null hypothesis that it is insignificantly different from zero.

E. Consider the case of a sample of size 20 of a variable $x$ distributed normally with mean 8 and variance 4. The usual estimator of the variance of $x$ has a divisor of $N-1$. Two alternative estimators use divisors of $N$ and $N+1$.

Explain in detail how to conduct a Monte Carlo study to investigate the relative merits of these three formulas.

F. Suppose the classical linear regression model applies to the money demand function $m = \alpha + \beta y + \delta r + \varepsilon$ and you have 25 observations on income $y$ and on the nominal interest rate $r$ which in your data are positively correlated. You wish to compare the ordinary least squares $\beta$ estimates including, versus omitting, the relevant explanatory variable $r$.

1. Explain in detail how to do this with a Monte Carlo study.
2. What results do you expect to get? Why?

G. Suppose the classical normal linear regression model applies to the money demand function $m = \alpha + \beta y + \delta r + \varepsilon$ and you have 25 observations on income $y$ and on the nominal interest rate $r$ which in your data are negatively correlated. You regress $m$ on $y$ (erroneously omitting $r$) and use a $t$ test to test the null hypothesis that $\beta = 1$ at the $\alpha = .05$ significance level.

1. Explain in detail how to conduct a Monte Carlo study to find the type I error of this $t$ test.
2. What results do you expect to get? Why?

H. Explain in detail how you would undertake a Monte Carlo study to examine:

1. the validity of the textbook formula for the variance of the sample mean statistic;
2. the payoff to incorporating extraneous information in an OLS regression;
3. how inference using OLS is biased when the errors are heteroskedastic;
4. the relative merits of OLS and estimated generalized least squares when the errors are first-order autocorrelated;
5. how OLS is biased in the presence of measurement errors;

6. the relative merits of linear and logit regression in a qualitative choice model;
7. the risk function of a pretest estimator; and
8. the power curve of a Lagrange multiplier test versus a Wald test or a likelihood ratio test.

I. Explain how to undertake a Monte Carlo study to examine the relative merits of ordinary least squares and two-stage least squares in the simultaneous equation system

$$D: Q = \alpha_0 + \alpha_1 P + \alpha_2 Y + \alpha_3 A + \varepsilon_d$$
$$S: Q = \beta_0 + \beta_1 P + \varepsilon_s$$

where $Q$ and $P$ are the endogenous variables quantity and price, and $Y$ and $A$ are the exogenous variables income and advertising.

**Typical Student Errors**
There are several generic errors that students tend to make when describing Monte Carlo studies for Questions D, E, F, G and I above.

**Question D**
Bias is estimated using the average of the 400 $\beta^*$ values, so the variance of the bias estimate should be calculated using the formula for the variance of the sample mean statistic, in this case estimated as 0.01/400. Many students just use 0.01.

**Question E**
1. The results here are sensitive to sample size, with the bias of the formulas dividing by $N$ and by $N+1$ disappearing as the sample becomes larger. Students should note that their choice of sample size is important here but many do not.
2. Some students become confused by the fact that this question is looking at the bias and variance of estimators of variance and are careless in the way in which they word their exposition.
3. Looking at only bias and variance misses the fact that dividing by $N+1$ in this example happens to produce the smallest MSE; sometimes students neglect to look at MSE.
4. Students have a tendency to estimate MSE by summing their estimate of variance and the square of their estimate of bias. This is not quite as good as estimating MSE directly – by finding the average of the squared difference between the parameter estimate and the true parameter value.

## Question F

1. Some students use two data-generating mechanisms and so create two sets of data, one with a nonzero coefficient on the interest rate and then another, inappropriate set with a zero coefficient on the interest rate.
2. Some students do the Monte Carlo study for one estimator separately, then repeat it for the other, drawing new error terms. Although this is not incorrect, it does not exploit the efficiency to be gained from comparing the two estimators using the same errors.

## Question G

1. Because the Monte Carlo study is to find the type I error of a test, the null hypothesis, that $\beta = 1$, must be true in the data. Many students neglect to ensure that this is the case by using $\beta = 1$ when generating data.
2. Some students think that the researcher failing to include $r$ as a regressor means that the data-generating process has a zero coefficient on $r$ and so they erroneously generate data with the coefficient on $r$ set equal to zero.

## Question I

1. A common mistake is failure to note that only the supply equation is identified so that the Monte Carlo study must be confined to investigation of the estimation of the supply equation's parameters.
2. A second common error is not to generate the $P$ and $Q$ values such that they have been generated as the equilibrium values of the simultaneous equations. To do this students need to employ the reduced form expressions, including the reduced error expressions, when generating the $P$ and $Q$ values.

## Appendix 7.B: Alternative Forms of Resampling

Throughout this chapter I have argued for the use of descriptions of Monte Carlo studies to enhance teaching of econometrics. The purpose of this appendix is to discuss how this suggestion fits into the related literature on resampling. As defined by Simon and Bruce (1991, 28) resampling is "Using the entire set of data you have in hand, or using the given data-generating mechanism (such as a die) that is a model of the process you wish to understand, to produce new samples of simulated data, and to examine the results of those samples." They claim (and cite confirming empirical evidence) that by teaching students in terms of resampling rather than in terms of mathematical formulas, better understanding of statistical concepts and a higher success rate in finding numerical answers are achieved. Boomsma and Molenaar (1991) and Albert and Berliner (1994) are interesting critiques.

Before discussing how my Monte Carlo suggestion fits into this literature it is necessary to describe the three fundamentally-different ways of conducting resampling experiments to find sampling distributions. I exposit them below in the context of an ordinary least squares (OLS) regression of $y$ on $x$, sample size $N$.

## Monte Carlo

Sampling distributions of statistics of interest are calculated by drawing errors from a known distribution, using them in conjunction with a known data-generating mechanism to create new data, and recalculating the statistics. Its major drawback is that any conclusions it reaches may be sensitive to the error distribution assumed. The essence of a Monte Carlo study should be clear from earlier examples, so I will not review the procedure here. What will be of relevance is how it differs from the two alternative procedures described below.

## Bootstrapping

Bootstrapping is a special case of Monte Carlo, with two main variants. The first variant begins by calculating the OLS estimates and their associated $N$ residuals. Then a Monte Carlo study is conducted using the OLS estimates as the true parameter values and using the residuals as the pool of errors from which one draws (with replacement) errors when constructing $y$ values. In effect, the error distribution is chosen as discrete, with equal probability on each of the $N$ residual values. The big advantage of the bootstrap is that it does not rely on a questionable assumption regarding the distribution of the true errors, allowing the distribution of the residuals to serve as a proxy for this unknown distribution. This variant of bootstrapping is squarely in the tradition of Monte Carlo studies; it does exactly what a Monte Carlo study does but changes the nature of the bowl of errors used in constructing the repeated sample $y$ values. The big disadvantage of this method is that it must be the case that each of these residuals is equally likely to be attached to each observation, something that may not be true. An example would be a case of heteroskedasticity when large errors are more likely to be attached to observations having true errors with larger variances.

To deal with problems such as this heteroskedasticity, a second variant of the bootstrap is employed. In this approach, each value of the dependent variable along with its associated independent variable values is placed in a vector to form a set of $N$ such vectors. A new sample of size $N$ is created by drawing with replacement from this set of $N$ vectors and the OLS estimator is calculated. By repeating this process several times, a sampling distribution can be calculated. The big advantage of this approach is that it circumvents the problem of all errors not being equally likely to be attached to each observation – in these repeated samples each error stays with its associated dependent and independent variable values.

This variant of the bootstrap has two big disadvantages. First, no known true parameter value is associated with this repeated sampling process so that although the variance of the estimator in repeated samples can be calculated, its bias cannot. Second, this procedure changes the meaning of the sampling distribution. Earlier the sampling distribution reflected how the drawing of error terms affects our estimates, given the values of the explanatory variables drawn when we obtained our sample. This second bootstrap procedure produces a sampling distribution that must be interpreted differently. It reflects how our estimates are affected by the drawing of both the values of the explanatory variables and their associated error terms, assuming the values of the explanatory variables drawn when we drew our sample are typical of explanatory variable values that could have been obtained. The difference between these two types of sampling distributions can be of consequence. Suppose, for example, we are interested in examining the determinants of public expenditure in cities of population greater than 20,000 in the state of Washington. The city of Seattle is very different from all other Washington cities. It would not be possible for more than one city with Seattle's characteristics to appear in the sample, but exactly that could happen in this second bootstrap procedure, producing a misleading sampling distribution.

Bootstrapping is becoming very popular in applied econometric work. Jeong and Maddala (1993) provide a good survey for econometricians.

## Randomization Tests

A third resampling method, found in the context of hypothesis testing, consists of shuffling the existing data in some suitable fashion, calculating a test statistic and repeating this procedure to build up an estimate of the sampling distribution of this test statistic. For example, suppose the null hypothesis is that the slope of $x$ is zero. If the slope of $x$ is zero, then it should make no difference which $x$ value is paired with $y$ when running a regression. By shuffling the $x$ values several times and rerunning the regression to produce several $t$ statistics, one can estimate the sampling distribution of the $t$ statistic and see if the $t$ statistic produced by the actual ordering of the data is unusual. In this case, the meaning attached to the sampling distribution is different yet again. It tells us how the $t$ statistic differs whenever the $x$ data are shuffled.

Randomization testing does not appear much in econometrics; for discussion of its conceptual difference from traditional econometric thinking, and analysis of its use in econometrics, see Kennedy (1995) and Kennedy and Cade (1996).

## Why Choose Monte Carlo?

There are several major differences between Monte Carlo and the other two resampling methods.

1. Bootstrapping and randomization are designed to produce information specifically tailored to the sample at hand, whereas Monte Carlo produces information regarding an assumed-known data-generation mechanism.
2. Because of point 1 above, bootstrapping and randomization can be used as techniques to undertake hypothesis testing for a given sample, whereas Monte Carlo can only be used to describe the character of a statistical procedure if that sample had been generated by a known data-generating mechanism.

3. Monte Carlo encompasses bootstrapping and randomization in the sense that if we wanted to know the character of a bootstrapping or randomization procedure in a known setting we would investigate via a Monte Carlo study.
4. The meaning of a sampling distribution is not necessarily the same in these three types of resampling methods.
5. There are some situations, such as the heteroskedasticity case for Washington state discussed earlier, in which neither bootstrapping nor randomization can be employed.
6. In many situations it is quite difficult to deduce how to perform a bootstrap or a randomization test, but in all cases a Monte Carlo procedure is straightforward.

To some extent these differences speak for themselves. My choice of Monte Carlo exercises to ensure that students learn the resampling concept was not intended to denigrate bootstrapping or randomization - they clearly have special advantages (and disadvantages). Monte Carlo studies are used in econometrics mainly to investigate the properties of an estimator or test in the context of a specific data-generating mechanism. Because much of textbook econometric theory is concerned with just this issue, Monte Carlo studies are of particular value in teaching econometric theory. Bootstrapping and randomization are better viewed as inference techniques and introduced to students as such.

My suggestion that students be asked to describe how to perform a Monte Carlo study to investigate an econometric issue should be interpreted as a means of enhancing student understanding of the resampling concept and the rationale behind the use of specific econometric techniques, rather than introducing them to a resampling technique (such as bootstrapping or randomization) which itself is a means of conducting inference. Simon and Bruce, in their statistical package Resampling Stats, are interested in showing how bootstrapping or randomization can be used to circumvent traditional statistical formulas in undertaking statistical inference. The strength of this approach is that, as the title of Simon and Bruce (1991) implies, it allows students more easily to produce answers to questions of "everyday statistical work" such as what is the probability that three of four children will be girls, or what is the probability that a basketball player who averages 47 percent success in shooting will miss eight of his next 10 shots? When we move into the world of the econometrician and ask about things like the properties of two-stage least squares or Lagrange multiplier tests, this approach becomes problematic. For example, one must begin with the mathematical formula in question, exactly what Simon and Bruce wish to avoid.

But what I suggest does share one major theme with Simon and Bruce. They state (1991, 29):

> *The first step in using probability and statistics is to translate the scientific question into a statistical question. ..... Though this step is difficult, it*

*involves no mathematics. Rather, this step requires only hard, clear thinking. You cannot beg off by saying "I have no brain for math!" The need is for a brain that will do clear thinking, rather than a brain for mathematics......But resampling pushes you to do this thinking explicitly.*

What I propose is a means of pushing students to do clear, hard thinking about econometrics.

## REFERENCES

Albert, J. and M. Berliner. 1994. Review of the resampling method of teaching statistics. *American Statistician* 48 (2): 129-31.

Boomsma, A. and I. W. Molenaar. 1991. Resampling with more care. *Chance* 4 (4): 25-9.

Jeong, J. and G. S. Maddala. 1993. A perspective on application of bootstrap methods in econometrics. In G. S. Maddala, C. R. Rao and H. D. Vinod (eds), *Handbook of statistics, Vol. 11*, pp. 573-610. Amsterdam: North Holland.

Kennedy, P. E. 1995. Randomization tests in econometrics. *Journal of Business and Economic Statistics* 13 (1): 85-94.

_____. 1998. *A guide to econometrics*, 4th ed. Cambridge, Mass.: MIT Press.

Kennedy, P. E. and B. S. Cade. 1996. Randomization tests for multiple regression. *Communications in Statistics - Computation and Simulation* 25 (4): 923-36.

Simon, J. L. and P. C. Bruce. 1991. Resampling: A tool for everyday statistical work. *Chance* 4 (1): 22-32.

CHAPTER **8**

# USING SPORTS TO
# TEACH ECONOMICS

**John J. Siegfried**

**Allen R. Sanderson**

The measurable impact of spectator sports on gross domestic product (GDP) is trivial. The gross revenues of a Major League Baseball (MLB) team, for example, are similar to those of a large supermarket.[1] The revenues of MLB as a whole constitute only 0.05 percent of GDP. Such comparisons, however, fail to capture the important role of sports in American society.

A typical half-hour evening television newscast contains about three or four minutes of sports news, roughly 20 percent of the substantive broadcast. The usual daily newspaper devotes one of only four or five sections exclusively to sports. Many more people discuss the challenges facing the local college football team with friends and family than ponder the fortunes of the neighborhood grocery store. There is undoubtedly a lot of interest in sports by Americans in general, and by students in particular. In our opinion, students are more likely to engage in the deeper thinking that leads to retention if they are interested in the subject being discussed.

The advantages to using sports examples to teach college economics go beyond simply attracting students' interest. Economics is often taught by analogy (McCloskey 1990). Students are more likely to gain an understanding of a point if they can connect personal experience to the analogy, and a lot of young

Americans have had substantial experience either playing or watching sporting events. Thus, students are more likely to grasp a lesson on marginal vs. average revenues or costs from an analogy to how the scoring average of a high school basketball player changes after a terrific game than from a rendition of the effect of an additional passenger on an airline's marginal and average cost per passenger-mile.

Periodic changes in sports leagues' rules, like the shift in property rights over the future services of players from team owners to the players themselves or the use of a designated hitter or an additional referee, produce natural experiments that illustrate economics in action. The frequent occasions for decisions by owners, managers, and players offer a virtual experimental laboratory for analysis (and, some might say, even complete with rats).

The plethora of data available about the individual inputs and outputs of sporting teams (as well as the interest of professional economists in sports) has produced a substantial empirical literature that compares actual behavior to that predicted from economic models. Furthermore, many contemporary examples and data are easily accessible for classroom use because of the intense coverage of the "business of sports" by newspapers and magazines.

Both of us teach principles of economics and a specialized undergraduate course on the economics of sports. In this chapter we relate some of the examples from sports that we use to illustrate important economics principles and some of the lessons we have learned from these experiences. We are certainly not the first to think of using sports as a vehicle to teach economics (Bruggink 1993; Merz 1996); there are dozens of specialized courses on the economics of sports being taught in America's colleges and universities, and almost all introductory economics textbooks use sports to illustrate some basic principles. The examples that follow vary in applicability and level of analysis from the introductory course to intermediate theory and applied field courses, but all should be within the grasp of motivated undergraduate students.

## I. PRINCIPLES OF ECONOMICS IN SPORTS

### Relative Prices

Press reports regularly claim that baseball ticket prices have soared beyond the reach of average fans, suggesting that it now costs a family of four more than $100 to attend a typical MLB game.[2] Whether something is considered dear or inexpensive depends on several factors: (1) the rate of its price increase over some time period compared to a yardstick such as the Consumer Price Index (CPI), (2) its price relative to the price of available substitutes, and (3) its price relative to a measure of ability to pay, such as the wage rate or income. On each of these criteria, average baseball ticket prices are cheap, and getting cheaper. An example like this is an excellent way to introduce students to relative prices, changes in the price level, and changes in purchasing power. Ask them what would be the role of a price system if each individual price in the economy tracked the CPI perfectly.

Measured against inflation, the average admission price to a major league baseball game fell or remained constant for most years from 1950 to the early 1990s. Ticket prices have risen relative to the CPI in the last few years, but the inflation-adjusted price was still lower in 1993 than in 1950. In the late 1990s, the average ticket price to a Major League Baseball game is still under $11.

Relative to the prices of many other forms of entertainment (i.e., substitutes), baseball ticket prices are lower and have risen less rapidly over time. Professional basketball, football, and ice hockey tickets are several times more expensive. Restaurant meals, amusement parks, rock concerts, and theater tickets also cost considerably more than a baseball ticket. Museums, movies, and a walk in the park are exceptions (and a good topic for discussion). Over time, real incomes in the U.S. have increased, so in terms of purchasing power or standard of living, the price of a baseball ticket relative to one's ability to obtain it also has declined.

## Marginal Analysis

One of the core concepts in economics is decision making at the margin, and the distinction between marginal, average, and total values. Examples from the world of sports can help students understand and appreciate this concept. For example, Chicago White Sox slugger Frank Thomas had been in Major League Baseball for seven years when he entered the 1997 season with a .326 lifetime average. He hit .347 that year. What did this *marginal* year do to his cumulative average?

Many athletic contests are decided "at the margin." Just one missed tackle in the National Football League (NFL) or one missed free throw in the Women's National Basketball Association (WNBA) can cost a team a win. A second baseman signaling to the shortstop whether the next pitch is a fastball seldom makes a difference, but the one time it does during a season can put a team into the playoffs. Swimmers, skiers and runners try to save precious seconds by the aerodynamic design of their clothing or equipment because the difference between winning a race and finishing second is often measured in hundredths of seconds, as 1998 Olympic gold medalist Picabo Street illustrated in Nagano, Japan.[3]

The public often questions values in a culture that rewards young athletes with multi-million dollar contracts yet balks at paying elementary and secondary school teachers, to whom we entrust society's best hope for the future, a relative pittance. This issue is perfect for the transition from the traditional water – diamond paradox, which most students grasp and appreciate, to a contemporary illustration. It is relative scarcity at the margin, not total value, that determines price. It is simply easier – and less expensive – to find one more person who can teach the fourth grade or high school history well than it is to find someone who consistently can hit .300 (or skate like Tara Lipinski). The fact that we spend about $2 billion a year on baseball but over $400 billion annually on elementary and secondary education suggests that our values are reasonably respectable.

Fans and commentators often criticize athletes who exhibit eccentric, anti-social, and/or even illegal behavior on or off the court or field of play. Dennis Rodman in the National Basketball Association (NBA), Lawrence Phillips in the NFL, and Pete Rose in baseball are but a few examples. Our employers would fire most of us for similar stunts. Apart from the fact that some of this behavior may increase the demand for tickets (there is evidence, for example, that fighting in the National Hockey League (NHL) attracts fans (Jones et al. 1993)), the point to emphasize is that these individuals receive large economic rents because there are few perceived substitutes for them. In contrast, because there are close substitutes for the typical worker, he or she earns little economic rent. Thus behavior that the boss perceives as inappropriate can be met with immediate dismissal. In sports, however, termination likely means the destruction of considerable economic rent, which is one reason why the unexpected dismissal of Latrell Sprewell by the Golden State Warriors for choking his coach in November 1997 attracted so much attention.

## Demand

Basic microeconomic models posit that the quantity demanded of a particular good or service is inversely related to its price, *ceteris paribus*. Factors held constant include the price and availability of substitute and complementary goods, income, tastes, expectations, and population. Sports offers a convenient way to get students to think about *ceteris paribus* issues.

For example, the quantity demanded for baseball is a function of the admission price. Other considerations that must be held constant to properly estimate the effect of price on attendance include: the quality of the home team and opponent; how closely the teams are matched; the time the game is played; weather conditions; promotions (such as pre-game souvenirs or post-game fireworks); the location and quality of the venue; competing events or entertainment alternatives; per capita income and the local unemployment rate; and the population within driving distance of the game.

In addition to the concept of holding other things constant, an instructor can also explore elasticities: How sensitive are fans to ticket prices; would this sensitivity vary with the price level; how income elastic is the demand for baseball, bowling, tennis or cricket? A related demand concept that we find more difficult for students to grasp is the derived demand for a factor of production. Players' salaries are determined by demand derived from the demand to watch particular sports and by the employment alternatives available to players. The profit-maximizing price is what the market will bear, based on the anticipated demand for the sport. Players' salaries do not determine ticket prices, no matter how often owners allude to their rising payrolls to justify price hikes. The demand for players, and the level of their salaries, is derived *from* the overall demand to watch the sport in person or on television and to purchase logo merchandise.[4]

## Efficiency

Many resource allocation decisions in sports affect efficiency. We focus on just one of them, the allocation of playing talent across teams, in order to illustrate the importance of matching the quantity supplied to the quantity demanded for maximizing social welfare.

Professional team sports leagues take steps allegedly designed to balance the level of playing skills among competitors. They allocate players new to the league on the basis of a "draft" that awards the most promising players to those teams that have recently enjoyed the least success on the playing field.[5] Currently the National Football League, Major League Baseball, and the National Basketball Association limit the total player payroll of teams in an effort ostensibly to prevent "wealthy" teams from securing a disproportionate share of the most talented free-agent players.

Economists have long recognized (Rottenberg 1956) the futility of efforts to balance team playing talent when the contracts of players can be transferred among teams. As the Coase theorem reminds us, in the absence of significant transaction costs, resources move to their most valuable use regardless of initial ownership. If a talented baseball player is valued more highly in New York than in Kansas City because there are more New Yorkers willing to pay to see the Yankees win than there are Kansas City residents willing to pay to see the Royals win (or, even with similar populations, if New York residents value winning more than do residents of Kansas City) the player's contract will be transferred from Kansas City to New York for a price between his value at the two locales. Transfers like this would occur regardless of whether the property rights over the player's services reside with his original team (as in the days when a "reserve clause" granted perpetual ownership rights to the team that first signed a player unless it transferred those rights to another team) or with the player himself, as is the case for those veteran players who qualify for "free agency" today.

Because of player trades and sales, player drafts do not tend to promote a balance of playing skills among teams. Player drafts may subsidize weak teams by granting them initial property rights over players. The extent of the subsidy depends on the time required before a player can become a free agent. Free agency for players does not promote a balance of playing skills among teams either. Wealth-maximizing players will sell their services to the team willing and able to pay the most for those services, a demand derived from the players' expected contribution to the team's performance and the willingness and ability of local residents to pay for better performance.

For the sake of economic efficiency, this failure to balance competition is fortunate. The argument that balanced competition is desirable rests on the false belief that fans value only one characteristic of games, namely uncertainty of outcome. Fans are clearly not indifferent to the level of uncertainty of outcome (Knowles, Sherony, and Haupert 1992), but they also value winning, and the response varies by geographic area (Porter 1992). Although an imbalance in team playing-skills reduces the uncertainty of games and thereby the demand for those games, the greater willingness to pay for winning by fans of certain teams than by fans of other teams can mean that the efficient level of competitive balance is far from perfectly even.[6] Imbalance leads to more winning by teams situated where people get more satisfaction from winning, and less winning by teams whose fans in the aggregate care less about it. Whenever the difference in the value of winning to the fans in two locations exceeds the loss in value associated with less evenly matched games, efficiency is promoted by moving playing skill from the team located where winning is valued less to the team located where winning is valued more.[7] It is also unlikely that severe imbalance of playing talent would be efficient. As playing-skills become more unequally distributed the uncertainty of games diminishes, the marginal utility of winning more games to the fans of the more successful teams diminishes, and the marginal utility of winning more games to the fans of the less successful teams grows, both acting to slow the payoff from further unequal allocations of playing skill.

## Surplus

Efficiency is achieved when our economic resources are devoted to those activities that create the greatest value for consumers. This basic economic concept is difficult for students to comprehend. Getting the allocation right is relatively more important if the value of resources when they are devoted to their best use substantially exceeds the value that could be created if they were allocated to their second best use. This difference is surplus.[8] It is large when the demand for the output is high and the opportunity cost of the resources is low, as is common in sports. The essence of resource allocation is maximizing consumers' plus producers' surplus.

Many people confuse aggregate revenues with surplus, the *net* value created by getting the allocation decision correct. The 1994-95 Major League Baseball players' strike provides an opportunity to illustrate this difference. Some television news programs reported the "economic loss" from the strike as the amount of ticket and television revenue that would have been received by teams if the cancelled games had been played, *plus* an estimate of how much fans would have spent on hotels, restaurants, parking, etc. while attending games. Ask students if this is a good estimate of the social welfare loss of the strike.

There are at least two (potentially offsetting) errors in using forgone revenues as a measure of social welfare. Each emphasizes an important economic concept. First, revenues fail to include the consumers' surplus lost to the strike. Thus the "economic loss" due to the strike may exceed forgone revenues. To the extent that sports consumers are FANatics, and have inelastic demands, this forgone consumers' surplus could be quite large. Second, the use of forgone revenue to measure economic loss ignores the possibility that the striking players and/or their families may value their newly created leisure time above zero. This value is the area under the (short-run) marginal cost curve. It should be subtracted from total revenue to obtain an accurate estimate of the net economic loss caused by the strike. The value of leisure time created by the strike might have been quite high because it is rare for players to have much time with their families during the summer.[9]

What is really needed to estimate the economic cost of the strike is a measure including all benefits, both those accruing to the consumers as surplus and those captured by the teams, and excluding the alternative value of the released resources (of which the players are the largest component). Taking these considerations into account, Chris Douglas (1996) estimated the contemporaneous economic cost of the 1994-95 baseball strike at $813 million dollars, about $10 million per day, while forgone revenues were only $8 million per day. Forgone spending on hotels, food, souvenirs and parking contributed almost nothing to the social welfare loss of the strike because for the most part these services are provided in highly competitive markets with quite elastic supply and demand. Fans simply drank their beer elsewhere in late summer of 1994. Little surplus was lost by their relocation. Zipp (1996) has a good empirical account of these issues.

## Strategy

Game theory now appears as a separate chapter in some introductory economics texts and is being infused throughout many other course in the economics curriculum. Basic concepts of game theory – think ahead, put yourself in your rival's shoes, backward induction, indirect effects, dominant and dominated strategies – are enormously useful in everyday life.

Most sporting events are zero-sum games. As Martina Hingis gains a point, Venus Williams loses one. As the Green Bay Packers gain four yards, the Dallas Cowboys lose four yards. The concepts of game theory are usually introduced with zero-sum games. Their symmetry simplifies the analysis of pure strategy games, allowing more attention to the fundamental ideas. Also, the concept of preventing your rival from being able to take advantage of your own strategy by making her indifferent among her alternative strategies is an intuitively appealing basis for teaching mixed strategies that evaporates for variable-sum games.

Although the existence of multiple equilibria is probably the most disconcerting characteristic of games for veteran economists, the absence of counterintuitive results often creates a mental obstacle for the rookie student. Because of their experience with sports, many students believe they "know how to play the game." Producing counterintuitive results in this context is persuasive evidence that there is something useful to learn from serious study of economics. A simple exercise with a mixed strategy equilibrium game demonstrates the importance of taking indirect effects into account, which is a key element of "thinking like an economist."

The payoff matrix in Figure 8.1 reports the success of a baseball batter against a pitcher. For simplicity, the pitcher has only two pitches, a fastball and a curve, and the batter knows that is the pitcher's complete repertoire. The batter is

**Figure 8.1: Baseball Game Payoff Matrix (hitter's batting average reported in cells)**

|  |  | Batter | |
|---|---|---|---|
|  |  | Guess Fastball | Guess Curveball |
| Pitcher | Throw Fastball | .600 | .200 |
|  | Throw Curveball | .200 | .400 |

relatively more successful against fastballs. When he guesses the pitcher will throw a fastball and the pitcher does throw a fastball, he bats .600. When he guesses correctly that the pitcher will throw a curve, however, he hits only .400. When he guesses incorrectly what will be thrown, he always bats just .200. The goal of the pitcher is to minimize the batter's average and the goal of the batter is to maximize it.

The pitcher knows that if he is predictable, the batter has a substantial edge. If the pitcher were to throw only one type of pitch, it would be a curve, but the batter still would be successful forty percent of the time. There is no dominant strategy for either the pitcher or batter because the best pure strategy of each depends on the pure strategy undertaken by the other. There is no pure strategy Nash equilibrium in this game.

There is a mixed strategy Nash equilibrium, however. If the pitcher throws fastballs $p$ percent of the time so as to ensure that the batter cannot take advantage of the pitcher's mix between fastballs and curves, then the batter must be indifferent between guessing fastball, guessing curve, guessing 50 percent fastballs and 50 percent curves, or guessing any other combination available to him. Thus the batter's expected payoff when guessing any combination of fastballs and curves must be the same. If it is not, he will select the strategy that gives him the higher expected batting average and thus take advantage of the pitcher. The calculations are easiest with the batter's pure strategy alternatives. The expected payoff to him from guessing fastball is $\{.600p + .200(1 - p)\}$; his expected payoff from guessing curve is $\{.200p + .400(1 - p)\}$. The value of $p$, the percentage of fastballs thrown, that equalizes the two expected payoffs is $1/3$.[10] The expected batting average of the batter is .333. Students need to be reminded that while the pitcher's optimal strategy is to throw 1/3 fastballs and 2/3 curves, the actual delivery of the pitches must be unpredictable.

Now comes the fun. Suggest to the students that you have a tip for the batter: "choke up" on the bat. The effect of this is to raise the batter's success when he is expecting a curve but the pitcher delivers a fastball. Fewer of these pitches now "blow by" the batter. The batting average in the upper right cell of Figure 8.1 rises to .300. Ask students what the pitcher should do now that the batter is better at hitting fastballs (when he was expecting a curve). The majority will respond that the pitcher should throw more curves. Then solve for the mixed strategy equilibrium.

The new equilibrium mix for the pitcher is 40 percent fastballs, an *increase* from 33.3 percent prior to the batter "choking up" on the bat, and opposite the usual student prediction. The new expected batting average is .360, a rise of .027, as would be expected when the only change was a batting improvement. Throwing *more* fastballs after the batter improved his hitting against fastballs will puzzle some students because they will fail to take into account how the batter will change his optimal strategy with his new found skill. The batter's original optimal guessing mix was one-third fastballs. After the tip to "choke up" on the bat, his optimal mix is to guess fastball only one-fifth of the time. He guesses curve more frequently after the tip because the tip has helped his batting *when he guesses curve*. So he guesses curve more frequently, 80 percent rather than 67 percent of the time. The pitcher, in turn, adjusts his optimal mix by favoring fastballs because now the batter is guessing curve more frequently, and the pitcher always does worse when actually pitching what the batter is expecting. So the pitcher throws 40 percent fastballs rather than 33.3 percent fastballs. This exercise helps students appreciate the importance of thinking about how their rival might react to a change in circumstances as well as how they should adjust their own behavior. [11]

## Monopoly

There are numerous examples of monopoly power in sports. Most professional sports teams have market power over local ticket sales because their geographic distance from other teams in the same league creates substantial costs to a consumer who would try to substitute live performances of another team in the face of a price increase. Teams don't have to worry about other suppliers moving into their territory because all of the professional sports leagues have restrictions on team movements, especially those that would place a relocating team near another franchise. In addition, the entry of new teams is strictly limited by the existing teams, who have authority to grant or refuse entry into their league. In a business where new entrants must rely on the cooperation of existing firms to produce their product (who will they play if the incumbents refuse?) there is not likely to be entry from hostile new competitors. [12]

Although expenditures on sports obviously come at the expense of expenditures by consumers on other goods and services, and most likely at the expense of other entertainment options, evidence also suggests that consumers do not even view different sports as particularly good substitutes.[13]  Studies of the demand for tickets to professional team sporting events find elasticities of demand at the average price approximating -1.0 (Demmert 1973; Scully 1989), which suggests that team owners maximize profits rather than alternatives such as team playing success.  Students can be shown how a profit-maximizing team with very low marginal costs would maximize profits by setting ticket price so that the elasticity of demand is close to one.  Marginal costs are certainly minuscule for additional patrons to an individual game, and also quite low for additional games during a season.  Perhaps the most interesting application of monopoly to sports involves league decisions to expand.  Absent the contrived scarcity of teams that evolves from limitations on expansion, the price of franchises would be modest.  Who would be willing to pay $200 million for an existing franchise when one could get a new one for free?  Whereas existing franchises might have some goodwill value, new franchises do not.  Yet recent prices for expansion franchises in football, baseball, and ice hockey have been close to prices at which the ownership of incumbent teams has been transferred, suggesting that the lion's share of the franchise price represents the scarcity value of a franchise rather than established goodwill.

How, then, would leagues determine the optimal rate of expansion to maximize the entry fees they collect from expansion franchises?  The entry fees are distributed among the existing members of the league.  No expansion generates no fees.  Rapid expansion reduces the willingness of prospective owners to offer high fees for an expansion franchise, because more expansion franchises are then anticipated over the horizon.  Between these extremes is an expansion rate that maximizes the net present value of league entry fees.  Leagues must expand slowly enough to keep some franchise hungry cities and potential owners chomping at the bit, in effect creating the artificial scarcity symptomatic of all monopolies.  This scarcity scares bidders into inflating their offers for fear of otherwise being rationed out of the market.  But leagues also must expand fast enough to ensure that the number of vacant cities that could support a team does not approach a number that could support an entire new league.  Although an incumbent league can prevent the hostile entry of individual teams by refusing to play them, it cannot similarly block the entry of an entire independent league.  Indeed, in 1960 the American Football League (AFL) initiated operations that were so successful that it eventually challenged the existing NFL.  Of course, once both leagues recognized the effects of competition on owners' profits, they merged.

Franchise owners often plead their case to Congress.  Both the NFL and the NBA secured legislation that allowed them to merge with competing leagues.  The NFL also persuaded Congress to pass the Sports Broadcasting Act of 1961, permitting teams in professional sports leagues to sell their broadcast rights collectively. (Universities are not covered by the Sports Broadcasting Act and thus, in 1984, were ruled in violation of the antitrust laws for similar behavior.)

Congressional pleadings invariably include owners' claims of poverty. Most professional sports teams are privately owned, and not required to release financial information. For the most part the teams have asked the public to take it on faith that owning a professional sports team is not profitable. Economists find these claims disingenuous in light of the rapid rate of increase of franchise values, averaging 15 percent annually for the four major team sports (Scully 1995, 132). Why, we might ask, would smart business people, who have earned fortunes in other industries pay ever increasing prices for an asset that is expected to generate only losses for the foreseeable future? This conundrum provides an opportunity to discuss with students the source of asset values and the possibility of nonpecuniary returns, as well as the honesty of professional sports franchise owners.

## Monopsony

For many years professional sports franchises were able to buy (players' services) low and sell (tickets) high. They enjoyed monopsony power in the purchase of their primary input – players – through an agreement among the teams in a league not to hire a player from another team unless the owner of that team voluntarily relinquished rights to him (usually by selling or trading him to the team that most desired his services). They sold their tickets in markets insulated from competition with other teams in the same sport and sold national broadcast rights collectively as monopolists.

The linchpin of their financial success was their monopsony power over players. Beginning with the emergence of players' unions in the 1960s and exacerbated by strikes, union contract settlements, and periodic legal skirmishes, the monopsony power of professional sports teams over veteran players has been drastically curtailed. Each of the leagues still drafts new players, who may play only for the team that selects them (or the team to which the draft rights are sold or traded). This continues to depress the earnings of rookie players below competitive market rates. It is perpetuated through the complicity of veteran players who write the draft rules into their union contract, thus exempting the draft from the antitrust laws. Veteran players gain by the exploitation of rookies to the extent that funds that would otherwise go toward meeting competitive market salaries for rookies are available for negotiations between teams and their veterans (White 1986).

The dissipation of market power over veteran players has provided a natural experiment to test the predictions of the monopsony model. Statistical studies of salaries show convincingly that when draft and player-retention schemes are relaxed, large increases in player compensation result (Raimondo 1983; Scully 1989; Quirk and Fort 1992; Kahn 1993). Compensation has grown most rapidly when either courts or collective bargaining weakened the draft and retention schemes, and has grown faster as players have won more relief from these institutions. Over the past quarter century professional basketball players' salaries have risen fastest, baseball players' second fastest, and football players' slowest (Staudohar 1989). The rapid increase in football player salaries in the 1990s, following the introduction of true free agency for veteran NFL players in 1993, further corroborates the connection between salary levels and competition in the labor market for players.

As monopsony power over their labor inputs has eroded, professional sports teams have turned increased attention to their second most costly input – a facility in which to stage their games. Each of the four major professional team sports leagues operates under a provision similar to the NFL's Rule 4.3, which requires approval of a supermajority (75 percent in the NFL) of the owners for franchise relocation. This voting requirement provides a strategic advantage to both incumbent teams negotiating a stadium contract extension with their existing landlord, and teams negotiating with a stadium in a location to which they propose to relocate. An incumbent tenant can threaten to relocate and also to form a coalition to block any other franchise from replacing it, thus creating monopsony power for the team in renegotiating its facility lease. A relocating team can credibly threaten to block the relocation of any other team that competes with it for a stadium lease because it needs to form only a submajority coalition to do so, thus deterring competitive bidding for the facility with which it is negotiating.

The result of franchise relocation restrictions in professional sports leagues is a balance of bargaining power tilted toward tenants – that is, team owners. The exploitation of this monopsony power in the stadium and arena market in the past decade is illustrated by the shift in stadium and arena financing. In the 1950s a majority of professional sports facilities was privately owned and financed. Today almost all stadiums and arenas are constructed with public funds and leased to teams at trivial rents. As the leagues' monopsony power over players has declined, professional sports teams have taken advantage of the country's obsession with sports by demanding free facilities from communities that believe a professional sports franchise is needed to acquire the image of a "major league" city, and see building a stadium as the best way to get one (Noll and Zimbalist 1997).

## Collusion and Cartels

Both professional and intercollegiate sports are replete with collusive agreements that illustrate the fundamental principles of cartels. We focus on activities of the National Collegiate Athletic Association (NCAA). Featuring the NCAA to teach about cartels has two advantages. First, many students are enrolled at institutions that are members of the NCAA, and take delight in evaluating and criticizing their college or university. Second, the NCAA is not exempt from the antitrust laws prohibiting collusive conduct as are Major League Baseball, national television broadcasting contracts of all professional sports leagues, and the league mergers in basketball and football.

The case for collective behavior in the organization of sporting contests among colleges and universities originated with two private market failures – a public good problem and an externality. The first was the necessity to develop standard rules for football, and the second was the need to control player violence that helped individual teams win games, but was destroying public interest in college football in the late 19th century. Individual colleges were caught in a prisoners' dilemma. They all agreed that college football would be better off with less violence, but any team that unilaterally cleaned up its act would suffer on the scoreboard. Collective action was required.

The NCAA was founded in 1905.[14] Once it succeeded in controlling violence, the organization expanded into economic regulation. Its most important market restrictions were developed after World War II, when members agreed to limit player compensation to tuition, room and board (initially called a "Sanity Code," as if paying players were insane) and to centralize the sales of rights to televise live college football games.

In the 1950s the NCAA developed a system to detect and punish cheating on the agreements, and extended its control of output by limiting the number of games in football and men's basketball. Punishment for cheating (e.g., broadcasting a game in competition with the exclusive NCAA broadcast, or compensating a player beyond tuition, room and board) could be severe, because the NCAA controlled all college sports and a violation in one sport could spawn sanctions in all.

NCAA sports are ripe for a cartel. There appears to be a quite inelastic demand, and entry is difficult.[15] These characteristics ensure substantial rewards to a successful cartel. It is relatively easy to police the behavior affecting some parts of the cartel agreement (e.g., agreement not to televise live football games in competition with the game sold collectively), and institutional arrangements have been devised to limit cheating on other aspects of the cartel agreement (e.g., investigations of and sanctions for exceeding the agreed limit on payments to players).

The restriction of output and limitations on the price of the most important input – the players – enhance net revenues sufficiently that institutions face strong incentives to field successful sports programs. The natural outcome has been a costly expansion of competition in unregulated areas, for example, recruiting. The NCAA reacted by imposing limitations on some forms of nonprice competition, such as limiting the number of coaches, the number of scholarship players, and player recruitment activities. In addition to direct efforts to control costs, the NCAA also enjoys external support for its efforts to protect the revenues produced by cartel restrictions from being squandered via rent-seeking competition (e.g., amateurism is "good" [for players, but apparently not for coaches] on moral grounds). But not all outlets for competitive pressure have been capped. Universities still compete for players by building bigger and better (than the competition) facilities.

In contrast to professional sports teams, which historically monopsonized player markets by means of an agreement not to hire players who were allocated to other teams, there is no "draft" of players into college sports. The NCAA controls the player market not by creating market power for individual teams, but rather by establishing a maximum wage below the competitive equilibrium for the entire market. This provides a pedogical opportunity to analyze price controls without resorting to the usual New York City rent controls, or usury laws. The gap between a player's marginal revenue product and the cost of tuition, room and board illustrates the incentive facing coaches, athletic directors and boosters to offer clandestine payments to college athletes and to overindulge in complementary factors of production such as coaches, stadiums, or training facilities as a means of competing for the best athletes.

The NCAA should be recognized as a cartel of colleges and universities, whose behavior is more closely parallel to OPEC than Mr. Chips. The fact that the members are not-for-profit institutions does not dampen their incentive to maximize revenues, for those revenues can be put to uses that enrich those in control. The frequent claims that athletic departments are in poverty are difficult to accept when so few major programs are terminated. Apparently many of the benefits do not show up on athletic department financial statements, providing an opportunity to discuss external benefits with your students.

## The Role of Government
Sports examples can be used to explain the role of government in a market economy. For example, under public interest rationales for government we consider market imperfections – using antitrust laws to create or maintain competition; dealing with natural monopolies; improving efficiency when there are capital market imperfections; internalizing externalities; providing public goods; and equity issues. The empirical record of government involvement in sports has been far from favorable to competition – baseball's antitrust exemption, the Sports Broadcasting Act, condoning the NCAA cartel, sanctioning mergers between competitive leagues, constraining labor mobility, and so forth; instructors can invite students to come up with examples – positive or negative – that fall under one or more of the public interest rationales for government intervention. Also, one need not search far to find illustrations of the use of government to promote private interests in sports.

The recent controversies surrounding public financing of stadiums and arenas provide an excellent context for discussing the role of government. Why do cities offer teams "free" places to play more frequently than similar assistance to cultural organizations, bowling alleys, or movie theaters? Do the grounds for public participation fall under public interest or private interest criteria? What are the redistributional consequences, given the average wealth levels of owners, players and fans vs. taxpayers in general (or, depending on how the stadium is financed, the incidence of sales taxes or property taxes or of lottery revenues)? Is a stadium or arena a public good? Would freeriding occur? Does a major league sports team create positive (e.g., favorable image, entertainment options) or negative (e.g., congestion, bad role models) externalities? Are sports leagues natural monopolies?

Finally, is league control of entry, relocation, labor relations, etc., a good substitute for direct government control if there is, indeed, a public interest reason not to rely on competitive markets?

## II. ADDITIONAL ILLUSTRATIONS

Space prevents us from including detailed descriptions of the many various applications of economic principles to sports. In this section we briefly identify a number of other possibilities.

Sports is a fertile field for examples of *comparative advantage*. Babe Ruth was a superb pitcher for the Boston Red Sox before he was converted to a right fielder in order to keep his bat in the daily lineup. (In his last three years as a pitcher for the Red Sox he was a combined 64-31.) Although he had an absolute advantage in pitching over many other players, his comparative advantage was in hitting (Scahill 1990).

After some thought, most students accept the notion that *free exchange can benefit both traders*, though when it comes to U.S. trade with Japan they often believe that only Japan benefits. The sports counterpart is that some commentators and fans believe that if two teams engage in a player trade, only one benefits. They find it hard to believe that at least *ex ante* both teams *expected* to gain from the transaction. Every city and every sport have lists of famous "bad trades," where the home team's general manager exposed his incompetence.

This topic opens up related applications of exchange, including *Pareto optimality* (when we've exhausted all opportunities for mutually beneficial gains), the fact that trade value depends upon the marginal values and opportunity costs (such as what do I have already, in terms of point guards or outfielders, and what do I have to give up?), and diminishing marginal returns or gains. The advantage of *agents* as negotiators whose broader reputation is at stake and who can insulate the player from communicating with a general manager is also relevant. In spite of loathing they receive from owners and the media, agents' comparative advantage presumably is to perform functions that lower transaction costs. The agent market is characterized by relatively free entry and price-taking behavior, not unlike real estate agents.

Instructors can employ a simple sports example to illustrate many concepts associated with *production*. A discussion might ensue about what constitutes the objective function or output for a team owner – is it victories, the margin of victory (i.e., point spread), championships, attendance, revenues? Traditional inputs in the production process are players, owners, and managers/coaches, but there are others such as training, grounds keepers, computers and technology, the stadium, promotions and gustatory amenities. As a team employs higher quality inputs – that is, acquires better players – its expected number of wins and attendance rise, but after some point the rate of increase begins to diminish, and it is conceivable that total attendance and/or revenues could even decrease if a team were so dominant that its contests became predictable and boring.

Sports offers convincing examples of the principle of *specialization and division of labor*, and it has become more evident over time. The "olden days" often saw more multi-sport players, both in college and in the professional ranks, than exist today. To excel at the highest level of performance, athletes (and musicians and other performing artists) simply must start earlier and practice longer. Time split between two major activities entails a large opportunity cost for each. Even within a sport, say football, one used to see one athlete play more than one position – both on offense and defense, or as a position player and a punter or field goal kicker. Football rosters now contain many more specialty players – pooch punters, nickel backs, long snappers, etc. Baseball relies more and more on specific role positions – a designated hitter (in the American League), long and short relievers, and even base-stealing specialists. Young girls must now choose between gymnastics and figure skating even if they exhibit considerable talent in both sports. Roger Banister, who broke the four-minute mile barrier in 1954 while he was a full-time medical student, and other earlier track stars were really amateurs. They trained part-time, whereas now track is a full-time occupation for world class runners.

The economics of reselling tickets ("scalping") provides another refreshing alternative to New York rent ceilings as an example of a *price ceiling*. In locations where scalping is illegal, the price ceiling is zero. Arizona added an interesting twist to scalping recently, legalizing it within a specially marked area outside the arena or stadium at a specified time. With all the scalpers together in one place along with all the buyers, the area looked like the floor of the Chicago Board of Trade, and the market power of scalpers who preyed on buyers ignorant of lower prices on the other side of the venue was dissipated (Happel and Jennings 1995).

The market for used baseball players illustrates problems caused by *asymmetric information*, *adverse selection*, and the *"winner's curse."* Pitchers who are signed as free agents spend more time on the disabled list than those who re-sign with their original team. This can be explained by asymmetric information. Healthy pitchers are re-signed by the original teams, leaving only "lemons" for the "used-pitcher" market. Further exacerbating the problem of disappointing free-agent signings is the winner's curse, caused by a player signing with the team bidding for his services that makes the most overly optimistic estimate of his future productivity (Cassing and Douglas 1980). Teams try to protect themselves against these possibilities by scouting, requiring physical examinations and adding performance incentives to player contracts.

The structure of sports leagues locks teams into a classic *prisoners' dilemma*. Winning is a zero-sum game. Attendance rises with winning, and so revenues depend on a team's success on the playing field. Thus, each team faces an incentive to sign quality free-agent players, even though, when all teams sign free-agents, *nothing* different happens to collective win-loss records. Indeed, the aggregate "output" of the league in terms of games won cannot increase as long as the schedule remains fixed. As a result, each team's expenses rise, revenues remain constant, and profits decline. In order to escape this prisoners' dilemma leagues have devised various schemes such as reserve clauses and reverse-order player drafts, the latest of which are aggregate player payroll ceilings (inappropriately called "salary caps").

For most young students a wise investment decision is to remain in school through college or even completion of a graduate or professional degree. The forgone income for a six-to ten-year period is rewarded by higher earnings over a forty- or fifty-year horizon. Many textbooks discuss and display these earnings streams and suggest how one would calculate an *internal rate of return*. For someone contemplating a career as a professional athlete, the age-earnings profile looks much different – earnings could start before high school (for a figure skater or tennis star) or as late as one's mid 20s (for a baseball player), and may virtually truncate around age 30. A good question for students to ponder is the rate of return at which it makes sense for a young person with reasonably attractive educational and nonathletic career options to devote herself or himself to athletic training. Given such a short earnings period, one can understand why a talented athlete would choose to forgo some or all of college, especially if there is an opportunity to return later.

An example of *opportunity cost* is the case of Jeff Fosnes, the star forward on Vanderbilt's 1974 Southeastern Conference champion basketball team. Fosnes was drafted in an early round of the NBA draft. He opted for medical school, however, comparing the expected earnings of a 50-year-old physician with those of a 50-year-old NBA player. For him the opportunity cost of a professional basketball career was too high because at the time medical schools did not admit "older" students. If Fosnes had "gone pro," he would not be a physician today.[16]

The quality of play and the athletic quality of players in professional sports today is better than ever, and economics has a lot to do with it. Why? Because more opportunities for fame and fortune have lured a higher percentage of a growing (domestic, and international, and, since Jackie Robinson, racially integrated) population into sports. Today's athletes are bigger, stronger, faster; they are in better physical condition; they start training earlier in life and put in more hours of practice. Thanks to free agency, they also get to keep a higher percentage of the revenues they generate. Salary levels attainable by these top performers produce strong incentives for them to stay in shape and to play better. When one could lose his job as a major league shortstop 40 years ago and return to his local community at a wage roughly comparable to what he earned stopping ground balls, the financial inducements to stay in shape were not overwhelming; today, however, when an average player's sports income exceeds $1 million a year, the sacrifice from returning to an ordinary job is enormous.

In a market economy, *economic profits* arise from several factors – hard work, chance, ownership of a specialized resource, entrepreneurship and business acumen, imperfect information, collusion with rivals, barriers to entry, or government protection. Many of these sources reflect a short-run imbalance that eventually is competed away, but some endure. Students can speculate about which factors apply to professional sports. For professional sports leagues and team owners, continued public protection from rivals, allowed collective action in selling broadcast rights and limiting expansion and team relocation, financial entry barriers[17] and infusions of taxpayer dollars for new facilities may produce an expectation of continued profitability despite owners' protests that they are losing money. Finally, the direct financial rate of return from owning a sports franchise might be lower than for alternative investments because of the nonpecuniary benefits of ownership – it's fun and it bestows instant celebrity status on the owner (presumably a positive attribute).

Sports also can be used to illustrate the principle of *discounting* or *present value*. An obvious application is to players' multi-year contracts. The media invariably reports the undiscounted sum of the annual salaries over the life of the contract. So a four-year contract that pays $2 million, $2.5 million, $3.0 million, and $3.5 million annually for 1999, 2000, 2001, and 2002 is reported as an $11 million contract, when its initial net present value at an eight percent annual investment opportunity cost is only $9.7 million (if the salaries are paid at the beginning of each respective year).

Economists have a role to play in *distributional issues*. We can unmask the winners and losers from particular policies, especially when many of the effects are indirect and the distributional impacts are obscured. For example, in a study of the income levels of consumers of different products based on the 1994 Consumer Expenditure Survey (CES), Timothy Peterson (1997) discovered that the weighted mean income of consumers of tickets to sporting events was 78 percent above the average consumer's income. Such information can help people assess the distributional consequences of proposals to subsidize sporting facilities from tax revenues collected via regressive state and local sales taxes. Although it is not clear who benefits most from such subsidies – team owners, players, or fans – none of them is eligible for food stamps.

## III. DO'S AND DON'TS

This list of guidelines should help instructors who use sports to illustrate basic principles of economics.

- Do remember that not all students are sports fans.
- Do remember that students come with different levels of understanding of league and team names, star players, and knowledge of the histories and strategies of various games.

- Do bear in mind the instructor-student age gap when selecting examples and illustrations; think Tiger Woods and Martina Hingis rather than Jack Nicklaus and Chris Evert.
- Do use current media accounts and data for both illustrations and measurement purposes.
- Do encourage students to be creative in the application of economic theory to the "wide world of sports."
- Do let students shine when they know more than you do about a particular game or its rules or history.
- Don't rely exclusively on North American sports examples and U.S. male sports figures; instead diversify.[18]
- Don't get caught up in the facts, personalities, or the rules of particular sports.[19]
- Don't overdo it on sports jargon.
- Don't forget it's an economics course, not a sports course.
- Don't rely too heavily on sports examples; choose your spots carefully.
- Don't let the sports examples stand on their own; tie them into economic theory.

## IV. CONCLUSION

In this chapter we have tried both to convey the usefulness of using sports in teaching economic theory to undergraduates and to illustrate some of the ways this can be done. Our coverage is not exhaustive in depth or breadth, but it should give instructors a start. Other economics topics that can be dealt with through sports examples include: risk and uncertainty; union behavior; income and substitution effects as they apply to the supply of labor; racial and gender discrimination; the structure of the competition and expected outcomes, such as more likely repeat champions in tennis than golf; and externalities.[20]

One could teach an entire introductory (or intermediate level) price theory course using nothing but baseball examples. Although we do not advocate such specialization, it is nevertheless our contention that a dose of sports illustrations can contribute toward making the course more enjoyable and productive for both instructors and students.

## NOTES

* The authors thank T. Aldrich Finegan and the editors for comments that improved the chapter.

1. A comparison based on the 1992 Census of Manufactures showed that the average revenues of a major league baseball team were approximately 95 percent of the average

revenues of one of the 700 largest supermarkets in the United States.

2. The usual tally of a family's outlay for a game includes tickets, soft drinks and beer, hot dogs and desserts, parking, and souvenirs. Although a family may indeed purchase all of these items on a given evening, (a) they are not *required* to buy anything beyond the admission tickets, (b) the food substitutes for what would have been eaten at a restaurant or prepared at home, and (c) the souvenirs are not likely to be purchased on repeat trips to the ballpark.

3. Fans or commentators frequently complain that a particular baseball player "can't hit," when in fact the difference between an average hitter – someone with a .260 average – and a player on the verge of stardom and a multimillion dollar contract – someone who can hit .300 – is only one hit a week.

4. The lucrative television contracts obtained by the NFL in early 1998 from CBS, ABC, Fox and ESPN, which added more than $30 million per team in annual revenues over the next several years will not lower ticket prices just because owners and leagues now have more money. Ticket prices will remain high – or go still higher – as a reflection of strong demand to watch football. NFL player salaries will now increase, both because of revenue-sharing arrangements and because salaries are derived from the overall demand for football. This is an excellent example of the order of causality.

5. The reverse order draft provides an opportunity to discuss the frequent conflict between strong incentives and equality of either opportunities or outcomes. For example, why reward a team that performs badly with the first player in the subsequent draft? Why not make it draft last, or demote it to minor league status and replace it with the best minor league team for the next season, as is done in British professional soccer? What are the pros and cons of such approaches and why might different leagues in different circumstances choose different incentives?

6. Another disadvantage of equally balanced competition is the increased likelihood that the outcome of a contest will be determined by chance – an unusual bounce of a ball or an official's error.

7. A slightly different competitive balance issue concerns not whether a team from a home territory that values winning highly wins a larger proportion of its games, but rather whether it tends to win relatively more games played in front of its home crowd. In the NBA, for example, where the home team retains virtually all of the gate receipts, scheduling (e.g., arduous road trips) appears to give an edge to home teams. It is not surprising, then, that the NBA has the highest home court winning advantage among the four major professional sports in North America.

8. Be sure to distinguish for students the two different meanings of the word "surplus" in economics. We label an excess of quantity supplied over quantity demanded as "surplus" and also call the area between the demand curve and opportunity cost "surplus." The latter is the more pervasive use by economists, but students are likely to think the former is the only important use.

9. Players on strike are not unemployed. In U.S. labor statistics they are counted both as in the labor force and employed.

10. Set the two expressions equal to each other and solve for $p$.

11. For another application of game theory to baseball see Merz (1996), who discredits Roy Blount Jr.'s (1993, 68) allegation that the great Giants' centerfielder Willie Mays, who never led the league in doubles, often retreated to first base when he realized he could get to second (but not all the way to third) after a hit into the gap. Blount

contends that Mays returned to first because lefthanded pull hitter Willie McCovey followed him in the Giants' batting order for 13 years.  With Mays on first base, the first baseman had to move to the bag to hold Mays close, opening a bigger hole for McCovey on the right side of the infield, while if Mays had gone on to second rather than retreating to first the opposing team would have walked McCovey intentionally.  If McCovey got a hit, Mays could then easily make it from first to third with the Giants ending up with men on first and third rather than first and second bases.  Merz explains how this alleged strategy of Mays is dominated by going to second no matter what the opposing pitcher does when McCovey comes to bat.  Furthermore, why is the first baseman holding Mays on the bag to reduce the probability of a steal of second when Mays just returned from second to first voluntarily?  This is an example of how to infer intentions from observable behavior, the economist's stock-in-trade.

12. The prospects for entry in professional team sports also differ substantially from other franchise industries because of the monopoly nature of the four major team sports in North America.  If, for example, McDonald's, Pizza Hut, Amoco, or Crown Books determines not to place a franchise in St. Louis, Burger King, Papa John's, Texaco, or Barnes and Noble may enter the St. Louis market.  But if the NFL decides not to locate a franchise in St. Louis, there is no comparable professional football league whose entry into the St. Louis market can satisfy that demand.

13. See, for example, Noll (1974) for a series of studies of different sports in which the presence of another sport in the same community does not appear to affect attendance.

14. Portions of this section are from Siegfried (1994) and are used with permission of the copyright holder, Federal Legal Publications, Inc.  For an extensive analysis of the NCAA as a cartel see Fleisher et al. (1992).

15. Entry may be difficult into NCAA sports, but it is easier than entry into professional sports leagues.  College teams that wish to upgrade to Division I status (the highest level of competition, and the only level that generates substantial revenues) have numerous teams they can approach as prospective opponents.  In contrast to professional sports, collegiate teams attempting to join a major conference also have alternatives, as there are more than a half dozen major college athletic conferences.

16. The first Heisman Trophy winner, Jay Berwanger of the University of Chicago, faced similar salary offers from the NFL and business when he graduated in 1936.  He selected business.

17. Because individual teams can't enter the industry, to be a credible threat requires sufficient capital to form an entire new league with a minimum of eight teams.

18. One of the authors, for example, always employs examples of players from his institution's successful women's basketball team when using the effect of a player's points in the most recent game on her scoring average to explain the relationship between marginal and average values.  Tennis examples using Martina Navratilova and Chris Evert are featured prominently in Dixit and Nalebuff's *Thinking Strategically* (1991).

19. Some years ago a student attempted to enroll in the Economics of Sports course taught by one of us.  That course requires intermediate microeconomic theory as a prerequisite.  The student did not meet the prerequisite, but insisted he would have no difficulty because he "knew more about sports than anyone else."  When he was denied admission to the course (a review of his record in principles confirmed that he surely did not "know more than anyone else about economics") he muttered that there must be something seriously wrong with a course on the Economics of Sports if a thorough

knowledge of sports was not sufficient background to take it. If he had realized the power of the core of economics principles and understood the way in which economists apply those few powerful ideas to a myriad of issues, he might have recognized that a discipline founded on the idea of "have tools, will travel" relies mostly on the tools.

20. One could also tie in Peltzman's well-known 1975 study of offsetting driver behavior with regard to seat belt usage with a sport's proposition that better and more protective equipment for NFL players doesn't reduce injuries – they just run at each other harder and attempt riskier behavior.

## REFERENCES

Blount, R. Jr. 1993. Plink-fumba-baraumba-boom. *Sports Illustrated* 79 (August 9): 64-74.

Bruggink, T. H. 1993. National pasttime to dismal science: Using baseball to illustrate economic principles. *Eastern Economic Journal* 19 (Summer): 275-94.

Cassing, J., and R.W. Douglas. 1980. Implications of the auction mechanism in baseball's free agent draft. *Southern Economic Journal* 47 (July): 110-21.

Demmert, H. G. 1973. *The economics of professional team sports*. Lexington, MA: Lexington Books.

Dixit, A., and B. Nalebuff. 1991. *Thinking strategically*. New York: W. W. Norton.

Douglas, C. 1996. The economic cost of the baseball strike. Senior Honors Thesis, Vanderbilt University (April).

Fleisher, A. A., B. L. Goff, and R. D. Tollison. 1992. *The National Collegiate Athletic Association: A study in cartel behavior*. Chicago: University of Chicago Press.

Happel, S. K., and M. M. Jennings. 1995. Herd them together and scalp them. *The Wall Street Journal* (February 23): A-14.

Jones, J. C. H., D. G. Ferguson, and K. G. Stewart. 1993. Blood sports and cherry pie: Some economics of violence in the National Hockey League. *American Journal of Economics and Sociology* 52: (January): 63-78.

Kahn, L.M.. 1993. Free agency, long-term contracts and compensation in major league baseball: Estimates from panel data. *Review of Economics and Statistics* 75 (February): 157-64.

Knowles, G., K. Sherony, and M. Haupert. 1992. The demand for major league baseball: A test of the uncertainty of outcome hypothesis. *The American Economist* 36 (Fall): 72-80.

McCloskey, D. N. 1990. *If you're so smart*. Chicago: The University of Chicago Press.

Merz, T. E. 1996. Willie Mays: Meet John Nash. *Journal of Economic Education* 27 (Winter): 45-8.

Noll, R. G. 1974. Attendance and price setting. In R.G. Noll, ed., *Government and the sports business*. Washington, D. C.: The Brookings Institution.

_____ and A. Zimbalist, eds. 1997. *Sports, jobs, and taxes*. Washington, D.C.: The Brookings Institution.

Peltzman, S. 1975. The effects of automobile safety regulations. *Journal of Political Economy* 83 (August): 677-726.

Peterson, T. 1997. Public subsidies for professional sports events are a subsidy for the wealthy. Senior Honors Thesis, Vanderbilt University (December).

Porter, P. K. 1992. The role of the fan in professional baseball. In *Diamonds are forever: The business of baseball*. Washington D.C.: The Brookings Institution.

Quirk, J., and R. D. Fort. 1992. *Pay dirt: The business of professional team sports*. Princeton N.J.: Princeton University Press.

Raimondo, H. J. 1983. Free agents' impact on the labor market for baseball players. *Journal of Labor Research* 4 (Spring): 183-93.

Rottenberg, S. 1956. The baseball players labor market. *Journal of Political Economy* 64 (June): 242-58.

Scahill, E. 1990. Did Babe Ruth have a comparative advantage as a pitcher? *Journal of Economic Education* 21 (Fall): 402-10.

Scully, G. W. 1989. *The business of major league baseball*. Chicago: The University of Chicago Press.

_____. 1995. *The market structure of sports*. Chicago: The University of Chicago Press.

Siegfried, J. J. 1994. Review of *The National Collegiate Athletic Association: A study in cartel behavior*, by Fleisher, A. A., B. L. Goff, and R. D. Tollison, in *The Antitrust Bulletin* 39 (Summer): 599-609.

Staudohar, P. D. 1989. *The sports industry and collective bargaining*. Ithaca N.Y.: ILR Press.

White, M. D. 1986. Self-interest redistribution and the National Football League Players Association. *Economic Inquiry* 24 (October): 669-80.

Zipp, J. F. 1996. The economic impact of the baseball strike of 1994. *Urban Affairs Review* 32 (November): 157-8.

# CHAPTER 9

# USING LITERATURE AND DRAMA IN UNDERGRADUATE ECONOMICS COURSES

**Michael Watts**

When George Stigler began to serve as an editor of the *Journal of Political Economy*, the back cover of the journal began to feature literary passages dealing with economic concepts, issues, and themes.   Many prominent economists have used literary allusions and quotations in some of their journal articles, textbooks, other publications.   In fact, it seems such a simple thing to do – find passages and work them into a presentation.   But in a recent survey (Becker and Watts 1996) it was found that very few economists use literary examples in teaching any kind of undergraduate course.

## I.  TO USE, OR NOT TO USE, LITERATURE AND DRAMA

One reason for economists' failure to employ literary passages is, naturally, the cost of finding appropriate passages; and certainly as a near-universal rule, courses in literature and drama are not part of the current graduate training of economists (Hansen 1991; Kasper et al. 1991; and Krueger et al. 1991). There is also the issue of devoting scarce class time to such material, instead of graphs, equations, and standard lectures that do not feature such "extraneous" material. Finally, as Veblen and some of his followers have suggested, there is the risk of appearing pedantic to our students, who themselves are not likely to be much better versed in literature and drama than they are in economics.[1]

In this chapter, I present the major reasons why I believe such material can be used appropriately and effectively by structuring class discussions around short handouts or student presentations of dramatic scenes. I present three detailed examples of such assignments, and then briefly discuss two other formats for presenting this material in specially designed classes. The chapter concludes with a discussion of Do's and Don'ts for economics teachers to keep in mind when using literature and drama in their classes, and a brief assessment of the opportunity cost of using this approach. An extensive list of additional literary readings that can be used to enhance classroom discussions of economic concepts and issues is attached in Appendix 9.A. A list of discussion questions I have used to teach a single class session (90 minutes) focusing on a series of readings from literature and drama is provided in Appendix 9.B. I have used the questions provided there for individual literary passages in several different undergraduate economics courses.

## II. IF IT WERE DONE, WHEN 'TIS DONE, THEN 'TWERE WELL, IT WERE DONE QUICKLY...

My basic strategy in using literature and drama to teach economics in undergraduate classes is to use short, self-contained readings – no longer than a few pages, and often a page or less. Although I use brief quotations and simple examples from literature and drama in many classes, I only use these readings as part of two or three classes per semester. In such a format, the costs to both students and instructors who choose to use the approach are relatively modest. The benefits are, I believe, more numerous and substantial.

First, the literary readings encourage all students – even those who are intimidated by graphs, math, and the formal terminology of economics – to participate in class discussions. For that reason, I always use one of the readings as the basis for the first extensive class discussion at an early point in the course. I often use Robert Frost's *Mending Wall*,[2] as discussed below, because it deals with a basic institution of market economies, private property, that is not a concept that economists normally graph or measure and analyze in other quantitative ways. I want students to see that there are important issues to be considered about even the most basic institutions in the economy, and that these issues are related to many current public policy debates both in this country and internationally.   In other words, I want to show that there are reasons for economists and others to talk about these issues, and to stress the idea that the institutional and cultural frameworks in an economy have an effect on people's behavior and directly influence many of the perennial public policy debates in that economy, as well as debates involving different nations.

The first extensive class discussion sets the stage for later discussion sessions, and promotes better daily exchanges of questions and comments from students, not just participation in the special assignments such as those described in this chapter.   With most students and in most classes, of course, the flow of student questions and discussion doesn't come automatically or easily.   Unless you show students that you want them to participate in discussions, and (especially at the beginning of the course) give them assignments in which they can be comfortable participating, not much discussion is likely to take place.   Literary passages are, I believe, an exceptionally good way to initiate, encourage, and help sustain that process.

A second benefit of using some literary assignments and examples relates to the old idea – often stated but seldom acted upon by economists in terms of varying their lectures and presentation style[3] – that different students learn economics (or any subject) in different ways.   Some students learn best by listening and watching, some by processing information as they work through problem sets or other written assignments, some by participating in simulations and experiments, some by talking things over with other students and the instructor in discussions, and some by reading (or writing) about new concepts or issues in textbooks or other sources.   Lecturing and drawing graphs are sometimes essential in economics, and for a few outstanding lecturers that may even be sufficient as well as necessary.   For most instructors, however, and probably for all undergraduate courses with more than a few students, variety is the spice of effective and interesting teaching.   Literary passages can provide some of that variety at a relatively low cost  to economists who are widely read, or who have access to a set of prepared readings.   Those costs are much lower than, say, the start-up costs of learning how to do classroom experiments or simulations, although some of those activities can also be very effective in most undergraduate courses.

A third reason for using literary passages in economics courses is to demonstrate in a particularly effective way that there is a verbal, nontechnical intuition and logic that underlies economic analysis.   It is true that most literary authors don't know much economic theory, let alone the stylized facts and key empirical findings from the discipline.   They do, however, understand much of the common sense that underlies many economic models, and even some of the anomalies that periodically challenge that common sense.[4]   They express that intuition in different terms and from a different perspective than economists do, but that often means they express it in ways that are more accessible and interesting to noneconomists, including students.[5]   I believe the second example presented below, based on a very short passage from Frank Norris' *The Octopus*, dealing with the forces of supply and demand, illustrates this point.

The fourth reason for using literary passages relates to the theme of Lee Hansen's chapter in this volume. Effective writing is an important – though perhaps underdeveloped and underappreciated – skill for modern economists, and particularly for those who want to communicate with noneconomists. Not surprisingly, part of what Hansen does in trying to teach good writing is to have his students read, collect, and discuss examples of good writing by economists and journalists. I would simply add to those assignments a sample of literary passages, such as those listed in Appendix 9.A.

The fifth and final reason I will mention for using the literary passages relates most directly to passages from drama. It is very effective to have a group of students read sections from plays in class – two tried and true examples are excerpts from scenes in Neil Simon's *Prisoner of Second Avenue*, which is the third example presented in this chapter, and sections from the opening scene of Thornton Wilder's *Our Town*. I have also had students improvise scenes based on selected poems from Edgar Lee Master's *Spoon River Anthology* and a passage from William Faulkner's *The Hamlet*. Role playing is a form of active learning that can be used effectively by economists teaching undergraduate courses, and is easily superimposed on readings of dramatic passages. [6]

Based on student comments from course and instructor evaluations, it is clear that many students remember the classes featuring literature and drama longer and more fondly than they do my traditional lectures. Because I debrief literary activities to stress the same economic concepts and issues covered in traditional lectures, and use a limited number of these sessions in any given course, it is reasonable to think that the effects on the students' cognitive learning are small but probably positive.

Others have also published articles calling for the use of literature and drama in economics and in business-oriented classes. Recent examples include Bogart (1995) Dimand (1991), Rockoff (1990), and DeMott (1989). For references to earlier articles and books on the topic, see the references in Watts and Smith (1989).

I will now turn to three specific examples of literary passages that can be used effectively to teach about private property, supply and demand, and unemployment. As a group, like other such literary passages, and especially when combined with the approaches that are typically used in undergraduate economics classes, they can help students understand the economic way of thinking, and accept it as a part of what Alfred Marshall called "the ordinary business of life."

## III. PRIVATE PROPERTY IN ROBERT FROST'S *MENDING WALL*

Most economists and even many economics students are familiar with the statement, "Good fences make good neighbors." They are rarely familiar with Frost's poem, and the debate in that poem centering around this statement, which is repeatedly spoken by an elderly, tradition-bound man. According to the narrator of the poem, the old man "moves in darkness" like a "savage" and "will not go behind his father's saying," but likes having thought of it so much that he keeps repeating it. (All quotations from the poem are taken from Frost, 1939, 47-8.)

The narrator has a much more skeptical view of fences – which is to say of private property – and points out that forces of nature, animals, and humans (particularly hunters) often tear down walls. There is a humanistic and romantic basis for the narrator's skepticism:

> Before I built a wall I'd ask to know
> What I was walling in or walling out,
> And to whom I was like to give offense.

But the narrator also uses that idea to endorse a pragmatic evaluation of costs and benefits, which closely parallels Ronald Coase's discussion of when it will or will not pay to build a wall or fence. He says:

> There where it is we do not need the wall:
> He is all pine and I am apple orchard.
> My apple trees will never get across
> And eat the cones under his pines.

Considering the narrator's actions as well as his words, the fence mending is clearly an annual rite that he always performs. Furthermore, he admits that he questions his old neighbor in a sense of Spring-induced "mischief." So despite the narrator's rational and romantic doubts about some walls and the institution of private property, there is still a sense of respect for the tradition of maintaining walls, and we are left with the idea that there is both some community wisdom and personal comfort in the saying that is again repeated to end the poem, "Good fences make good neighbors."

This poem fits easily on one or two sheets of paper, and can be read and reread by most students in a period of a few minutes. I find it useful to have students first read the poem individually for five minutes to determine what is happening, and then discuss the positions that are expressed in the poem in small groups. When they go into these groups, I tell them to pick a spokesperson who will be called on in five minutes to list any economic concepts and issues they recognize in the poem, and to summarize in a few sentences what the poem is about. The result of these reports is usually to identify the concept of private property, and perhaps to recognize a few points from the debate between the neighbors. Asking whether the narrator of the poem views property as a natural or inalienable right reliably brings more students into the discussion, and while most students aren't familiar with seventeenth and eighteenth-century thinkers' concepts of natural rights, pointing out that Thomas Jefferson changed John Locke's "life, liberty, and property" to "life, liberty, and the pursuit of happiness" in the Declaration of Independence usually conveys enough of the idea for this discussion, particularly when contrasted with the young Pierre Proudhon's claim that "Property is theft."

Referring to the verses in the poem dealing with things in nature that try to tear down walls, and to the idea of knowing what walls keep in or keep out, establishes the narrator's position on these issues. The pragmatic, cost-benefit defense of property can then be presented, with some examples and questions based on Coase's examples. Finally, the goal of showing the relevance of these topics to current public policy issues can be met using short handouts, overhead transparencies, or simply some directed discussion of public policy issues, such as recent privatization reforms in industrialized, developing, and transition economies; the predictable overuse and pollution of publicly owned resources; and news stories about people in this country fighting to keep their property in the face of public building projects that allow the use of eminent domain laws. A quick search of electronic indexes and databases for news services or periodicals has never failed to find recent examples of all of these topics[7], and linking the ideas in Frost's poems to current issues and economic concepts makes for a memorable class. Procedurally, the activity demonstrates to students that you are serious about wanting their participation in class discussions.

## IV.  SUPPLY AND DEMAND IN FRANK NORRIS' *THE OCTOPUS*

Written in 1901, *The Octopus: A Story of California* dramatizes the plight of wheat farmers who are caught in the tentacles of a railroad monopoly at a time when grain prices, technological innovations, and even the climate and other forces of nature seem to conspire against the small, family farmer. Presley, the young hero of the novel, decides to take his revenge on Shelgrim, the railroad president. But when he confronts Shelgrim, Presley hears one of the shortest recorded lectures on supply and demand:

> ...(R)ailroads build themselves. Where there is demand sooner or later there will be a supply. Mr. Derrick, does he grow his wheat? The Wheat grows itself. What does he count for? Does he supply the force? What do I count for? Do I build the Railroad? You are dealing with

forces, young man, when you speak of Wheat and the Railroads, not with men. There is the Wheat, the supply. It must be carried to feed the People. There is the demand. The Wheat is one force, the Railroad, another, and there is the law that governs them – supply and demand. Men have only little to do in the whole business. Complications may arise, conditions that bear hard on the individual – crush him maybe – but the Wheat will be carried to feed the People as inevitably as it will grow. (The quotations here and below are from Norris, 1938, Book II, 285-6.)

Presley initially argues that Shelgrim, who is the head of the railroad, controls the company. Shelgrim responds that the only control he might have over the company would be to take it into bankruptcy, but then some other company would come and operate the railroad "as a business proposition." Similarly, he points out, an individual farmer could burn or give wheat away and incur bankruptcy. But, he asks, "Can anyone stop the Wheat? Well, then, no more can I stop the Road."

Presley has the reaction that all economics instructors strive to leave with their students after initial lectures on supply and demand: "This new idea, this new conception, dumbfounded him. Somehow, he could not deny it. It rang with the clear reverberation of truth."

Once again, this entire passage and even more can fit on one page, and students can easily read and consider the handout in five minutes. Other parts of the passage that I have not quoted here also stress the limited role that individuals play in these market forces and business decisions, so I begin the discussion by asking whether students agree with that idea or not. Some students respond by talking about the important roles individual workers, executives, or entrepreneurs can have in creating a new business or strengthening an existing one. Other students follow Norris and stress the power and impersonal nature of market forces, arguing that if one person had not invented some new machine or founded some company, someone else soon would have. It is not uncommon, given the wheat farming context of the passage from *The Octopus*, for a student to talk about the economic and technological forces that displaced so many workers and families from agriculture in the United States and other developed economies during the past century. I try to be sure that both of these perspectives are worked into the discussion, playing devil's advocate in cases when only one perspective is voiced, or when the students who support one view are more vocal and articulate than students on the other side of the debate.

In order for students in principles classes to have enough background to appreciate the idea of market forces, I typically schedule this activity after the introductory sessions on supply, demand, equilibrium price and quantity, shortages, surpluses, price controls, and shifts in supply and demand. Students can (and do) then use these ideas in their discussions, and frequently bring in examples of individuals or companies to support their arguments. Bankruptcies or near-bankruptcies that are narrowly averted are classic examples of these cases. Students often feel that executives who cause or avert bankruptcies have personally affected a company's fortunes, but other students (or I, if necessary) will point out that whether or not a bankruptcy occurs, many of the firms' assets remain in their current uses or occupations, but sometimes under different ownership or managers.

To extend the discussion and introduce the topics of market structures and market power, I ask whether the president of a monopoly has more discretion and power than the president of a firm with many equal-sized competitors. After some affirmative responses have been offered, I ask students to discuss in what ways. Even though students have not seen the formal monopoly models at this point, the discussion on these questions is usually neither extreme nor one-sided, and it often moves easily into the area of factor market topics such as employment, compensation levels, and even discrimination. In short, the discussion usefully reviews the material just covered on supply and demand, and builds interest in several upcoming topics. Students should feel comfortable in discussing the ideas and raising questions that deal with the underlying substance and importance of the models that are presented in class, not just questions about the lines and areas in the graphs that are used to help analyze those questions. That is not to say that I oppose the use of rigorous graphical analysis in principles courses. In fact, I regularly teach indifference curves and isoquants in those courses, which puts me in a minority of instructors. But the key pedagogical issue here is one of variety in effective teaching approaches.

## V.  UNEMPLOYMENT AND THE ECONOMIC WAY OF THINKING IN NEIL SIMON'S *THE PRISONER OF SECOND AVENUE*

The title character in this play, Mel, suffers a nervous breakdown after he is laid off. He finally tells his wife, Edna, that his unemployment is the result of a plot. She asks who is responsible, and he identifies "the human race! ...(T)he sudden, irrevocable deterioration of the spirit of man. ...(M)an undermining himself, causing a self-willed, self-imposed, self-evident self-destruction." (All quotations here are taken from Simon, 1972, 52-75.) Mel describes the humiliation of waiting in line for his welfare check in a shirt and tie, telling "some fat old dame behind the counter" that he did look for work that week, and did not turn down any offers to work. He also describes their ninety-one-year-old doorman, "with no teeth, asthma and beer on his breath," as giggling at him "because *he's* working." Apart from a powerful depiction of the psychic costs of unemployment, this short scene can also be used to discuss the idea of voluntary vs. involuntary unemployment.

A later scene presents Mel's brother and three sisters meeting with Edna to discuss what they can do to help Mel. After a hilarious discussion of estimating the costs involved and what a reasonable length of time for Mel to recover might be -- assuming the doctor is really as good as Edna says he is -- Mel's brother, Harry, agrees to provide any funds required to pay the psychiatrist. The sisters will contribute whatever they can afford. But shortly after that, when Edna suggests that these funds could be used instead as a down payment on a youth camp for Mel to run, or that she could sell some of her jewelry to get the funds for the youth camp and their funds could still be used for the psychiatric help, Harry and the sisters quickly withdraw their offer. Harry asks, "You mean we should pay to get Mel healthy so you can lose your money in a camp and get him sick again?" Edna pleads "(H)elp him!" and Harry answers "Not when he's sick. When he's better, we'll help him."

Using the dialogue on what resources Harry and the sisters can provide, what kind of help Mel needs most, and the alternative possible uses of funds to help with Mel's medical and employment problems, a very lively class discussion can be generated by asking students to identify which characters are, or are not, thinking like an economist. Then, to bring the discussion back to the topic of unemployment, comparisons between the characters' debates and the debates over the effectiveness of public policy programs actually used to assist and retrain unemployed workers in recent years can be made.

As noted earlier, because this reading is from a play, it is very easy to "stage" a reading or role play of these scenes in class, with students taking the various parts. I find that works most effectively if the students who are not reading parts do not receive the text until after the role playing has been completed.

## VI. BRIEF IDEAS FOR MORE EXTENSIVE TEACHING FORMATS USING LITERATURE AND DRAMA

I have offered a one-credit-hour class on Economics Through Literature and Drama for secondary social studies and English teachers, in which most of the references listed in Appendix 9.A were featured in discussions, direct readings, or participant presentations and improvisations. The evaluations in that course are probably the most favorable I have ever received from any group of students or teachers. A similar or longer class could easily be presented for traditional undergraduate students.

For the past several years, I have also presented an hour-and-a-half class on economics in literature and drama, featuring about 70 pages of readings and the series of discussion questions on particular readings that is reprinted as Appendix 9.B. The most general part of that assignment is to have students note, in the margins of the readings, any economic concept or issue that is illustrated in the passages. In team-taught courses with some latitude in topic coverage, this material has proven to be a well-received change of pace that reinforces the main themes of undergraduate instruction in economics, and helps students to see economics in another part of the world around them.

## VII. DO'S AND DON'TS IN USING LITERATURE AND DRAMA TO TEACH UNDERGRADUATE ECONOMICS

Most of the points in this list are relevant guidelines for any kind of classroom discussion. If you are not experienced in using classroom discussions, it would probably be helpful to read at least one of the general references on that topic, such as Hansen and Salemi (1997).

Important points to remember in using literature and drama to teach economics:

- Do be very selective in the readings you choose, both in terms of the number of readings used (which should normally not exceed three or four readings in a semester-long class) and the topics covered (which should be something you feel is important enough to warrant additional class time).
- Do try to vary the form of the literary readings (i.e., use poems, prose, plays) and the background, time period, and social perspectives of the authors you use. Such variety provides spice for these assignments, too.
- Do write out and carefully review the discussion questions you intend to use with the readings, whether or not you distribute the questions to your students. Have questions ready that will let you pursue several lines of inquiry, or at least discuss the reading and economic concepts in different order, depending on the students' responses.
- Do remember to discuss and debrief both the story content of the reading and the economic concepts or issues that are presented in it. Make sure the students understand what is happening in the reading, and any obscure (to undergraduates) terms, before discussing the economics content in the reading.
- Do try to involve all students in the discussion, through small group discussions of the readings before the general class discussion, if necessary.
- Do sometimes use role playing, readings, and improvisations to make the literary passages more active.
- Do encourage students to bring in other examples of literary passages on economic concepts and issues.
- Don't present the attitude that all or most literary authors present flawed economic analysis. Some do, but in many cases the literary authors simply choose to present issues from the standpoint of individual human interest stories or personal ethical dilemmas, rather than an analysis of economic

incentives, agents, and constraints. Many of the literary authors are surprisingly good at recognizing and accurately depicting the economic forces.

- Don't assume that students will be eager to discuss the literary passages without good leading questions from you. Students will have strong opinions on many of the passages, but they will often still want some direction from you about where you want the discussion to go. In other cases they may get lost in deciphering what really happens in the reading (particularly in poems written before this century, and with authors who make extensive use of symbolism or unorthodox perspectives and literary forms).

- Don't be afraid to set and enforce a limited time for the discussion of the passages.

- Don't be afraid to use lectures and graphs after the discussion period in order to extend or complete the debriefing of the reading.

- Don't pretend that you can explain all of the literary features of the passage in the same way a literature professor might. In fact, point out that you are using the readings to do very specialized things, with the result that your analysis of the events and the literary content of the reading may be limited, compared to the analysis that may be offered in literature classes.

## VIII. CONCLUSION

Used selectively, and indeed sparingly, literary readings can encourage and enhance discussions in most undergraduate economics courses. They are particularly helpful in reaching students who have an innate interest in literature and drama, or who tire of strictly graphical and mathematical presentations. For instructors, literary passages seem to make it easier and in some ways inescapable to participate in a discussion *with* students, rather than lecturing to them. As suggested in the first chapter of this volume, that is an area where many instructors could use more help and teaching materials that are structured to promote class discussions.

Used this way, the literary passages have a low opportunity cost, once appropriate literary passages have been identified and prepared. Because these readings offer examples of economic concepts or issues, instructors are most likely to substitute the literary passage and classroom discussion for some other kind of example. The more traditional examples and applications economists favor tend to be graphical analysis of some specific market or topic, empirical estimations relating to particular markets or topics, or public policy issues. I have certainly not eliminated all of those kinds of examples in my classes in favor of the literary passages, nor would I recommend that other instructors do so. The traditional examples offer more precise and quantitative kinds of analysis or results for students to consider. The literary passages have an advantage in developing the intuition that lies behind economic concepts and behaviors, and in the power of the expression and imagery used to present concepts and issues, which helps students understand and remember the material. At the margin, therefore, most economists could use literature and drama to add a touch of spice and variety to their undergraduate teaching.

## Appendix 9.A: Literary Passages With Economic Concepts

This list will help instructors find passages they might use in preparing lectures or other instructional materials. It is an expanded version of a similar table in Watts and Smith (1989). Two caveats are in order: 1) the list is obviously exemplary, not exhaustive; and 2) most of the works included have been published in several editions and by more than one publisher.

| Author | Title | Publisher | Date of Cited Edition | Pages | Economic Concepts |
|---|---|---|---|---|---|
| Adams, Henry | *Democracy* | Peter Smith Publishing Co., Gloucester, Massachusetts | 1965 | 3-9 | Public Choice |
| Anderson, Sherwood | *Winesburg, Ohio* | Viking Press, New York | 1958 | 8-12 | Specialization, Division of Labor |
| Bastiat, Frederick | "Petition from the Manufacturers of Candles...," In *Bastiat's Sophisms of Protection* | G.P. Putnam's Sons, New York | 1874 | 73-80 | Tariffs, Scarcity, Comparative Advantage |
| Baum, L. Frank | *The Wonderful Wizard of Oz* | University of California Press, Berkeley | 1986 | --- | Bi-Metallism, Monetary Policy |
| Bellamy, Edward | *Looking Backward* | Houghton, Mifflin and Co., Boston | 1890 | 65-75 85-99 | Utopian Socialism |
| | "The Parable of the Water Tank," in Bellamy's *Equality*, G. Ford and S. Monod, eds. | Greenwood Press, New York | 1969 | 195-203 | Comparative Systems |
| Boswell, Robert | *Mystery Ride* | HarperPerennial | 1992 | 143-146 | Money, Tastes and Preferences, Property Rights |
| Clancy, Tom | *Clear and Present Danger* | Berkley Books, New York | 1990 | 583 | Cartels, Supply and Demand, Price Elasticity |

| Author | Title | Publisher | Year | Pages | Comparative Systems |
|---|---|---|---|---|---|
| Dickens, Charles | *Hard Times* | W.W. Norton & Co., New York | 1969 | 195-203 | |
| Doig, Ivan | *Dancing at the Rascal Fair* | Harper & Row Publishers, New York | 1987 | 2-11<br>128-131 | Immigration, Risk<br>Entrepreneurship, Risk |
| | *English Creek* | Penguin Books | 1985 | 28-29<br>42-45<br>96-97 | Price Fluctuations, Risk, Business Cycles,<br>Structural Change, Marketing |
| | *Ride With Me, Mariah Montana* | Penguin Books | 1991 | 136-162<br>39-40<br>56-58<br>109-110<br>132-135<br>199-200<br>310-314 | Property Rights and Extinction<br>Occupational Hazards, Unions<br>Cost Minimization<br>Economies of Scale and Family Farming<br>Economic Losses<br>Economic Losses and Private Philanthropy |
| | *Bucking the Sun* | Scribner | 1997 | 33, 37-8<br>132-133<br>153<br>174-77<br>202-203 | Fiscal Policy and Keynes<br>Marketing and Pricing<br><br>Socialism and Radical Unionism |
| Dos Passos, John | *U.S.A.:*<br>"Tin Lizzie"<br>"Prince of Peace"<br>"The Bitter Drink" | Harcourt Press, New York | 1937 | 421-423<br>264-265<br>93-105 | Entrepreneurship, Economies of Scale<br>Entrepreneurship, Philanthropy<br>Conspicuous Consumption |
| Dreiser, Theodore | *Sister Carrie* | Random House, New York | 1927 | 321-328 | Specialization, The Extent of the Market |
| Emerson, Ralph Waldo | *Journals* | Houghton Mifflin, New York | 1912 | 169<br>377-379<br>528-529 | Entrepreneurship, Investment, Income<br>Distribution |
| Faulkner, William | *The Hamlet* | Random House, New York | 1940 | 371-380 | Property Rights, Contracts |
| Fitzgerald, F. Scott | *The Great Gatsby* | Charles Scribner's Sons, New York | 1953 | 39-41<br>174-177 | Human Capital |

| Author | Title | Publisher/Place | Year | Pages | Topics |
|---|---|---|---|---|---|
| Francis, Dick | *Banker* | Fawcett Crest, New York | 1982 | 19-23 80-82 | Banking, Investment, Risk |
| Franklin, Benjamin | *Autobiography* L. Labaree, R. Ketcham, H. Boatfield and H. Fineman, eds. | Yale University Press, New Haven, Connecticut | 1964 | 53-63 | Saving, Investment, Human Capital |
| | *Poor Richard's Almanac* | Mount Vernon, New York (Excerpts from the 30 Annual Editions Printed by Franklin) | 1936 | --- | Saving, Human Capital, etc. |
| Frost, Robert | *The Collected Poems of Robert Frost* "Mending Wall" | Halcyon House, New York | 1939 | 47-48 | Private Property |
| | *The Road Not Taken* "The Road Not Taken" | Holt, Rinehart & Winston | 1939 | 270-271 | Opportunity Cost, Normal Profits |
| Goethe, Johann W. | *Faust*, A. Swanwick, Translation | A.L. Burt, New York | n.d. | 211-214 | Money, Barter, Monetary Policy |
| Heller, Joseph | *Catch – 22* | Dell Publishing Co., New York | 1966 | 66-69 237-239 | Economic Systems, Entrepreneurship, Supply, Demand |
| | *Good as Gold* | Simon and Schuster (Pocket Books), New York | 1980 | 44-53 120-129 153-157 | Public Choice |
| Huxley, Aldous | *Brave New World* | Harper & Row, New York | 1946 | 264-271 | Technology, Freedom of Choice |
| Irving, Washington | "The Poor-Devil Author," in *The Complete Tales of Washington Irving*, C. Neider, ed. | Doubleday & Co., New York | 1975 | 277-291 | The Demand for Labor |

| Author | Title | Publisher | Year | Pages | Economic Concepts |
|---|---|---|---|---|---|
| Jonson, Ben | *Volpone*, in Stuart Plays, rev. ed., A. Nethercot, C. Baskerville and V. Heltzel, eds. | Holt, Rinehart & Winston | 1971 | 136-137, 149, 164 | Greed, Public Choice, Fraudulent Contracts |
| Junger, Sebastian | *The Perfect Storm: A True Story of Men Against the Sea* | W.W. Norton & Co. | 1997 | 1, 5, 13-16, 33-36, 41-50, 56-60, 66-76, 121-22 | The Economics of Commercial Fishing: Wages, Profits, Risk Premia, Prices, Supply and Demand, Externalities, Tragedy of the Commons, Regulation |
| Krakauer, Jon | *Into Thin Air* | Random House, New York | 1997 | 21-26, 66-67<br>64-65<br>76-77<br>131<br>149 | Pricing, Elasticity of Demand, Opportunity Cost, Barter, Externalities, Profit, Collusion, User Fees, Risk, Implicit Labor Contracts, Discrimination and Compensating Wage Differentials |
| Massinger, Philip | *A New Way to Pay Old Debts*, in Stuart Plays, rev. ed., A. Nethercot, C. Baskerville and V. Heltzel, eds. | Holt, Rinehart & Winston | 1971 | 714-715 | Monopoly Power, Economies of Scale |
| Masters, Edgar Lee | *Spoon River Anthology* | Crowell-Collier Publishing Co., New York | 1962 | 48, 73, 150, 169, 188, 240 | Specialization, Division of Labor |

| Author | Title | Publisher | Date | Pages | Concepts |
|---|---|---|---|---|---|
| Miller, Arthur | *Death of a Salesman*, in *The Portable Arthur Miller*, H. Clurman, ed. | Viking Press, New York | 1971 | 6–36 | Competition |
| | *All My Sons*, in *Arthur Miller: Collected Plays* | Viking Press, New York | 1957 | 114–115 124–127 | Market Forces, Economic Values |
| Milton, John | *The Mask of Comus* | Nonesuch Press, Bloomsbury | 1937 | 23–24 | Natural Resources, Scarcity |
| Norris, Frank | *The Octopus* | Houghton Mifflin Co., Boston | 1938 | 395–407 | Markets, Competition, Income Distribution |
| Orwell, George | *The Road to Wigan Pier* | Harcourt, Brace & Co., New York | 1958 | 22–26 78–82 96, 100 | Productivity, Technology, Occupational Safety, Cyclical Unemployment |
| Pope, Alexander | *The Poems of Alexander Pope*, J. Butt, ed.: | Yale University Press, New Haven | 1963 | | |
| | "Imitations of Horace," | | | 570–596 | Economic Incentives, Income Effects and Risk |
| | *Moral Essays: Epistle III, To Allen Lord Bathurst* (Second Epistle, Second Book) | | | 651 | Traditional and Economic Values |
| | *The Dunciad: Book IV* | | | 778–780 786–791 | Specialization in the Physical and Social Sciences |
| Rabelais, Francois | *Gargantua and Pantagruel*, (Book III, Chapters 3–5 and 37) in *The Works of Rabelais* | The Bibliophilist Society, London | n.d. | 233–242 | Credit, Debt, Economic Incentives, Externalities |

| Author | Title | Publisher | Year | Pages | Topics |
|---|---|---|---|---|---|
| Rand, Ayn | The Fountainhead / Atlas Shrugged | Sears Readers Club, Chicago / Random House, New York | 1943 / 1957 | 736-744 / 410-415 / 475-484 / 745-749 | Freedom of Choice / Individualism, Economic Freedom and Efficiency |
| Remarque, Erich Maria | The Black Obelisk, D. Lindley, trans. | Harcourt, Brace & Co., New York | 1957 | 6-16 | Hyperinflation |
| Salinger, J.D. | Catcher in the Rye | Little, Brown & Co., Boston | 1951 | 110-111 | Conspicuous Consumption |
| Shakespeare, William | The Merchant of Venice, in Shakespeare: The Complete Works, G.B. Harrison, ed. | Harcourt, Brace & World, Inc. | 1968 | 583 / 604-608 | Risk Acceptance, Diversification, Contracts, Property Rights, Usury |
| Shelly, Percy Bysshe | "Song to the Men of England," in Adonais, G. Woodbury, ed. | Hough Publishing, Co., New York | 1901 | 364-365 | Labor Theory of Value, Exploitation |
| Simon, Neil | The Prisoner of Second Avenue | Random House, New York | 1972 | 57-75 | Unemployment |
| Sinclair, Upton | The Jungle | Doubleday, Page & Co., New York | 1906 | 160-162 | Consumer Safety, Regulation |
| Solzhenitsyn, Alexander | Cancer Ward | Farrar, Strauss & Giroux, New York | 1974 | 427-428 | Nationalized Health Care |
| Southern, Terry | The Magic Christian | Andre Deutsch, Ltd., London | 1959 | 19-20 / 22-30 / 65-76 | Individual Economic Values, Advertising, Consumer Sovereignty |
| Steinbeck, John | East of Eden | Viking Press, New York | 1952 | 480-481 / 540-545 | Market Forces, Economic Value |
| | Grapes of Wrath / In Dubious Battle | Viking Press, New York / Viking Press, New York | 1967 / 1968 | 49-53 / 26-29 | Unemployment, Business Cycles / Labor Markets, Unions |

| Author | Title | Publisher | Year | Pages | Topics |
|---|---|---|---|---|---|
| Stoppard, Tom | *Arcadia* | Faber and Faber: London | 1993 | 60-66 | Technological Change and Economic Progress, Marginal and Total Utilities of the Arts and Sciences |
| Swift, Jonathan | "A Modest Proposal…" in *Jonathan Swift*, A. Ross and D. Wooley, eds. | Oxford University Press, New York | 1984 | 492-499 | Population, Cost-Benefit Analysis, Economic Values |
| Tan, Amy | *The Joy Luck Club* | Ivy Books, New York | 1989 | 16-18 | Investing and the Random Walk Hypothesis |
| Twain, Mark | *A Connecticut Yankee in King Arthur's Court* | University of California Press, Berkeley | 1983 | 322-333 | Nominal vs. Real Values, Economic Education |
| Vonnegut, Kurt | *Welcome to the Monkey House* | Dell Publishing Co., New York | 1968 | 7-13 | Equality, Income Redistribution |
| Webb, Charles | *The Graduate* | The New American Library, Inc., New York | 1963 | 11-15 | Economic Values |
| Wilder, Thornton | *Our Town* | Coward McCann, Inc., New York | 1938 | 29-32 | Economic Values, Incentives, Economic Systems |
| Wolfe, Thomas | *From Death to Morning* | Grossett & Dunlap, New York | 1935 | 195-201 | Normal vs. Excess Profits |

## Appendix 9.B: Discussion Questions

Used in conjunction with handouts prepared from a subset of the items listed in Appendix 9.A, all of the following questions were covered in an hour-and-a-half class devoted specifically to economics in literature and drama, for undergraduate seniors in an honors seminar at Vanderbilt University. I have used the same questions for individual readings in various undergraduate courses at Purdue University.

General Assignment: In *all* of the assigned passages, note in the margins each of the economic concepts illustrated by the author. Also make a list of the general economic roles of government that are suggested across all of these readings, and compare that to a list of such functions found in any of the standard principles of economics textbooks. For some of the passages, these are the only assignments; for other passages, additional discussion questions are indicated below:

"Mending Wall," by Robert Frost
  1) In this poem, is private property regarded as a natural right, as John Locke argued, or as theft, as Pierre Proudhon argued?
  2) Would Ronald Coase favor building or maintaining the particular wall described in this poem?
  3) What is the speaker's attitude toward traditional economic relationships?

*The Hamlet*, by William Faulkner
  Does the Coase theorem hold in the situation described in this passage?

*Mystery Ride,* by Robert Boswell
  1) Is private property theft?
  2) Does private property encourage good or bad environmental practices?

*Catch-22*, by Joseph Heller
  1) Does Milo Minderbinder accept the concept of Pareto optimality? Does he practice it?
  2) List the nonmarket allocation systems that are (briefly) mentioned in this passage. How does Milo fare when he encounters one of those systems?

*Dancing at the Rascal Fair*, by Ivan Doig, and *Banker*, by Dick Francis
  1) Is entrepreneurship a separate factor of production?
  2) In these passages, are any or all of the characters entrepreneurs? Are all of them managers?

*Winesburg, Ohio*, by Sherwood Anderson
1) Identify all of the examples of specialization along the lines of comparative advantage that are provided in this passage.
2) Compare and contrast Anderson's views on specialization in this passage with those expressed by Adam Smith in the *Wealth of Nations*.

*The Octopus*, by Frank Norris, and "Poor-Devil Author," by Washington Irving
Is the economic analysis of supply and demand forces in these passages:
      a)  accurate, and b) reasonably complete?

*From Death to Morning*, by Thomas Wolfe
How do economists determine a reasonable or fair rate of profit? Are their discussions on this issue much different from those of Wolfe's characters?

*The Joy Luck Club*, by Amy Tan
1) How do economists determine a reasonable or fair rate of profit?
2) Is the stock market an efficient market?
3) Can unfair profits be earned on the stock market, or by playing *mah jong*?

*Democracy*, by Henry Adams, and *Good as Gold*, by Joseph Heller
Which Nobel laureate(s) in economics would have been least surprised by Mrs. Lee's and Professor Gold's experiences in Washington?

*U.S.A.*, "Tin Lizzie," by John Dos Passos,
1) Based on the description in this passage, does it appear that Henry Ford paid efficiency wages?
2) In this passage, does Dos Passos seem to be sympathetic to the nineteenth century Luddite and anti-enclosure movements?

*Atlas Shrugged*, by Ayn Rand
1) Use this passage, the earlier passages by Heller and Dos Passos, and Dos Passos' "Prince of Peace" segment on Andrew Carnegie, to illustrate at least two different characteristics or theories of entrepreneurship.
2) What would Rand likely say about the recent changes in the highest marginal tax rate for the federal income tax?
3) Have any economists or other literary authors used an image like Rand's draining water tank?
4) Does Rand approve of interpersonal comparisons of utility?

"A Modest Proposal...," by Jonathan Swift
Treating this piece as satire, have any modern economists expressed similar reservations about the basis for, or the practice of, cost-benefit analysis?

## NOTES

1. Most students taking economics courses do so to meet requirements associated with their major, not because they take the courses as electives. It is, however, an assumption that students in economics courses are less familiar and comfortable with literary works than other students who, as a group, are also poorly read in literature and drama.

2. When I do not use *Mending Wall*, I often use Frost's *The Road Not Taken* to discuss the concept of opportunity cost and foreshadow the ideas of competitive equilibrium and normal profits, because although Frost's narrator in that poem takes the road "less traveled by" he also points out "Though as for that, the passing there had worn them really about the same."

3. Or so it seems from the Becker and Watts (1996) survey data on economists' classroom teaching methods presented in Chapter One of this volume.

4. Any economist offended by this idea would do well to recall Adam Smith's discussion about the few innate differences between philosophers and street porters.

5. Proponents of recognizing and developing better rhetorical approaches in economics make many of these same points, and argue for the use of history and biography in teaching economics along very similar lines (McCloskey 1985; Klamer, McCloskey and Solow (1988).

6. See van der Meulen Rodgers (1996) for a discussion of role playing in courses on international and development economics.

7. I most often use articles from *The Economist*, *The Wall Street Journal*, or *Business Week*, all of which have home pages on the World Wide Web. In some cases there are charges for searching the archive issues of these sources on the net, however, so to find articles in these publications I most often use electronic indexes or CD-Rom databases that are accessible to me on servers maintained by the Purdue and Krannert Libraries and the Krannert Computing Center. The most useful databases and indexes for me have been ABI/Inform Research, EconLit, the Business Periodicals Index, and the Social Sciences Index.

## REFERENCES

Becker, W. and M. Watts. 1996. Chalk and talk: A national survey on teaching undergraduate economics. *American Economic Review* 84 (2): 448-53.

Bogart, W.T. 1995. Looking backward at feasible socialism: Using Bellamy to teach Schumpeter. *Journal of Economic Education* 26 (4): 352-6.

DeMott, B. 1989. Reading fiction to the bottom line. *Harvard Business Review* 67 (May/June): 128-34.

Dimand, M. 1991. Marginal comment: Reservations about *Murder at the Margin*. *Journal of Economic Education* 22 (4): 383-6.

Frost, R. 1939. *The collected poems of Robert Frost*. New York: Halcyon House.

Hansen, W.L. 1991. The education and training of economics doctorates. *Journal of Economic Literature* 29 (3): 1054-87.

_____ and M. Salemi. 1998. Improving classroom discussion in economics courses. In W. B. Walstad and P. Saunders (eds.), *Teaching undergraduate economics: A handbook for instructors*. New York: Irwin-McGraw-Hill.

Kasper, H. et al. 1991. The education of economists. *Journal of Economic Literature* 29 (3): 1088-109.

Klamer, A., D. N. McCloskey and R. Solow (eds). 1988. *The consequences of economic rhetoric*. New York: Cambridge University Press.

Krueger, A.O. et al. 1991. Report of the commission on graduate education in economics. *Journal of Economic Literature* 29 (3): 1035-53.

McCloskey, D.N. 1985. *The rhetoric of economics*. Madison, WI: University of Wisconsin Press.

Norris, F. 1938. *The octopus: A story of California*. Garden City, New York: Sun Dial Press. [First published in 1901.]

Rockoff, H. 1990. The *Wizard of Oz* as a monetary allegory. *Journal of Political Economy* 98 (4): 739-60.

Simon, N. 1972. *The prisoner of Second Avenue*. New York: Random House.

van der Meulen Rodgers, Y. 1996. A role playing exercise for development and international economics courses. *Journal of Economic Education* 27 (3): 217-23.

Watts, M. and R. Smith. 1989. Economics in literature and drama. *Journal of Economic Education* 20 (3): 291-307.

CHAPTER **10**

# ACCEPTANCE SPEECHES BY THE NOBEL LAUREATES IN ECONOMICS

**William J. Zahka**

There are several reasons why the Nobel prize winning economists are worthy of consideration in teaching economics.  First, there is the variety of their fields of interest.  The Nobel prize five-member selection committee seems to vary its choice by area of economic specialty, by nationality, by economic ideology and political beliefs.  The economic environment and the state of the world economy at the time of selection appear to be factored into the decision-making process. The areas of economics covered include macroeconomics, microeconomics, history of economic thought, developmental economics, econometrics, financial economics, game theory, input-output, and international economics.  Thus, the lectures offer the instructor a broad range from which to choose.  Second, the laureates gain increased influence simply because they are selected.  They are asked to advise governmental agencies, to address business organizations, and to talk to collegiate student groups.  As a result of their increasing visibility, they become role models to younger economists.

Used as a teaching tool, the lectures can broaden the horizons of both the teacher and the students. Instructors will also find that use of the Nobel lectures adds both rigor and relevancy to the course.

## I. GENERAL APPROACH

The general procedure for using the Nobel lectures can be viewed as addressing five questions:

| | |
|---|---|
| Purpose. | Why use the Nobel prize lectures? |
| Selection. | Which lecture or lectures best fit the course? |
| Preparation. | What kind of background material is needed? |
| Presentation. | Who will present what to whom? |
| Evaluation. | How well did it all work? |

I will discuss these questions in order and in the next section offer a seminar example of their use.

### Purpose

The Nobel lectures, like any other teaching material, should contribute to the overall purpose of the course. The first area where the lectures are especially useful is content. This embraces the wide range of topics in the lectures, the stress on an interdisciplinary approach and the use of mathematics. The second area is skill development. This involves the reading of the lecture, orally presenting the material and preparing a written report. Nobel lectures can also be assigned as a "team" project involving a number of students. The last area is role models. Students are able to examine the economic thinking of the laureates and in the process develop their own economic reasoning ability. The Nobel lectures can also serve as a springboard for students to consider a career as a professional economist.

### Selection

There are two concerns in selecting a lecture: relevance and level of difficulty. The list of laureates and topics in Table 10.1 helps to narrow down the choices by giving a simplified view of both aspects. By looking down the topic column, you can quickly identify lectures in the general area of interest. A glance to the right-hand columns will give you an idea of the level of difficulty. Note that the highly difficult lectures are not necessarily off limits to less advanced students, although I emphasize the more accessible work of Buchanan, Hicks, Lewis, Schultz, Simon, Solow and Stigler. The Nobel lectures are published in *Les Prix Nobel* for the year in which the prize was awarded. In addition, they are reprinted in selected economic journals (see **Sources for the Lectures** section).

## Table 10.1: Nobel Economic Laureates, Title of Nobel Lecture, Topic and Level of Difficulty

| Name | Year | Title | Topic | Difficulty Level | | |
|------|------|-------|-------|------|------|------|
| | | | | Least | More | Most |
| Maurice Allais | 1988 | An Outline of My Main Contributions to Economic Science | Micro-economics | X | | |
| Kenneth Arrow | 1972 | General Economic Equilibrium: Purpose Analytic Techniques, Collective Choice | Micro-economics | | X | |
| Gary S. Becker | 1992 | The Economic Way of Looking at Behavior | Micro-economics | X | | |
| James Buchanan | 1986 | The Constitution of Economic Policy | Micro-economics | X | | |
| Ronald H. Coase | 1991 | The Institutional Structure of Production | Micro-economics | X | | |
| Gerard Debreu | 1983 | Economic Theory in the Mathematical Mode | Micro-economics | | | X |
| Robert W. Fogel | 1993 | Economic Growth, Population Theory and Physiology: The Bearing of Long-Term Processes on the Making of Economic Policy | Economic History | | X | |
| Milton Friedman | 1976 | Inflation and Unemployment | Macro-economics | X | | |
| Ragnar Frisch | 1969 | From Utopian Theory to Practical Applications: The Case of Econometrics | Econo-metrics | | | X |
| Trygve Haavelmo | 1989 | Econometrics and the Welfare State | Econo-metrics | X | | |
| John C. Harsanyi | 1994 | Games with Incomplete Information | Micro-economics | | | X |
| Friedrich Von Hayek | 1974 | The Pretence of Knowledge | Micro-economics | X | | |
| John Hicks | 1972 | The Mainspring of Economic Growth | Micro-economics | X | | |
| Leonid Kantorovich | 1975 | Mathematics in Economics: Achievements, Difficulties, Perspectives | Micro-economics | X | | |
| Lawrence Klein | 1980 | Some Economic Scenarios for the 1980's | Econo-metrics | X | | |

## Table 10.1: Nobel Economic Laureates, Title of Nobel Lecture, Topic and Level of Difficulty (Continued)

| Name | Year | Title | Topic | Least | More | Most |
|------|------|-------|-------|-------|------|------|
| Tjalling Koopmans | 1975 | Concepts of Optimality and Their Uses | Econometrics | | X | |
| Simon Kuznets | 1971 | Modern Economic Growth: Findings and Reflections | Economic Development | X | | |
| Wassily Leontief | 1973 | Structure of the World Economy | Input-Output | | X | |
| W. Arthur Lewis | 1979 | The Slowing Down of the Engine of Growth | Economic Development | X | | |
| Robert E. Lucas, Jr. | 1995 | Monetary Neutrality | Macroeconomics | | X | |
| Harry Markowitz | 1990 | Foundation of Portfolio Theory | Microeconomics | | X | |
| James Meade | 1977 | The Meaning of 'Internal Balance' | International Economics | X | | |
| Martin M. Miller | 1990 | Leverage | Microeconomics | | X | |
| James Mirrlees | 1996 | Information and Incentives: The Economics of Carrots and Sticks | Microeconomics | | X | |
| Franco Modigliani | 1985 | Life Cycle, Individual Thrift, and the Wealth of Nations | Macroeconomics | | X | |
| Gunnar Myrdal | 1974 | The Equality Issue in World Development | Economic Development | X | | |
| John F. Nash, Jr. | 1994 | The Work of John Nash in Game Theory | Microeconomics | | | X |
| Douglass C. North | 1993 | Economic Performance Through Time | Economic History | X | | |
| Bertil Ohlin | 1977 | 1933 and 1977 -- Some Expansion Policy Problems in Cases of Unbalanced Domestic and International Economic Relations | International Economics | X | | |
| Paul Samuelson | 1970 | Maximum Principles in Analytical Economics | Microeconomics | | X | |
| Theodore Schultz | 1979 | The Economics of Being Poor | Economic Development | X | | |

**Table 10.1: Nobel Economic Laureates, Title of Nobel Lecture, Topic and Level of Difficulty (Continued)**

| Name | Year | Title | Topic | Difficulty Level Least | More | Most |
|------|------|-------|-------|-------|------|------|
| Reinhard Selten | 1994 | Multistage Game Models and Delay Supergames | Micro-economics | | | X |
| William Sharpe | 1990 | Capital Asset Prices With and Without Negative Holdings | Micro-economics | | | X |
| Herbert Simon | 1978 | Rational Decision-Making in Business Organizations | Micro-economics | X | | |
| Robert Solow | 1987 | Growth Theory and After | Macro-economics | X | | |
| George Stigler | 1982 | The Process and Progress of Economics | History of Economic Thought | X | | |
| Richard Stone | 1984 | The Accounts of Society | Macro-economics | | X | |
| Jan Tinbergen | 1969 | The Use of Models: Experience and Prospects | Econo-metrics | X | | |
| James Tobin | 1981 | Money and Finance in the Macroeconomic Process | Macro-economics | | X | |
| William Vickrey | 1996 | (Died three days after announcement of the award.) | | | | |

## Preparation

There are two general approaches to using the Nobel lectures. The first is as supplementary material within a course based on other methods, traditional or otherwise. The wide range of topics covered in the lectures makes it likely that there will be a relevant lecture or two for almost any undergraduate course. Incorporating the lectures is not unlike using other outside readings, but there are some unique features that merit special attention. Let the students know beforehand the level of difficulty of the lecture, as well as new terms and concepts they will encounter in the reading.

The second, more challenging approach uses the lectures as the basis for the course. One type of course for which this can be effective is a survey of modern economic thought. It is also possible to build more specific courses around certain topics where there are a number of related lectures. For example, my course in economic development used the lectures of Kuznets, Lewis, Meade, Schultz and Solow.

In preparing to use a lecture, instructors have to consider their teaching objectives and personal guidelines. I have found that the lectures can be used for all of the economic electives I teach. The final choice of the lectures depends on what will provide the students with new insights and a challenging assignment. The length of the lecture and the amount of mathematics used in the lecture help to determine whether to assign the reading to an individual or to a "team." In my courses, each member in a team has to present their allocated pages to the class. Visual aids are also expected where applicable. Teams also prepare a handout to the class to outline the key ideas they gathered from the lecture. As a prelude to the assignment, I point out the new areas of research and new topics. A rather long lecture warrants additional time because of the in-depth research of the laureate.

Preparation time is most important for the instructor to determine the best strategy to be used in using the Nobel lectures as a teaching tool:

- Do background reading beyond the lecture itself to provide a frame of reference to answer questions the students may ask about the laureate as well as the Nobel lecture.
- Give yourself plenty of time to do your research on the laureate, contributions to the literature and the citations to his publications.
- Give the library plenty of lead time to get the journals on reserve with the Nobel lecture or to order *Les Prix Nobel* from the publisher. Recent laureates have sent copies of their lecture to me prior to being published in *Les Prix Nobel* or the journal.

## Presentation

Have each student pass out to the class a one to two-page summary or outline of the lecture. Depending upon the student's computer literacy, some students use Powerpoint or other presentation software to present their reports. Others use transparencies. Be sure to let the students know the maximum time allowed for their reports. Twenty minutes is an optimal time limit. The presentations count toward their final grade, a course requirement as stated in the syllabus. Twenty percent of the final grade works out quite well as a motivator. Assign the dates that students will give the reports in plenty of time so that they will be able to read the lectures, to compose their thoughts and decide upon the method they feel most comfortable with to present their report. I have yet to have a student who did not go beyond the call of duty to present the assignment.

## Evaluation

For evaluating class participation, I look for the following:

- Ready to participate in discussion; had they read the lecture?
- Able to grasp the key points from the lecture

- Able to see the relevance of the lecture to other economics courses
- Able to see links to current events

For evaluating the term paper, I consider:

- Depth and relevance of the material on the laureate's background
- Understanding the reason for the laureate's selection for the prize
- Presentation of the essence and the logic of the lecture
- Ability to hold the interest of the class, as evidenced by questions from their peers

## II. SEMINAR EXAMPLE FOR USING NOBEL LECTURES

For an example of how I use the Nobel prize lectures, I have chosen a seminar course on contemporary economic thought. The course lends itself to the extensive use of the lectures. The instructional methods, however, are similar to those that would be used if a single lecture were used to give depth in a course with a different focus.

### Purpose

Using the Nobel lectures in a seminar on contemporary economic thought serves a number of purposes. The primary benefit is the content of the lectures, but another reason for using the lectures is that many of them deal with the thought processes the laureates used to arrive at their breakthroughs. Because the students in this seminar were mainly economics majors, this aspect of working in the field has considerable personal interest. A third purpose in working with the lectures is to give the students experience working with difficult material. Students who only read textbooks, which use carefully chosen vocabulary, visual aids, and clear organization to make learning easy, are not well prepared to read most articles written by economic specialists. Working with the Nobel prize lectures gives students a chance to develop techniques for mastering material that hasn't been predigested. Other purposes are to show the value of an interdisciplinary approach and identify potentially productive areas for future research. The lectures also provide the student with an overview of the history of economic thought. Many of the laureates refer to the contributions of past economists, such as Adam Smith and David Ricardo, and their positive impact on economic analysis. Students realize that the development of economics involves an evolutionary process. Today's economists build upon the foundations of their predecessors.

## Selection

The texts used in the seminar were Breit and Spencer (1990), *Lives of the Laureates*, and W. Sichel's (1989) *The State of Economic Science: Views of Six Nobel Laureates*. Students were assigned to read the autobiographical sketches and the laureates' viewpoints on economic issues before reading the Nobel lectures. The book selections show the students the reasons why the laureates chose economics for their profession and the importance of mentors in the laureates' intellectual development. The sketches conclude with material such as their dates of birth, education, academic affiliations and lists of their major publications. All this information is useful in a class discussion that provides a panorama of the laureate's background.

The selection of the Nobel lectures for the seminar course is based on the topics covered. Samuelson's lecture serves as the cornerstone of the seminar, to show the students the breadth of his contributions to economics. Friedman's lecture follows, because his topics – inflation and unemployment – are always relevant. Discussions of Samuelson's and Friedman's biographical backgrounds and lectures provide an ideal setting to discuss differences in their political ideology and thus their opposing approaches to resolving economic issues and problems. The remaining seven lectures of Arrow, Buchanan, Hicks, Klein, Lewis, Solow and Stigler introduces students to the laureates' contributions to history of economic thought, development economics, econometrics, macroeconomics, microeconomics, growth theory, and public choice.

Another concern in selecting lectures is the level of difficulty. The seniors in this course can handle the material with guidance. Allowance should be made for the students' overall preparation. Lectures are rated for level of difficulty in Table 10.1. Students can be asked to determine if the ratings result from mathematical, statistical or conceptual rigor or from the degree of abstraction.

To complement the course, Dr. Lawrence Klein, the 1980 Nobel laureate, was invited to speak to the class and answer questions. His presence, along with his insights into the present state of the economy, helped make the course come alive. In addition, Dr. Franco Modigliani, the 1985 Nobel laureate, spent a day on campus during the semester. His lectures reinforced the theme of the seminar.

## Preparation

In preparation for a class I researched and read other articles and books by the laureates to give me a better perspective of their background and many contributions to economics. I also read the citations of the award and the biographical sketch the laureate prepared for publication in *Les Prix Nobel*. (Copies of the library's *Les Prix Nobel* and economic journals with the relevant lectures were also placed on reserve in the library for the student's use.)

During the first meeting of the seminar, I asked each class member for their suggestions or techniques to get the most out of the lectures.  The end results were the following:

1.  What is the significance of the title of the lecture?
2.  What did I "expect" to learn from the lecture?  (ex ante)
3.  What did I "learn" from the lecture (ex post) (such as: new economics terms, concepts, economists and their contributions to economics)?
4.  How can I apply the knowledge gained from the lecture to other courses?
5.  What new insights did I gather from the lecture?
6.  Did my judgment change on the economist's stature after reading the lecture?
7.  Was I challenged by the lecture?  If so, by what?  If not, why not?
8.  How much history of economic thought is used and/or referred to in the lecture?
9.  How do concepts from other disciplines relate to economics (e.g. physics to economics)?
10. For what type of audience did the laureate prepare this lecture?
11. What other courses should I take to broaden my economics background?
12. Was the lecture stimulating and of interest?  Why or why not?
13. How did the laureate try to solve the economic triad of what to produce, how, and for whom?
14. Is a working knowledge of mathematics, geometry, calculus and statistics important to understanding this lecture?
15. How did the laureate, earlier in his career as a teacher, influence the intellectual development of one of his students, (who many years later was himself chosen to be a laureate)?

In addition, for each lecture, I prepared a set of questions for discussion and a list of optional library research topics to focus attention on significant aspects of the lecture.  Three lectures are illustrated to capture the thrust of the type of research and reading that can be expected from the class.

**Lecture Example:** Paul Samuelson's 1970 Nobel prize lecture: *"Maximum Principles in Analytical Economics"*

## Questions for Discussion:
1.  What is the thrust of the lecture?  Why do you think Samuelson chose this topic for his lecture?
2.  What does he mean by Maximum Principles?  by Analytical Economics?
3.  Discuss the influence of Joseph Schumpeter while Samuelson was a student at Harvard.
4.  Who were the following: Pigou?  Veblen?  Davenport?  Von Neumann?

5. What is the LeChatelier's principle? How does Samuelson relate it and physics to economics?
6. What is "revealed preference" theory? How did Samuelson derive this theory?
7. What are indifference curves? How does Samuelson use them in his lecture?
8. How do operations research and linear programming differ?

### Library Research Assignment (Optional)
1. Randomly peruse *The Collected Scientific Papers of Paul A. Samuelson*, Vol. 1 (1966) ed. by Stiglitz, J., Cambridge, Mass. M.I.T. Press. Do you see any correlation between his past writings and his Nobel lecture. Which ones?
2. Read the preface and chapter one in Paul A. Samuelson's (1947) *Foundations of Economic Analysis*, Cambridge Mass., Harvard University Press. What did you gather from these pages? How do they relate to the lecture?
3. What factors does Samuelson feel will help a person become a Nobel laureate?

**Lecture Example:** Theodore Schultz 1979 Nobel prize lecture: *"The Economics of Being Poor"*

### Questions for Discussion:
1. Define the following terms: (a) developed country, (b) developing country, (c) first world countries; (d) second world countries; (e) third world countries.
2. What is Schultz's solution to the population "problem"?
3. What does the author mean by the "economics of being poor"?
4. Discuss the influence of Thomas Malthus and David Ricardo to the theory of economic development.
5. What does Schultz mean when he says the quality of population and the quantity of population are substitutes? What shape of indifference curve analysis would you use to show perfect substitutability?
6. Discuss the "investments" that are included in the discussion of health and human capital theory.
7. Discuss some of the economic implications of longer life spans caused by improvements in health.
8. "Education accounts for much of the improvements in population quality." Discuss.
9. What role do the "highly skilled" play in the process of economic development? Cite examples and empirical evidence.
10. How does Engel's Law relate to a study of "economics of being poor"? Discuss.

## Library Research Assignments (optional):

1. Research five recent journal articles that Schultz has published since receipt of the Nobel prize in 1980. Has he changed his focus of research?
2. Read Sir Arthur Lewis' Nobel Laureate lecture (1980 co-recipient with Theodore W. Schultz), "The Slowing-down of the Engine of Growth," *American Economic Review*, September 1980, pp. 555-564. How does Lewis' approach to the study of economic development differ from that of Schultz? In what ways are they similar?

**Lecture Example:** George Stigler's 1982 Nobel prize lecture: *"The Process and Progress of Economics"*

## Questions for Discussion:

1. Distinguish between the pre-scientific stage of economics and the scientific stage.
2. Describe the three approaches on how to have "new ideas" accepted.
3. Discuss the contributions to economics of the following:
   a) Coase (b) Malthus (c) Becker (d) Cantillon
4. What event truly made economics begin the "age of economic science"? Discuss.
5. Discuss the four major current areas of research in industrial organization.
6. Discuss Stigler's contributions to "economics of information."
7. Why does Stigler believe that the most fundamental of economic problems is the theory of value?
8. Explain the law of diminishing returns. How does it fit into the theme of this lecture?
9. Why do economists resist new ideas? Were Keynes' ideas quickly accepted? Smith? Cournot? Why or why not?

## Library Research Assignments (optional):

1. Trace the theory of value from Plato through the "marginal revolution of the 1870s."
2. Stigler was a prolific writer. Read one of his books that is of interest to you, then write a book review.
3. Read and summarize Stigler's presidential address to the American Economic Association, "The Economist and the State," *American Economic Review*, March 1965, pp. 1-18.

## Presentation

Lindbeck's (1985) article "The Prize in Economic Science in Memory of Alfred Nobel," in the *Journal of Economic Literature* serves as the starting point for the course. It introduces the students to the impetus for the creation of the

Nobel Prize in Economic Science, to selection criteria for laureates, and to the difficulties involved in the committee's deliberations on the selection.

The plan of action is to spend one week per laureate. With a Monday-Wednesday-Friday teaching cycle, half of the first meeting is spent discussing the biography of the laureate. This provides the students with the laureate's background. One aspect includes discussion of where the laureate attended undergraduate and graduate school, the influence of his professors on graduate school selection, courses to take, and topic chosen for a dissertation. In many cases the laureate acknowledges specific teachers who had a great effect on his intellectual development. A second biographical aspect is why the laureate chose economics as his major field of study. For example, in many cases, personally experiencing the Great Depression was the deciding factor. The third aspect is that the students can learn from the laureate's experiences to make them better economists. The latter part of the first, and the second and third class meetings is devoted to the Nobel prize lecture.

*Term Paper:* For the seminar on contemporary economic thought, a term paper is required from each student. Because these were advanced students, I leave the length of the paper to their discretion. However, because a large portion of their grade depends upon the quality and depth of research, most conclude that approximately thirty pages is needed. With the experienced students, the instructor may wish to specify the length of papers.

The students choose a laureate who is not covered during the class. Their papers include a biographical sketch of the laureate and an analysis of his contributions to economics, which requires extensive library research. The paper must also include use of the tools of economic analysis students have learned in their upper level economics classes.

*Oral Reports:* Twelve students presented twenty minute oral reports on their term papers. Each student had to prepare a one page abstract or an outline for the class to refer to as the student gave his/her presentation. Two reports were scheduled per class meeting during the last two-and-a-half weeks of the semester.

*One Minute Oral Highlight:* During the last meeting, each student was asked to give an unannounced extemporaneous oral report on the highlight of their research of one-minute length. I explained that they were not warned because I intended:

- to show the students the importance of being able to think on their feet and to organize their thoughts.
- to begin to develop their confidence, so that in a similar situation they would have had a previous experience.
- to compare their performance to their peers'. Those who were not satisfied with their presentation could enroll in a course in public speaking.

## Evaluation

Students read and discussed in class nine selected laureate lectures covering a broad spectrum of economics.    In addition, based on their in-depth library research, students gave presentations on Becker, Modigliani, Schultz, Simon, Stigler, Stone, Tinbergen and Tobin.    In total seventeen lectures were interpreted and assessed in much greater detail than could be done from using a conventional textbook in history of economic thought.    Finally, familiarity with the laureates gave the students inspiring role models at the beginning of their professional careers.

To assign grades, I look at the depth and breadth of the term paper's coverage of the laureate.  I evaluate the written outline or abstract of the student presentation in addition to the oral report.  Also considered is the ability of the student to keep the attention of the class during the presentation.  I use a "team" approach for long or technical lectures.   This approach also helps students to develop their interpersonal skills as they decide who will read and summarize their respective pages, as well as their oral skills when they present their report in class.  In the "team" report, I look for the amount of cooperation between the members of the team and the smooth flow of the information from the members. Those members who did not carry the full weight of their responsibility will be quite evident during their presentation.


## III. SOME DO'S AND DON'TS IN USING THE NOBEL LECTURES AS A TEACHING TOOL

- Do explain to the class the reason that you are using the lectures as supplementary material in the course.
- Do prepare a set of questions or point out areas they should be looking for when they read the lecture.
- Do introduce terms or concepts that you think they should be familiar with.
- Do have the students bring into class concepts or terms that are new to them.
- Do provide to the class your viewpoints and a summary of the main points that should have been gleaned from the lecture.
- Do point out whether the lecture is strictly written in an essay form or requires the use of mathematics.
- Do review with the class key points in the laureate's educational background or other points of interest that had an influence on the laureate's field of study.
- Do point out the role that mentors played in the laureate's intellectual development.
- Do use the references at the end of the lecture as sources for term paper assignments and/or library assignments.

- Do look at the diversity of topics and economic issues that are presented in the lectures.
- Do point out the lecture has a focus and a message that the laureate wants to convey to the reader in the acceptance speech.
- Do consider the lectures in lieu of the chapter where the lecture will provide a more in-depth viewpoint of a topic being discussed in the chapter.
- Don't let the students convince you that the contents of the lecture will be beyond their grasp and comprehension. Remind them that they have the academic background; emphasize the benefits of work with challenging material.
- Don't let the extra several hours required to incorporate specific lectures to chapters in the textbook be an obstacle. Reading and taking notes on a short, nontechnical lecture will take approximately an hour. A rather lengthy and technical lecture will take two to three hours. However, the knowledge and insights that you will glean from the lectures will exceed the time and effort involved. The marginal benefits will far exceed the marginal costs.
- Don't let the complexity of some of the lectures prevent assigning them. Students with a grasp of higher mathematics can present the lecture in class as an oral report. It will be a useful learning experience for the student and possibly help some of the other class members realize the importance of mathematics as a language.
- Don't forget to order copies of *Les Prix Nobel* or to place the journals with the respective lectures on reserve at the library.
- Don't expect that the students will read the lecture in the same manner as you do. They do not have your background. Be prepared to help them understand the things that may be obvious to you.

## IV. CONCLUSION

The Nobel prize lectures are especially good teaching tools as they provide a more personal perspective and a broader viewpoint on the laureates' areas of expertise than would be found in their journal articles. Articles, by their very nature, are technical and narrow in focus. In the Nobel lectures, the laureates try to summarize their own work, to suggest solutions for the pressing economic issues of the time, to evaluate the contributions of other economists, and to trace their mentors' influences on their own intellectual development. Analyzing the Nobel lectures provides interesting insights into how the laureates regard their work, how they believe economic theory can best be applied, and what they consider the most fruitful areas for future research.

## SOURCES FOR THE LECTURES

Arrow, K. 1974. General economic equilibrium: Purpose, analytic techniques, collective choice. *American Economic Review* 64(3): 253-72.

Becker, G. 1993. The economic way of looking at behavior. *Journal of Political Economy* 101(3): 385-403.

Buchanan, J. Jr. 1987. The constitution of economic policy. *American Economic Review* 77(3): 243-50.

Coase, R. 1992. The institutional structure of production. *American Economic Review* 82(4): 713-9.

Debreu, G. 1984. Economic theory in the mathematical mode. *American Economic Review* 74(3): 267-78.

Fogel, R.W. 1994. Economic growth, population theory and physiology: The bearing of long-term processes on the making of economic policy. *American Economic Review* 84(3): 369-89.

Friedman, M. 1977. Inflation and unemployment. *Journal of Political Economy* 85(3): 451-72.

Frisch, R. 1981. From utopian theory to practical applications: The case of econometrics. *American Economic Review* 71(December supplement): 1-16.

Hicks, J. 1981. The mainspring of economic growth. *American Economic Review* 71(December supplement): 23-9.

Koopmans, T. 1977. Concepts of optimality and their uses. *American Economic Review* 67(3): 261-74.

Kuznets, S. 1973. Modern economic growth: Findings and reflections. *American Economic Review* 63(3): 247-58.

Leontief, W. 1974. Structure of the world economy. *American Economic Review* 64(6): 823-34.

Lewis, W. A. 1980. The slowing down of the engine of growth. *American Economic Review* 70(4): 555-64.

Modigliani, F. 1986. Life cycle, individual thrift, and the wealth of nations. *American Economic Review* 76(3): 297-313.

North, D. 1994. Economic performance through time. *American Economic Review* 84(3): 359-68.

Samuelson, P. 1972. Maximum principles in analytical economics. *American Economic Review* 62(3): 249-62.

_____.1983. My life philosophy. *American Economist* 27(2): 5-12.

Schultz, T. 1980. The economics of being poor. *Journal of Political Economy* 88(4): 639-51.

Simon, H. 1979. Rational decision-making in business organizations. *American Economic Review* 69(4): 493-513.

Solow, R. 1988. Growth theory and after. *American Economic Review* 78(3): 307-17.

Stigler, G. 1983. The process and progress of economics. *Journal of Political Economy* 91(4): 529-45.

Stone, R. 1986. The accounts of society. *Journal of Applied Econometrics* 1(1): 5-28.

Tinbergen, J. 1961. The use of models: Experience and prospects. *American Economic Review* 51(December supplement): 17-22.

## REFERENCES

Breit, W. and R. Spencer, eds. 1990. *Lives of the laureates: Ten Nobel economists.* 2nd ed. Cambridge, Mass.: MIT Press.

Lindbeck, A. 1985.  The prize in economic science in memory of Alfred Nobel. *Journal of Economic Literature* 23 (March): 37-56.

Nobel Foundation. 1969 to 1995, each year. *Les prix Nobel.* Stockholm: Almqvist & Wiksell International.

Samuelson, P. 1947. *Foundations of economic analysis.* Cambridge, Mass.: M.I.T. Press.

Sichel, W. 1989.  *The state of economic science: Views of six Nobel laureates.* Kalamazoo, Mich.: W. E. Upjohn Institute.

Stiglitz, J. ed. 1966. *The collected scientific papers of Paul A. Samuelson.* Cambridge, Mass.: M.I.T. Press.

Zahka, W. 1990.  The Nobel prize economics lectures as a teaching tool.  *Journal of Economic Education* 21 (Fall): 395-401.

# CHAPTER 11

# USING CASES AS AN EFFECTIVE ACTIVE LEARNING TECHNIQUE

## Stephen Buckles

"There are three main objectives to the elementary course in economics: to master economic principles; to acquire skill in applying the principles to reality; and to learn to analyze policy issues systematically. The usual textbook and the usual course overemphasize the first, under emphasize the other two" (Fels and Buckles 1981, v). This observation was originally made by Rendigs Fels in reference to the introductory course, but it applies almost equally well to economics courses at all undergraduate levels. Lee Hansen has proposed five objectives for economics majors (Hansen 1986, 150-151). The use of case studies as a teaching tool reinforces the development of three of those objectives: displaying command of existing knowledge; displaying ability to draw out existing knowledge; and utilizing existing knowledge to explore issues. Cases can help students learn to apply principles to the stories they read in newspapers and magazines and see on television news. Cases can also teach students how to analyze economic policy issues. Case studies can be used effectively at a variety of levels: introductory courses, intermediate theory, and senior seminars in applied areas and policy.

The term "case study" has been applied to a wide variety of teaching materials and methods. In this chapter, the case study method means the identification of real (current or historical) examples that require the application of economic concepts and principles to understand better the economics and in some instances to apply concepts in such a way as to recommend economic policy. The appropriate emphasis is upon requiring application and analysis. Cases then are more than just examples used to illustrate a point within a lecture. The case study method may be used within lectures as a demonstration of analysis by the teacher, but the most effective use of the technique is asking students to analyze data and to develop explanations and solutions on their own. The key part of the case study definition is active student involvement.

The case method presents real-world problems in which students are expected to apply the theoretical knowledge and analytical methods they have acquired. Cases often include relevant and irrelevant data. Cases may include weak or incorrect analysis. In cases involving policy choices, there are often no right or wrong answers; students will need to use value judgments in making final decisions. The purpose is to develop skills and abilities to apply economics. Cases ask students to reason for themselves, not to restate facts and data. Standard lectures may assist students in learning definitions and descriptions of theories. Cases are opportunities for practice in "thinking like economists".

In this chapter, I discuss the benefits and costs of using case studies in economics teaching, present a variety of possible sources and formats for case studies, suggest challenges in designing cases, and give three examples of how cases may be used in classes including an example of role playing. The Do's and Don'ts list for case writing and use should be helpful to those who try the case method.

## I. WHY USE CASES?

Learning theory tells us that higher levels of understanding require active involvement in application and use of concepts (e.g., see Becker 1997). Cases, unless use is limited to inclusion as parts of lectures, require active involvement and application. Active involvement in the learning process seems to help particularly when learning how to solve complex problems. In addition, cases offer opportunities for repetition and reinforcement of concepts already studied, thereby increasing the likelihood of retention (McKeachie et al. 1994).

Lecturing can be motivating when one's style is enthusiastic; it can model a style of analysis; and it can present material and facts that are not available in other forms. Active student involvement is more effective in motivating students if the instructor's style is not enthusiastic. Active learning can change attitudes and develop problem solving and critical thinking skills (McKeachie et al. 1994).

Learning theorists have long told us the extreme importance of motivation. Students enjoy real-life examples and develop a greater appreciation for the relevance of concepts. Actual current economic events are brought into the classroom in cases, and that helps fill in gaps created by students' lack of real-world experience. As a result, the motivation to learn may be enhanced (Bonwell and Eison 1991).

In business schools the case method was first used because of the lack of sufficient theory. Business schools could only give students practice in solving many varied business problems. Cases were designed to "enable students to discover and develop their own unique framework for approaching, understanding, and dealing with business problems." (Barnes, Christensen, and Hansen 1994, 42) In fact, an increasing use of mathematics and social science theory in business schools has contributed to a decrease in the use of the case method (Barnes, Christensen, and Hansen 1994, 39-40). In contrast, a well-developed body of theory has existed in economics for some time. Economists have tended to explain the theory through lectures in classes as their primary activity. This is quite different from the classic Harvard Business School case approach where little theory is being applied and cases are used as a means of generating practice in thinking and analyzing problems. The use of case studies within economics (and now in most business school courses and in other social sciences) allows us to reinforce understanding of theory by repeating and reviewing basic concepts and providing practice in using that body of theory to solve problems.

Students also gain skills in solving problems with missing data and/or conflicting theories. They learn to function in an uncertain world. Because of this uncertainty, it often pays to use straight-forward cases or simplified examples at the beginning of a course, particularly an introductory one.

## II. COSTS OF USING CASES

Cases require continual updating of reading material to maintain currency and interest. This is probably more true in macroeconomics courses where names of policy makers and economic data change often. Microeconomic cases on particular markets often have a longer life.

In most instances, cases require significant class time. If the cases are being substituted for lectures introducing a number of concepts, this coverage may have to be accomplished through increased reading and outside preparation. (A summary of the literature on these costs can be found in Bonwell and Eison 1991.)

For many of us, preparing the discussions to accompany cases requires more faculty time than preparing a lecture on the same topics. The costs are borne mostly by the instructor. The benefits are gained mostly by students. This explains some of the reluctance on the part of faculty to use cases.

## III. SELECTING AND PREPARING MATERIALS FOR CASES

Source materials may come from newspapers, magazines, radio programs, TV news shows, government documents, and position papers from think tanks and political candidates and parties. Good sources are national public radio and public television, which make their program transcripts available. Stories can be as simple as those relating interest rates and stock prices found in almost every daily newspaper, every day. Or as common as the regular announcements of unemployment, inflation, productivity, and growth figures. Or as tailored to student interests as price indexes of campus-purchased food developed by a student newspaper. Or the hundreds of newspaper stories describing changing sales and prices - concert ticket sales, ticket prices to sporting events, or college tuition. Or a full-fledged debate about major policy issues - recent examples include NAFTA, mergers and acquisitions, increasing competition in the telecommunications industry, deregulation and increasing competition among electric power firms, decisions by the Federal Reserve to raise or lower the target federal funds rate, or the size of federal budget deficits. Case materials may be as brief as a paragraph or as long as several pages. Harvard Business School cases are as long as forty pages of text. Editing to distill primary documents helps focus student effort and discussion, but if part of the goal is to train students in differentiating between relevant and irrelevant data and analysis, too much editing may be counterproductive.

## IV. WRITING QUESTIONS

After selecting the core materials, the important next step is writing questions to guide student thought and class discussion. The case method is not more widely used partially because of the difficulty in writing effective questions and answers. Finding good material is relatively easy, but writing questions that are interesting, that direct student thought to an informed, careful analysis, and that are within the abilities of the students in undergraduate courses is time consuming and difficult.

I have divided cases into problem cases and policy cases, following a model Rendigs Fels developed in his work with case studies (Fels and Buckles 1981). Problem cases are intended to train students to use economic principles to get a better understanding of the economics and arguments they encounter in newspapers, magazines, daily news, and informal discussions. The goal of this type of case is to explain the economics principles behind the examples and to use economics to better understand the problems.

Questions in this kind of case should begin by asking students to provide an overview of the facts or problems in the reading. Students should next be asked to identify the relevant economic concepts and principles, probably best done in a brain-storming technique so that concepts are identified before they are actually used in analysis. The next questions guide the student through the application of the concepts. An example is provided later in this chapter in the case on Girl Scout cookies. As students gain more skills, fewer questions with less direction can be provided.

Policy cases present current problems that may require changes in economic policy. The questions ask students to identify and apply concepts in a systematic way and then to make policy recommendations. Rendigs Fels developed a practical outline for approaching policy cases (Fels and Buckles 1981, 119). His five-step procedure for analyzing policy issues is: 1) define the problem; 2) specify goals, policy options, and relevant economic principles; 3) analyze the consequences of each of the principal options; 4) use these results to evaluate the alternatives, ranking them according to each goal; and 5) decide which alternative is best in light of the evaluations finished in step four and the relative importance of each of the goals. This procedure can be used to guide students through the difficult task of analyzing policy issues logically and coming to intelligent positions. The five-step method is applicable to a variety of issues in and out of economics. It is simple enough to teach beginning students, while at the same time it provides a sound framework for orderly thinking.

When used during class time, the first two steps often take too much time. Teachers might consider summarizing the first two steps themselves in a lecture format or asking students to come prepared to present the first two steps. The third and fourth steps can be handled through discussions leading to a ranking of each policy option according to each specified goal. Discussion of the fifth step depends upon the tradeoffs among goals and may be best settled with some discussion followed by a vote. However, a caution is appropriate. A common failure in using cases is for the instructor to demonstrate how theory is applied rather than to use case studies to develop the students' own skills and judgment, and to never really involve students in an active manner.

## V. FORMATS

A variety of case formats will actively engage students. One of the easiest and most effective methods is as an active learning technique separating parts of a lecture within a single class period. This provides an opportunity to involve students in applying concepts or principles just discussed, thereby breaking up the class period and creating a more interesting class. Cases can also be used as demonstrations of applications of theory by an instructor presenting a brief synopsis, presenting a set of questions to guide the analysis, and then proceeding to answer the questions within the context of a lecture.

Small groups can be assigned the task of addressing questions within a case. The assignment can be for prior preparation, or for shorter cases, actually completed in small groups during the class period. The analysis can be done by each group and then presented to the class as a whole. Or different parts of a case can be discussed by each group. If each group is asked to do the same case, class discussion and involvement will be best if it is likely that different answers will result, as in a policy case. Alternately, each group can be assigned different cases to discuss in class. One advantage of small group discussions of cases is that students, who are hesitant in larger groups, will be more likely to speak out and actively participate. Students can be asked to write position papers addressing the case. Cases can also be used as exam questions. Students can be asked to debate policy issues. The debate can be structured by assigning students to different sides based upon different interpretation of data, different applications of theory, or different goals.

Role playing is an effective alternative to small group discussions. Role playing motivates students and can be fun, but it can also be threatening to some students. It may involve only two students or committees of students backing up individual presentations. Students are assigned roles such as presidential advisers, members of Congress representing varying constituencies, labor, management, or resource owners. Roles can be assigned at random, which can be very threatening to students, but is also a tremendous motivation for completing reading assignments. Some instructors find that allowing students to have some choice of roles is a more productive approach. In either case, students need time to prepare their roles – either prior to class, in a few minutes discussion within small groups, or simply with a few minutes of work alone. The assignment and descriptions of the roles should be clear enough to let the students know who they are supposed to be, otherwise students may go off on tangents that consume class time and lead the discussions in unproductive ways. A play with a specific script, however, reduces creativity and opportunities for students to explore their own abilities to analyze and solve problems.

Debriefing is one of the most important parts of case studies in general, and role playing in particular. As much or more time should be devoted to the debriefing as to the role playing itself. Students in the role of observers can summarize or explain why attitudes and results were reached. The role players themselves can be asked to interpret their actions and summarize lessons learned.

## VI. THREE EXAMPLES OF CASE STUDIES

The first example is a problem case designed to demonstrate the relevance of simple theory to beginning students. The second example can be used as a problem or a policy case. It is a role play adapted from an article that itself could be the basis of a case. The third example is an involved policy case, selected to illustrate the challenges of putting together interesting, effective cases. This reading ages quickly and needs additional data and analysis to answer all possible questions. Note that these three cases are quite different in purpose, content, and method.

## Case 1 – Price Elasticity

### Girl Scouts Hike the Price of Cookies

The price of Girl Scout cookies is increasing from $ 2.50 to $ 3.00 a box. What will that do to sales, which start Friday?

Not much, hopes the local Suncoast Girl Scout council, which relies on cookie sales for 70 percent of its budget. Rising cookie prices falls into the economics lesson on "elasticity of demand." That's an unappetizing way to describe whether we're hungry (or charitable) enough to pay a higher price. If demand for a product is inelastic, that means most people will still buy, even if the price goes up. If demand for a product is elastic, more people stop buying if the price increases.

Most economists interviewed said that the demand for Girl Scout cookies is probably very inelastic. That's a fancy way of explaining what most cookie nibblers already know in their gut. If you're craving Thin Mints, a 50-cent increase in price isn't going to curb your buying.

"If you think of them as cookies, they are good cookies, but there are some very good substitutes in the store," said Dave Denslow, a University of Florida economist.

But most people buy more than cookies when the scouts knock on the door, Denslow said. "They are really selling the chance to contribute to these Girl Scouts and give yourself an excuse to eat these really rich cookies," he said.

So it's likely that the demand for the cookies probably will fall only slightly with the price increase, predicted one Girl Scout leader. "We will probably be able to increase revenues by increasing prices. Sales in terms of numbers of boxes of cookies will be fewer, but it will be a relatively small loss."

*St. Petersburg Times*, January 18, 1997, E1, E7 (Edited)

### Case 1 Questions
1. Summarize the problem. List the relevant economic concepts.
2. What will happen to the quantity demanded if the price is increased? (Was the Girl Scout leader who was quoted confusing demand and quantities demanded? Are there other corrections you might recommend to the journalist?)
3. If demand is elastic, what will happen to revenue? Explain why.
4. If demand is inelastic, what will happen to revenue? Explain why.
5. What will happen to profits in either case? Explain.

6. Do you believe that the demand for Girl Scout cookies is more likely to be elastic or inelastic? Why?
7. How should the Girl Scout Council determine what to do?

The questions should be distributed along with the article. Students can be asked to answer questions as homework or in a paper, or told to come to class prepared to discuss the answers. Class discussion can take a variety of forms. This case is designed to encourage students to think about the application of rather straight-forward concepts and the relationships among revenues, costs, and profits. Given several rather casual uses of terms, it is also an opportunity to discuss the importance of careful, exact wording when describing economic applications.

Students seem to enjoy actually using concepts in this manner. They particularly enjoy, although some are hesitant, correcting journalists and economists. Introductory students are able to answer questions one through four and six rather easily. Questions five and seven are more challenging and thought provoking. Question seven particularly stimulates a variety of proposals. Using this case early in the course also permits instructors to refer back to it when confronting more advanced applications later in the course.

### Case 2 – International Trade

This brief role play is based on an April 6, 1996 *Wall Street Journal* article. The arguments in the role play are mostly direct quotes from those interviewed in the article. The role of Ricki Lake has been added in an effort to attract students' attention. Other names have been changed. Use of a structured role play can get students used to acting out roles. But more important is the debriefing process – a process that can occur in small groups, class discussions, or through homework assignments. After doing a role play exercise in this fashion, students can be asked to role play based on articles describing a problem or policy, without a detailed guide to exact lines. A more elaborate role play exercise is described in van der Meulen Rodgers (1996). A more unstructured role play allows more flexibility and requires more input on the part of the students.

Cheap Imports From Mexico Are 'Killing Us'

**Narrator:** The setting is the Ricki Lake Talk Show and the guests for the show are Paul Mare and a NAFTA representative. In response to criticism that Ricki doesn't endorse quality programming, this is her attempt to dispel that image. There will be a debate with Ricki as facilitator. Two audience members are provided with questions to assist in expressing all opinions in the debate.

**Ricki:** Hi! My name is Ricki Lake and boy, do we have a show for you today. If tomatoes have been on your mind recently, this is the show for you. To my right we have Paul J. Mare, a Florida tomato grower. And to my left we have a representative from the current administration, and an individual who supports NAFTA, the North American Free Trade Agreement. So lets begin!

**Mare (in a loud, excited voice):** Well, I would like you all to know, in fact I would like the whole country to know, that something needs to be done to stop Mexican growers from selling tomatoes below cost. I have tried speaking with the President to convince him to impose quotas and increase tariffs, but the main villain behind the scene seems to be NAFTA. These Mexican growers are "killing us."

**Ricki:** Well now let's hear from the administration. What have you got to say to that?

**NAFTA (sounding superior):** Well Ricki, it is awfully convenient for Mr. Mare to yell such accusations, especially with this being an election year and all, but I think most everything he is saying is completely unjustified. First of all has he even thought about the fact that the increase in competition could be because of the decrease in the value of the peso by 40 percent.

**Mare:** The value of the peso doesn't make a difference.

**NAFTA:** Or that weather problems have hurt Florida growers in recent years, enabling the Mexicans to capture a greater share of the market? Maybe Mexico can produce tomatoes for less than you can. Or maybe Mexican tomatoes just plain taste better?

**Mare:** You don't even know what you are talking about. If you did, you would know that it doesn't really matter how tomatoes taste because they are condiments, seldom eaten alone! As far as the rest of your arguments go, the Mexicans are just trying to kick us when we're down, and if the government doesn't help us who will? They are absolutely murdering the state of Florida.

**Ricki:** O.K., O.K., we'll need to settle down; this is suppose to be good family programming. Now Mr. Mare, are you basically only interested in protecting your own profits?

**Mare:** That is completely unjustified. We just want to play on the same level.

**Ricki:** I think that I must have missed something. Why are you not playing on the same level now?

**Mare:** Now hear me out. I'm not saying that the government should stop all trade of summer tomatoes with Mexico, however, we should at least establish a standard basis of transportation. Right now, we ship our firm, unripe Florida tomatoes in ordinary boxes; the Mexicans hand-pack their vine-ripened tomatoes in cushiony trays that resemble egg cartons. We can't possibly afford to pack'em that way and still pay our workers a decent wage. I say let's just all use the same simple boxes.

**Ricki:** Let's hear from a consumer.

**Audience member:** Do you really consider that fair? What if you totally did away with the Mexican competition, then you and the other three large Florida growers would have a monopoly. What will happen to consumer prices then?

**Mare:** There is plenty of competition in the U.S. Prices would not go up.

**Audience member**: This question is directed toward the NAFTA supporter. I am a Florida state senator and I have looked into the eyes of proud farmers facing bankruptcy, choking back tears, as they tell of the plight of their crops, employees and creditors. Was this NAFTA's vision?

**NAFTA:** Once again I must ask, does the problem lie with NAFTA or elsewhere? I spoke with the chief Agriculture Department economist, and he says that though there may have been dips and spikes of tomato production in Florida, the general trend is undoubtedly upward. Explain that?

**Ricki:** Well I can see that lots of crazy emotions are flying around here. We will probably have to continue this another day and conclude this gut wrenching drama for now. Until then you all have food for thought. Remember I love you all, keep your heads up high, and reach for the stars. Until next time, Ricki Lake.

## Case 2 Questions

1. List the relevant economic concepts.
2. What is happening in the tomato markets?
3. Use supply and demand analysis to describe the American and Mexican tomatoes sold in the U.S. market.
4. What will be the likely result of tariffs? of quotas?
5. What is the purpose of the proposal for common box requirements?
6. Should we protect the American growers and workers?
7. Would the answers be different if the tomatoes were from California instead of Mexico? Why or why not?

The debriefing can consist of small groups taking sides in a debate or a discussion led by the faculty member. It could continue with questions from the audience if the students playing the parts are creative enough and understand the economic roles. The goals are to get students to think about the benefits and costs of free trade, nontariff barriers, and effects of the tariffs and quotas. Students may bring up questions focusing on the effects of lower wages in Mexico, better growing conditions, and higher quality tomatoes. More difficult issues include the falling value of the peso as a cause of the Florida tomato growers' problems. It has been this author's experience that the results of role playing and the discussion of cases will be improved if instructors are very clear in their own minds about the content goals of the experience.

## Case 3 – Economic Growth

The following reading is a policy case. It includes a number of related issues that could be discussed in classes at a variety of levels. If students are just beginning economics, it might be best to limit discussion to one of the issues, for example, the acceptance of a growth rate of 2.2 percent. The article is an op-ed piece written by a former managing director of Lazard Freres & Co. It is edited to help students focus on the primary issues in the article. In addition, I have removed references to specific political figures and dated statistics. Although the issues in macroeconomics cases do not change quickly, the individuals quoted, and those managing policy, and the data do change.

Recipe for Growth
by Felix G. Rohatyn

The American economy is now constrained by a financial iron triangle, in part created by the Republican majority together with the Clinton administration, from which it is difficult to break out and which is beginning to generate serious social tensions.

• The first leg of this triangle is the commitment to balance the budget in seven years. Even though there has never been a rational explanation for this time frame, it has now become part of the political theology. It would be [ ] dangerous for either party to depart from it....

• The second leg is [ ] the acceptance, by both parties and blessed by the Congressional Budget Office, that our economic growth rate will be 2.2 percent for the seven-year period. [ ] It implies that this rate of growth is the limit of what our economy is capable of without inflation. Since this view has the support of the Federal Reserve, the Treasury and the financial markets, it has become a de facto limit on economic growth. The markets and the Fed react to any appearance of acceleration with higher interest rates and the economy then falls back to 2.2 percent or below.

• The third leg of this triangle is the impact of technology and global competition on incomes and employment. [The] ever-increasing differentials in wealth and income among Americans of differing levels of education and skills, [are] creating serious social tensions and political pressures.

Unless we can somehow break out of this iron triangle, we could face serious difficulties, and the best hope for a break-out is to make a determined effort for a higher rate of economic growth. Only higher growth, as a result of higher investment and greater productivity, can make these processes socially tolerable. In order to deal constructively with the realities of technology and the global economy, Democrats and Republicans may have to abandon cherished traditional positions and turn their thinking upside down: Democrats may have to redefine their concept of fairness, while Republicans may have to rethink the role of Government.

**Economic Insecurity**
The American economy is growing very slowly despite occasional upward blips. Growth and inflation are both around 2 percent.[ ]

At the same time, the Dow Jones

Industrial Average is near its all-time high..., mergers and restructurings are still taking place at a record pace, and layoffs and downsizing are continuing as the inevitable result of global competition and technological change. [   ]

The social and economic problems we face today are varied. They include job insecurity, enormous income differentials, significant pressures on average incomes, urban quality-of-life and many others. Even though all of these require different approaches, the single most important requirement to deal with all of them is the wealth and revenues generated by a higher rate of economic growth. John Kennedy was right: A rising tide lifts all boats. Although it may not lift all of them at the same time and at the same rate, without more growth we are simply redistributing the same pie. That is a zero sum game and it is simply not good enough. [   ]

Bringing the rate of growth from its present 2 - 2.5 percent to a level of 3 - 3.5 percent would generate as much as an additional $1 trillion over the next decade. It could provide both for significant tax cuts for the private sector as well as for the

higher level of public investment in infrastructure and education required as we move into the 21$^{st}$ Century. It would obviously generate millions of new jobs. The present bipartisan commitment to balance the budget in seven years, based on the present anemic growth, is economically unrealistic and probably socially unsustainable. In all likelihood, higher growth is in fact the only way to achieve budget balance. The question is how to achieve it.

The conventional wisdom among most academic economists as well as the Treasury, the Federal Reserve Board and Wall Street is that our economy cannot generate higher growth without running the risk of triggering inflation. Not everyone shares that view. In particular, the leaders of many of this country's leading industrial corporations believe that we could sustain significantly higher growth rates based on the very significant productivity improvements they are generating in their own businesses, year-after-year.

*The Wall Street Journal*, Thursday, April 11, 1996, A18

## Case 3 Questions

1. How does Mr. Rohatyn define the problem?
2. Specify the economic goals relevant to the problem. What are the policy options? What are the relevant economic principles?
3. Analyze the policy options.
4. Rank order each of the policy options according to your goals.
5. Decide which alternative is best.
6. Why do some policy makers choose one alternative and others another?

## Case 3 Answers

The following are sample answers to the Case 3 questions and suggestions for using policy cases in the classroom.

1. The case actually includes three problems: the speed at which we plan to balance the federal budget; a de facto limit on how fast the economy can grow; and an increasing spread in the distributions of income and wealth.

   A case can be structured so that not all possible problems are discussed in class. The other problems can be assigned for homework or used in exams. Here, I have chosen to limit discussion to the growth issues. A full discussion of all three problems cannot be completed in a single period.

2. Economic goals might include a faster increase in real GDP, low inflation, low unemployment, more equal income distribution, and sufficient or even increased social spending by government. A simpler discussion for students new to the case method may be limited to the first three goals.

   *Policy options.* Increase growth in the money supply so that spending grows at a rate of 3 - 3.5 percent or leave monetary policy as it is. I have limited the policy options to two for ease of discussion and to save time in the class discussion. A full discussion might include additional options.

   *Relevant economic principles.* These include aggregate supply and demand; monetary policy; the nonaccelerating inflation rate of unemployment (NAIRU); and short-run tradeoffs between unemployment and inflation.

3. In discussing growth, the article seems to refer to capacity; however, it implies growth in spending when referring to the role of the Federal Reserve. A stimulative monetary policy may cause a rise in real GDP and a fall in unemployment in the short run. Some increase in inflation may be experienced. If the economy is currently producing at a level of output that is less than the NAIRU level of output, the economy may remain at the new higher level of real GDP. However, if the economy begins at a level of output that is equal to the NAIRU level of output, inflation may begin to accelerate and the attempts to cause an increase in real GDP will result only in more inflation. (The question of whether the economy could grow at an additional percentage point for ten years through more stimulative monetary policy is another discussion.)

4. There will be a difference in how each policy meets each goal depending upon where the economy is in relation to the NAIRU level of output. A ranking of each policy in the short run is shown in Table 11.1.

5. Given the results in the grid, the policy choice depends upon how one values the goals. In the long run, the policy makes sense only if we are not at the NAIRU level of output. If the increase in real GDP and the reduction in unemployment are more important goals to achieve than holding down inflation, then the correct policy is increased money supply growth.

## Table 11.1: Policy Ranking Grid

| Policy | Goals | | |
|---|---|---|---|
| | Increase in real GDP | Unemployment | Inflation |
| Increase money supply growth | 1 | 1 | 2 |
| Maintain money supply growth | 2 | 2 | 1 |

6. Different policies may be recommended as a result of differing values, i.e., weighting the goals differently, different assumptions about the data (the NAIRU level of output), or different conclusions about the theory.

Policy cases reinforce learning of theory by asking students to use the theory in real problems. Policy cases can demonstrate how differences in values, in understanding of current data, and in theory cause us to reach different conclusions and make different policy recommendations. These three cases represent a typical problem case, a more elaborate, part-problem, part-policy case presented as a role play, and a rather involved policy case. Each can be used to reinforce concepts and to provide practice in thinking. Each can be referred to later in courses in efforts to reinforce already learned concepts and to provide a context upon which to build and tie new concepts.

## VII. DO'S AND DON'TS

These suggestions should assist instructors who chose to adopt the case method.

- Do select articles carefully – look for what will interest students, yet have sufficient substance.
- Do reward students for reading prior to class by giving students the opportunity to demonstrate that they have prepared.
- Do give a prepared list of questions to students as assignments are made.
- Do tell students to outline or write out answers before coming to class.
- Do prepare your sample answers to the questions to see if the questions can be answered and to plan your discussion.
- Do construct questions so that answers are not so obvious that no discussion occurs.
- Do provide sufficient information to allow significant analysis.
- Do identify the goals of the case. What is it you want your students to learn?
- Do remember – writing quality questions is the hardest part.
- Don't ask only (or even many) factual questions.
- Don't assume an effective discussion can take place with no or little preparation on the students' parts.

- Don't assume an effective discussion can take place with no or little preparation on the professor's part.
- Don't use the same format for all cases. That is, don't always lecture or lead the discussion in the same way. Use brief problem cases, more involved policy cases, and role plays.
- Don't assign lengthy articles where only part is relevant.
- Don't consistently use articles where mistakes are made.
- Don't include too much data and descriptive analysis for the time allowed.

## VIII. CONCLUSION

In this chapter, I have discussed the efficacy of using case studies in teaching undergraduate economics. Books of prepared cases are available at a number of levels. More current news stories can be turned into cases by following some of the guidelines provided in this chapter. The chapter offers suggestions as to how to select and edit material, write questions, and use the cases in classes. Cases provide opportunities for the enhancement of motivation, repetition and review of principles, and development of critical thinking skills. At the same time, the use of cases in classes means less time available for lecturing and may result in a smaller number of concepts being explained in class. These benefits and costs are similar to other forms of active learning. For most of us, case studies are worth trying.

## REFERENCES

Barnes, L. B., C.R. Christensen, and A.J. Hansen. 1994. *Teaching and the case method,* 3rd edition. Boston: Harvard Business School.

Becker, W. E. 1997. Teaching economics to undergraduates. *Journal of Economic Literature* 35 (September): 1347-73.

Bonwell, C.C. and J.A. Eison. 1991. *Active learning: Creating excitement in the classroom.* ASHE-ERIC Higher Education Report No. 1. Washington, D.C.: George Washington University.

Carlson, J.A. and D.W. Schodt. 1995. Beyond the lecture: Case teaching and the learning of economic theory. *Journal of Economic Education* 26 (Winter): 17-28.

Fels, R. and S. Buckles. 1981. *Casebook of economic problems and policies: Practice in thinking,* 5th edition. St. Paul: West Publishing.

Hansen, W. L. 1986. What knowledge is most worth knowing - For economics majors. *American Economic Review* 76 (May): 149-52.

Marks, S.G. and M.G. Rukstad. 1996. Teaching macroeconomics by the case method. *Journal of Economic Education* 27 (Spring): 139-47.

McKeachie, W.J., N. Chism, R. Menges, M. Svinicki, and C.E. Weinstein. 1994. *Teaching tips: Strategies, research, and theory for college and university teachers,* 9th edition. Lexington, MA: D.C. Heath and Company.

Rukstad, M.B. 1992. *Macroeconomic decision making in the world economy: Text and cases,* 3rd edition. Ft. Worth, Tex.: Dryden.

van der Meulen Rodgers, Y. 1996. A role-playing exercise for development and international economics courses. *Journal of Economic Education* 27 (Summer): 217-23.

Velenchek, A. 1995. The case method as a strategy for teaching policy analysis to undergraduates. *Journal of Economic Education* 26 (Winter): 29-38.

CHAPTER **12**

# ENGAGING STUDENTS IN QUANTITATIVE ANALYSIS WITH THE ACADEMIC AND POPULAR PRESS

### William E. Becker

Applications of quantitative methods in economics are not universally viewed as unique. For example, in what may be the most influential textbook in statistics, Sir Ronald Fisher (1970) bluntly stated:

> The science of statistics is essentially a branch of Applied Mathematics, and may be regarded as mathematics applied to observational data. (p. 1) Statistical methods are essential to social studies, and it is principally by the aid of such methods that these studies may be raised to the rank of sciences. This particular dependence of social studies upon statistical methods has led to the unfortunate misapprehension that statistics is to be regarded as a branch of economics, whereas in truth methods adequate to the treatment of economic data, in so far as these exist, have mostly been developed in biology and the other sciences. (p. 2)

The argument that statistics should be taught as applied mathematics by mathematicians implies that the identification and context of problems or issues in the social sciences are irrelevant or so trivial that intuition is sufficient – after all, anyone can specify a regression equation in which a dependent variable is explained by a set of independent variables.   Yet Fisher's statement also indicates that it was the special nature of biological data that gave rise to the development of specific methods of analysis by biometricians.  If there are data characteristics in issues confronted by biologists and other researchers in the natural sciences that require insights gleaned from the discipline, isn't this also true for economics and the other social sciences?[1]

There are unique features of the problems and issues in economics that suggest special methods of analysis.   For example, although mathematician Daniel Bernoulli proposed an equation for utility in 1738, it was the Victorian economists who independently fashioned utility into an explanation of how markets behave and how buyers and sellers reach agreement on price in a simultaneous manner.   Bernoulli dealt with the level of utility as a number. Jeremy Bentham in 1789 and the other eighteenth and nineteenth century economists that followed thought in terms of preferences, enabling them to build a theory of supply, demand and equilibrium (Bernstein 1996, 189).   In 1923 John Von Neumann conveyed something important to mathematicians but it wasn't until he worked with economist Oskar Morgenstern in the 1940s that he realized that more than mathematics was involved in the theory of games.   In their headline grabbing article in *Science* (1981), as well as their numerous other writings, psychologists Amos Tversky and Daniel Kahneman provide ample evidence that more frequently than most of us admit decision makers do not behave in accordance with the objectivity of mathematics.   Economists (Thaler 1993, 1995) show, however, that the Prospect Theory of Tversky and Kahneman (1992) does not say behavior is random and erratic, even though decision making is not rational by Bernoulli's or Von Neumann's mathematical standards.   Together with other social scientists, economists have found that human choices are orderly even though they may be only "quasi-rational."

As demonstrated by articles in *Science, The New York Times*, and other popular presses, debates within the sciences are of interest to the general public and students alike.  The nature of the problems and issues addressed, as well as the nuances of the theories and methods of analyses advanced by economists, set economics and economists apart (as seen, for example, in the "Trends" and "Viewpoint" sections of *Business Week*).   The rationale for teaching quantitative methods in an economics department rests on our ability to show these discipline-related applications.[2]   One way we can do this is by using examples, problems, and case studies that incorporate events reported in the newspapers, magazines, and journals that economists and students of economics are or should be reading.   In this chapter I illustrate how students can be engaged in headline situations that make clear the importance of learning quantitative methods for use in economics.

## I. HOW WE TEACH

Following the completion of micro- and macroeconomics principles courses, in which the majority of students are enrolled to fulfill requirements for other majors, economics majors take two intermediate micro and macro courses, a course in statistics/econometrics, and some field courses that may or may not include more quantitative methods (Siegfried et al. 1991). Although students in our statistics and in some of our econometrics courses may be predominantly noneconomics majors, they are there because of an interest in or requirement related to economics and business.

In a national survey, Becker and Watts (1996) found some differences between the way statistics and econometrics courses are taught and the way that other economics courses are taught. In particular, problem sets are used more in statistics and econometrics than in other undergraduate economics courses. Curiously, however, those applications are not based on events reported in newspapers, magazines and journals that should be of interest to students of economics and business.

Some instructors can set problems raised by their own research and consulting, problems students can expect to see on their jobs. After all, as argued in the introduction to this chapter, the rationale for teaching statistics and econometrics outside a mathematics department rests on a belief that there is something special about economic analyses. Although the calculation of a mean and a median is the same in medicine and economics, a discussion of the average duration of economic expansions since World War II is more pertinent to those majoring in economics than a discussion of average blood pressure or average time to dementia with mad cow disease. The importance of economic theory is often lost when mathematicians attempt to make situations real, as seen for example in the "Chance Course" (Snell and Finn 1992) where a potpourri of statistical applications are presented with no discipline-grounded analyses.

To teach students to apply the tools of statistics to actual situations and data encountered by economists, there is little justification for examples involving the drawing of balls from urns, flicking of spinners, tossing of coins, or contrived card and dice tricks. Yet these methods of generating data continue to be found in the activity-based teaching and assessment methods advocated by mathematics educators (Scheaffer et al. 1996; Gal and Garfield 1997). Students need to be involved in working exercises, considering case studies and solving problems. This implies replacing the urns with preselection pools from which individuals are hired, replacing the coins with surveys in which individuals face multiple-choice responses, and replacing examples from genetics with examples from quality control. If games of chance are employed to demonstrate risk, use actual situations involving lotteries or other financial decisions students see in the popular press.

Basic and more advanced quantitative methods can be made "real" with reference to the popular press. But simply assigning students to find applications and relevant data in newspaper articles is too unstructured as a starting point. As demonstrated in Becker (1997), the mini-case study approach introduced by Fels (1974, and presented in this volume by his coauthor Stephen Buckles) can be modified to lead students into analysis. Short case studies enable instructors to demonstrate a specific form of analysis while giving students an opportunity to observe how concepts and theories are used to examine a diverse array of issues. With short, focused case studies students do not get lost in extraneous verbiage as they begin the study of statistics and econometrics. Students need to see some pearls and learn where to look for them before going to the ocean.

Few economists have published or given courtroom or boardroom testimony in all areas found in statistics and econometrics courses. The popular press and academic journals can be used as surrogates for missing credentials and experience, although we may feel more comfortable and find it easier to work with contrived problems and fake data. The differences between fairy tales and fact, however, are apparent to students. Consider, for example, two shortened versions of questions taken from different final examinations given in the 1996 and 1997 spring semesters at Indiana University.

Q 1996: Economic theory suggests that the greater the number of pages in a book, the greater its price. As a novice economist, you want to test for a significant relationship between price ($y$, in dollars) and number of pages ($x$). You run a regression and obtain

$$\hat{y} = 1.041553 + 0.009907x$$

If a book contains 900 pages, the predicted price of that book would be

    A. $8.92     B. $9.96        C. $675.24       D. $936.01

Q 1997: A real estate report in the *WSJ* (February 28, 1997) gave the "top 10 condominium sales in New York City." The estimated relationship between condo sale price ($y$, in millions of dollars) and condominium size ($x$, in square feet) is given below. Based on this regression, was the condominium at 353 Central Park West ($y = 1.6$, $x = 2733$) a good buy?

$$\hat{y} = -0.8456 + 0.001085x$$

A.  No, because its actual price ($1.6 million) was less than its predicted.
B.  Yes, because its actual price was less than its predicted ($2.12 million).
C.  No, because its residual ($y - \hat{y}$) is negative; a good buy has a large positive residual.
D.  Yes, because its actual and predicted prices per square foot are relatively low.

Both exams had over 40 multiple-choice questions with similar average scores of about 65 percent correct. The use of cited sources gives a sense of realism to the 1997 exam. Questions such as Q1996 provide no references and are obviously contrived: a 900-page book priced at $9.96 must seem ludicrous to students who buy textbooks.[3]

Exam questions, homework assignments, and other student activities reflect the manner in which a course is taught. I suspect that students who took the course represented by Q1997 walked away with better statistical skills and different impressions of their applicability than those completing the 1996 course. The Q1997 type of question makes clear that the course is aimed at applying statistics to economics.

Individual application questions can be used outside a formal exam structure to stimulate student interaction. For example, twelve times during the semester, typically as we move between topics, I project a single multiple-choice question on the screen of a 350-student lecture hall. Each student answers the question by marking A – E on a machine-scorable sheet distributed as they enter the hall. For a second question, "A. Certain" to "E. Doubtful" is marked as an expression of confidence. Students then discuss their answers with neighbors – the lecture hall is abuzz. After a few minutes, students continue the process with question three (a repeat of question one) and final confidence given in question four (as a repeat of question two). Student attendance and participation increased with the introduction of this activity because students get credit for attempting the four responses, as well as for selecting the correct response to number three.

I call the above question-based activity "a class-participation quiz." Its origin can be traced to Harvard University physics professor Eric Mazur. The need for such interaction among students in the learning process is made clear in the Harvard Assessment Seminars survey (Light 1992, 8). My participation quizzes are an attempt to get students interacting in a large class setting. I report this activity only to show that quizzes and tests can be use to advance communication skills and student interaction as they work to acquire quantitative skills, even in large lecture halls where such activity is usually considered inefficient, if not impossible.

## II. DESCRIPTIVE STATISTICS

Learning statistics often begins with calculations of descriptive statistics. The amount of experience students should have with computational formulas is debatable, but sooner or later they must be exposed to computer software that performs these calculations. Although writing equations on a blackboard is traditional, teaching statistics and econometrics without spending time in a computer lab is difficult to justify. Data from the press can be employed even for the most basic calculations. Small data sets enable hand calculations to verify what a computer program does. One such data set involves the duration of economic expansions (*Wall Street Journal*, November 15, 1996), from which the data in Table 12.1 were extracted. The article stated that "The nation's continuing economic expansion, now 67 months old, has far surpassed the previous postwar average (50 months) and few see the party ending anytime soon."(p. A1)

Students can be engaged in the analysis of these data via homework assignments or right in class with questions that require them to write short answers that can be discussed in class or graded – as in the minute paper (Angelo and Cross 1993, 148-53). Detailed answers can then be provided as needed. For example:

QUERY: First, does the "50-month average" pertain to the mean or median of the length of U.S. expansions since WW II? Second, what is your best estimate of the standard deviation of duration of U.S. expansions that occurred since WW II? Third, has the latest 67-month spell "far surpassed the previous postwar average?"

ANSWER: First, in November 1996, the *WSJ* could not have included the then current expansion in calculating the mean duration of expansions since WW II because that expansion had not (and as of June 1998 still had not) come to an end. That is, the length of the expansion still underway as of November 15, 1996, was unknown; we only know that it had been underway for 67 months up to November. After entering the 10 duration values into an Excel spreadsheet, the "Descriptive Statistics" routine can be used to get the descriptive statistics for the input data range. The resulting summary statistics appear in Table 12.2.

Notice that although the last cell of data contains the 67-month value for the current expansion (up to November 1996), only the prior nine expansions were used in the calculations of descriptive statistics. The mean duration of these nine expansions is approximately 50 months (49.89), as reported in *The Wall Street Journal*. This data set is small enough for students to calculate the mean with the formula

$$\bar{x} = \frac{\sum_{i=1}^{n} x_i}{n}$$

that provides a check on what the computer has done. If they mistakenly set $n = 10$ (which many do) the groundwork is set for the discussion of the truncated last spell.

Unlike the mean, a median for all 10 expansions can be determined even though the exact length of the last spell is not known. The median of all 10 spells is between 39 and 45 months regardless of how long this current expansion might last. Setting the median at 42 months shows five duration

## Table 12.1: Duration of Expansions Since World War II

| Beginning to End of U.S. Expansion | Duration (in months) |
|---|---|
| Oct-45 to Nov-48 | 37 |
| Oct-49 to Jul-53 | 45 |
| May-54 to Aug-57 | 39 |
| Apr-58 to Apr-60 | 24 |
| Feb-61 to Dec-69 | 106 |
| Nov-70 to Nov-73 | 36 |
| Mar-75 to Jan-80 | 58 |
| Jul-80 to Jul-81 | 12 |
| Nov-82 to Jul-90 | 92 |
| Mar-91 to Present | 67 |

Data Source:  National Bureau of Economic Research

## Table 12.2: Descriptive Statistics for Expansion Data

| Data | Descriptive Statistics | |
|---|---|---|
| 37 | Mean | 49.88888889 |
| 45 | Standard Error | 10.27056804 |
| 39 | Median | 39 |
| 24 | Mode | #N/A |
| 106 | Standard Deviation | 30.81170413 |
| 36 | Sample Variance | 949.3611111 |
| 58 | Kurtosis | 0.080068248 |
| 12 | Skewness | 0.955462191 |
| 92 | Range | 94 |
| 67 | Minimum | 12 |
| | Maximum | 106 |
| | Sum | 449 |
| | Count | 9 |
| | Confidence Level(95.0%) | 23.68398769 |

spells shorter and five duration spells longer than 42 months no matter how long this current expansion continues.  (Only the 39-month median for the first 9 spells is reported in Table 12.2, which again drives home the point that getting a computer program to produce numbers is not the same as knowing the appropriate statistics.)  Although *The Wall Street Journal* did not report it, students can see that the median is often the preferred measure of central tendency for duration data because it is less sensitive to the completion of spells.

Second, the standard deviation for the duration of U.S. expansions since WW II can only be calculated for the first nine spells (with students able to practice their math and check the Excel calculations as done for the mean). From the Excel printout we see that the standard deviation is 30.8117 months. Thus, the third question can be addressed: plus or minus one standard deviation from the mean duration covers a range from approximately 19.1 months to 80.7 months, from which we can conclude that as of November 1996 the current expansion was not an overly long one; however, by February 1998 it had become one.

## III. DATA ANALYSIS

When using data on the economy, it may be worthwhile to keep in mind a three-part feature in the *Washington Post* reported on the public's versus economists' views: "Good news for President Clinton: There is a core group of voters who agree with him that the economy is stronger than it was when he took office...Bad news for the president: They're economists – and nobody believes them anyway." (*Washington Post*, October 15, 1996, A1) Our low credibility likely affects our ability to teach data analysis. Teaching econometrics was not helped by Marilyn vos Savant's answer (*Parade Magazine*, September 5, 1997, 22) to a reader who asked how economists working with the same data reach different conclusions. She wrote that economists are like chefs who amaze us with the variety of stuff they cook up when given exactly the same ingredients, equipment and staff. But as students need to learn, it is often the sample data we work with that give rise to the differences in interpretation. High school natural science teachers as well as the news media do a good job of indoctrinating students in the need for "good scientific methods," but neither the science teacher nor the newscaster typically sheds light on problems in sampling and estimation.

Consider the "margin of error" for survey results reported by the news media. Readers and TV audiences must be expected to know what this information is because the journalist never elaborates. Curiously the survey margin of error calculation is not provided in most introductory statistics textbooks. In the introductory statistics course, I use reported survey statistics to show the calculation of the margin of error, $1/\sqrt{n}$. The discussion emphasizes the critical nature of two assumptions: 1) that there is a 50 percent chance that the respondent will select one alternative versus another on each of the questions in the survey, and 2) that the estimator is normally distributed so that a 95 percent confidence interval is approximately plus or minus two standard errors of an estimator. I emphasize that these are technical details but the more interesting questions are related to sampling methods, and the reliability and validity of the measurement instruments. Students, however, appear fascinated with the simplicity of the $1/\sqrt{n}$ calculation and Dan Rather's authoritative voice when he says "margin of error." In the more advanced econometrics class, I emphasize the problems of selection and nonresponse error. As in Hansen and Hurwitz (1946), students come to realize that the size of the sample alone may be a poor indicator of reliability.

Some instructors attempt to make the randomness in sampling real by having students do surveys. The use of experimental economics and games has also become popular in the teaching of economics, as described by Noussair and Walker in this volume. I question whether students see the reality in what they are doing unless there is a link to actual events outside the classroom experience. Self-reported data collected in classroom surveys or in the community are typically more appropriately used to show unreliable and invalid collection methods and opportunistic samples than a good source of data for work in a statistics course. For example, "what is your age?" is a question often put to students in a classroom to generate sample data from which descriptive statistics and multiple sample means are calculated to construct a sampling distribution of $\bar{x}$. Students typically respond with whole numbers (18, 19, 20 and 21) even though age is a continuous variable. Similarly, it is well known that when asked for academic performance measures students exaggerate (Maxwell and Lopus 1994). To tie them to the "real world," these classroom data collection problems can be likened to the efforts to establish the employment effect of the 1992 change in the New Jersey minimum wage law, as featured in numerous headlines. The debate over the use of wage data collected in phone interviews of restaurant workers in Pennsylvania and New Jersey versus payroll data supplied by a trade association is evident in the exchange of viewpoints and reader reactions found in *Business Week* (April 24, 1995 and May 15, 1995) and Gary Becker's column in *Business Week*, "How Bad Studies Get Turned Into Bad Policies" (June 26, 1995).

In introductory statistics students learn about counting (combinations and permutations) and probability distributions, but these are seldom tied to real-world applications. I try to solve this problem in the case of counting by asking students about the calculation of odds and probability in a letter from the Hoosier lottery that appeared in press releases:

> QUERY: The following letter was circulated by the Indiana State Lottery. How does its use of the word "odds" relate to the probability of winning?
>
> Dear Lotto Cash player,
>
> Thank you for your interest in the Hoosier Lottery's Lotto Cash game. You indicated that you had a question about how odds are

calculated for the game. Hopefully the following will provide you with the information you need.

The general formula for calculating lotto odds is as follows:

$$\text{Odds}(m) = \frac{\left(\dfrac{f}{p}\right)}{\left(\dfrac{p}{m}\right)\left(\dfrac{f-p}{p-m}\right)}$$

where f = field size, p = player picks, and m = number of matches.

The factors in the form of (x/y) are called binomial coefficients and are evaluated as follows:

$$\left(\frac{x}{y}\right) = \frac{x!}{y!(x-y)!}$$

A binomial coefficient provides a means of calculating the number of ways there are to draw *y* objects from a set of *x* objects (in this case the objects are lotto balls).

**x!** means *x* factorial and is evaluated as x(x-1)(x-2)...1. For example, 5!=5×4×3×2×1=120. Zero factorial is evaluated as 1.

In the case of the Hoosier Lottery's Lotto Cash game, the field size **f** is 44, the player picks **p** is 6 and the number of matches **m** may be 6, 5, 4, 3, 2, 1 or 0, depending on how many of the balls drawn by the lottery the player matches.

Using our formula for 6 matches, (the 6 of 6 grand prize) we get, Odds of 6 matches:

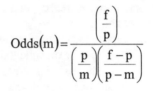

$$\frac{\left(\dfrac{44}{6}\right)}{\left(\dfrac{6}{6}\right)\left(\dfrac{44-6}{6-6}\right)} = \frac{\dfrac{44!}{6!(44-6)!}}{\dfrac{6!}{6!(6-6)!}\dfrac{38!}{0!(38-0)!}} = \frac{44 \times 43 \times 42 \times 41 \times 40 \times 39}{\dfrac{6 \times 5 \times 4 \times 3 \times 2}{1 \times 1}} = 7,059,052$$

We hope this has helped you with your calculations.

## THE HOOSIER LOTTERY

ANSWER: The "mathematical odds" of six matches is not 7,059,052. This is the size of the sample space, which is the denominator for the probability of winning with six matches. The probability of the prize associated with six matches is 1/7,059,052. The "gambling odds" of six matches is also not 7,059,052, although they are close. The gambling odds are

$$\frac{7,059,051/7,059,052}{1/7,059,052} = 7,059,051$$

Or 7,059,051:1, which is a real "long shot."

This demonstration of counting leads nicely to the binomial distribution, where I use situations such as that described on an *Insider TV* show (February 15, 1995): a tow truck operator is shown stealing items from one of four cars the TV show placed in a New York City tow area. A NYC official is quoted saying that no more than 1.0 percent of the cars that are towed and impounded have objects inside stolen. In a "think, pair, share" activity (as described by Bartlett in this volume) I ask students to assess the manner in which a one-in-four theft rate can be considered unusual if one in a hundred is expected. They come up with the question "how far above 0.04 is 1.00?" If the calculation is not forthcoming, I ask them for the probability of at least one car in four being burglarized if 0.01 is the probability of a burglary. The appropriateness of the binomial model and the magnitude of the resulting 0.039 probability are discussed. The debate over the TV show's conclusion versus the implications of this 0.039 probability is lively and quickly leads to a discussion of the difference between statistical significance and practical importance when working with small versus large samples.

As popularized by Huff and Geis (1954) and more recently demonstrated by Crossen (1994), efforts of the media to summarize the findings of research are often riddled with errors in data, calculations, and statistical reasoning. I am sure that we all have our favorite example. I try to avoid the outrageous because students can find those on their own after seeing the pearls. I prefer news clips requiring clarification that can be used to highlight subtleties of data analyses in economics. For example, an article that appeared in the *Washington Post* (January 29, 1995) calls attention to problems associated with nonlinear data transformation. The author implied that since 1990 the annual percentage returns of the American Heritage stock fund (31, 96, 19, 41, and 35) averaged 35 percent and concluded that this was "a wild ride! A fund's standard deviation is a whopping 18.5." I use these percentages to show students how to do log transformation with the Excel command "=LN(.)" (Table 12.3) and to recognize why geometric means are used. Their calculation in Table 12.3 reveals that the mean of the Ln(1+r) series is the median of the original 1+r series. They also see why simple rules of thumb [e.g., Ln(1+r) $\cong$ r] are not universally appropriate. This exercise provides an excellent introduction to the interpretation of regression coefficients in semi-log specifications [Ln($Y$) = $\beta X$ + $\varepsilon$] and problems of forecasting with this model $\{E[Ln(Y)] \neq [LnE(Y)]\}$. This understanding is critical for students of finance, macroeconomics, labor economics, and other areas in which heterogeneity in $Y$ may be the result of compounding.

As demonstrated by both Huff and Geis (1954) and Crossen (1994), the popular press is notorious for misleading graphical presentations. But the press can be used to give credibility to proper graphical techniques. For example, *Fortune* (October 27, 1997) ran a feature article on Yale professor Edward Tufte's (1983) book on displaying data, calling it the guide for those who work with numbers.

The job of the teacher is to use the popular press not as a whipping boy but as a support. Using errors found in the press for classroom demonstrations and discussions may backfire. Journalists may be viewed as more credible than academics, as suggested by the previously cited *Washington Post* quote: "They're economists – and nobody believes them." A teacher's criticism, no matter how legitimate, may fall on deaf ears. Furthermore, even if the teacher is successful in demonstrating the error, students may view this as more evidence of the irrelevance of econometrics - after all the journalist draws a large salary writing for a big name press and apparently didn't need to know statistics or econometrics to get his or her job! Furthermore, there is always the chance that we could make an error in our criticism. Many Ph.D.s wrote to

## Table 12.3: Financial Data and the Geometric Mean

|    | r    | 1 + r | Ln(1+r) |                                     |
|----|------|-------|---------|-------------------------------------|
| 1  | .19  | 1.19  | 0.17395 | =LN(C1)                             |
| 2  | .31  | 1.31  | 0.27003 | =LN(C2)                             |
| 3  | .35  | 1.35  | 0.30010 | =LN(C3)                             |
| 4  | .41  | 1.41  | 0.34359 | =LN(C4)                             |
| 5  | .96  | 1.96  | 0.67294 | =LN(C5)                             |
| 6  |      |       | 0.35212 | =AVERAGE(D1:D5)                     |
| 7  |      |       | 0.18986 | =STDEV(D1:D5)                       |
| 8  |      |       | 0.30010 | =MEDIAN(D1:D5)                      |
| 9  |      |       | 1.42208 | =EXP(D6)Geometric mean (1+r)        |
| 10 |      |       | 1.20908 | =EXP(D7)Std. Deviation (1+r)        |
| 11 |      |       | 1.35000 | =EXP(D8)Median (1+r)                |

Marilyn vos Savant at *Parade Magazine* claiming she was "the goat" in Monty's three-door game show problem. *The New York Times* gave front-page coverage to this "Let's Make a Deal" controversy. Morgan et al. (1991), Georges and Craire (1995), and other probabilists and game theorists finally had to admit that Marilyn was right.


## IV. STATISTICAL SIGNIFICANCE

The popular press need not be relied on for error-free reporting. We need it to establish what is newsworthy. For example, from high school science classes many students enter college with a belief in the need for replication and large samples to establish truth. They willingly regurgitate the need for random sampling and statistical significance, although they often confuse "statistical" with "scientific," "random" with "representative" and "significance" with "importance." The distinctions can be driven home with reference to articles such as "New Diet-Drug Data Spark More Controversy" *Wall Street Journal* (October 1, 1997) which reports on the FDA's never ending desire for replication:

> American Home Products Corp is challenging the validity of data that led to the recall of its diet drugs . . . 'Based on all the data we've received subsequently, we think that the 32% estimate is a very solid number,' says the FDA's Dr. Graham. He concedes its sample wasn't scientifically selected, but says 'there's less than a one-in-a-million chance that the results in our survey could have occurred by chance.'. . The FDA declines to say how many more echocardiograms it has reviewed but Richard Bowen, a diet doctor in Naples, Fla., says he has sent in at least an additional 60 . . . 'The second batch shows results similar to the earlier sample,' he says.(p. B1)

But what constitutes "similar" results in statistics? The aggregation of the five samples by the FDA showed 92 of 291 people who took the diet drug developed leaky heart valves. Dr. Graham's claim about a 0.000001 probability of getting the observed 92 heart problems, if sampling was random, implies a maximum expected value of 57.327, as seen in panel a of Table 12.4. The question to be put to students is which of the following hypothetical A or B samples show results more "similar" to that reported by the FDA? (Note: $32\% \cong 17/51$)

The problems with statistical significance can be driven home with several examples from the academic world. For example, Tversky and Kahneman (1982) demonstrate the importance of power and sample size in defining successful replications. They distributed a questionnaire at a meeting of psychologists, with the following inquiry:

## Table 12.4: Calculating Expected Incidences of Heart Trouble and Associated Probabilities of Observed Incidences

Panel a: Actual Events

| Largest implied pi | Number tested | X = x heart trouble | Expected number E(X) | Prob of x or more $1-P(X<x^*)$ |
|---|---|---|---|---|
| 0.197 | 291 | 92 | 57.327 | 0.0000010 |
| 0.197 | 291 | 92 | =A13*B13 | =1 BINOMDIST(C131, B13,A13,1) |

Panel b: Hypothetical Events

| Largest implied pi | Number tested | X = x heart trouble | Expected number E(X) | Prob of x or more $1-P(X<x^*)$ |
|---|---|---|---|---|
| A: | | | | |
| 0.197 | 51 | 17 | 10.047 | 0.0153479 |
| 0.197 | 51 | 17 | =A16*B16 | =1-BINOMDIST(C16-1,B16,A16,1) |
| B: | | | | |
| 0.197 | 597 | 166 | 117.609 | 0.0000011 |
| 0.197 | 597 | 166 | =A19*B19 | =1-BINOMDIST(C19-1,B19,A19,1) |

Note: The Excel commands for calculating the expected numbers and the probabilities of the observations are shown in the lower right-hand corners of each panel.

An investigator has reported a result that you consider implausible. He ran 15 subjects, and reported a significant value, $t = 2.46$. Another investigator has attempted to duplicate his procedure, and he obtained a nonsignificant value of $t$ with the same number of subjects. The direction was the same in both sets of data. You are reviewing the literature. What is the highest value of $t$ in the second set of data that you would describe as a failure to replicate?(p. 28)

Tversky and Kahneman reported the following results:

The majority of our respondents regarded $t = 1.70$ as a failure to replicate. If the data of two such studies ($t = 2.46$ and $t = 1.70$) are pooled, the value of $t$ for the combined data is about 3.00 (assuming equal variances). Thus, we are faced with a paradoxical state of affairs, in which the same data that would increase our confidence in the finding when viewed as part of the original study, shake our confidence when viewed as an independent study.(p.28)

I use this example from Tversky and Kahneman in the following set of classroom queries:

QUERY: Demonstrate how Tversky and Kahneman determined that the "$t$ for the combined data is about 3.00."

ANSWER: The first $t$, $t_1 = 2.46$, and second, $t_2 = 1.70$, can be solved for $\bar{x}_1$ and $\bar{x}_2$ and then $\bar{x}_3$ can be created as $\bar{x}_3 = 0.5(\bar{x}_1 + \bar{x}_2)$ and $t_3$ can be determined as

$$t_3 = \frac{(0.5)[2.46(s/\sqrt{15}) + \mu + 1.70(s/\sqrt{15}) + \mu] - \mu}{s/\sqrt{15}} = 2.94 \cong 3$$

QUERY: Why does this experiment demonstrate a lack of understanding of power and sample size?

ANSWER: For a fixed value of the hypothesized value of the population mean, increasing sample size results in an increase in the power of the test.

For another example of aggregation (meta-analysis) problems I make use of a question Jessica Utts (1991) posed at a History of Philosophy of Science seminar at the University of California at Davis:

Two scientists, Professors A and B, each have a theory they would like to demonstrate. Each plans to run a fixed number of Bernoulli trials and then test

$$H_0: p = 0.25 \text{ versus } H_A: p > 0.25$$

Professor A has access to large numbers of students each semester to use as subjects. In his first experiment, he runs 100 subjects, and there are 33 successes ($p = 0.04$, one-tailed). Knowing the importance of replication, Professor A runs an additional 100 subjects as a second experiment. He finds 36 successes ($p = 0.009$, one-tailed).

Professor B teaches only small classes. Each quarter, she runs an experiment on her students to test her theory. She carries out ten studies this way. (Results are shown in Table 12.5.)

I asked the audience by a show of hands to indicate whether or not they felt the scientists had successfully demonstrated their theories. Professor A's theory received overwhelming support, with approximately 20 votes, while B's theory received only one vote.(p. 367)

To help students see the influence of aggregation on statistical significance, I supplement Utts's question with a few of my own queries:

QUERY: What are each professor's aggregate results for their respective 200 subjects?

ANSWER: Professor A's and B's sample proportions are calculated to be 0.345(= 69/200) and 0.355(= 71/200) respectively with the aggregated data set each of size 200.

QUERY: What is the one-tail $p$-value for the combined trials of each professor?

ANSWER: Under the null hypothesis, the standard error is 0.0306186 for a sample of 200. The sample proportion 0.345 for the aggregated data set of Professor A yields a $p$-value of 0.0096 = 1-NORMDIST(0.345,0.25,A1,1). Similarly, based on the sample proportion 0.355 with the aggregated data set, Professor B's $p$-value is 0.0003 = 1-NORMDIST(0.355,0.25,A2,1).

QUERY: Utts led her audience to find a difference in the two professors' results, where statistical significance is found for Professor A, and not B, even though the proportion of successes is higher for Professor B. But are there differences in the two professors' aggregate results?

ANSWER: The aggregate $p$-values calculated in the above query are not greatly different from each other. In fact, the null hypothesis can be rejected at a typical 0.05 Type I error level for both professors. Both professors' aggregate results support their theories.

## Table 12.5: Attempted Replications by Professor B

| n | Number of successes | One-tailed $p$-value |
|----|----|----|
| 10 | 4 | 0.22 |
| 15 | 6 | 0.15 |
| 17 | 6 | 0.23 |
| 25 | 8 | 0.17 |
| 30 | 10 | 0.20 |
| 40 | 13 | 0.18 |
| 18 | 7 | 0.14 |
| 10 | 5 | 0.08 |
| 15 | 5 | 0.31 |
| 20 | 7 | 0.21 |

## V. TEACHING REGRESSION

Getting students to appreciate the unique feature of least squares regression is difficult. But their experience with test taking can help, as seen in the following query, where a publicly available problem from the 1993 United States National Achievement Test is reproduced from my business and economics statistics textbook (Becker 1997).

QUERY: A *Newsweek* (April 4, 1994) article reported on the desire of the U.S. Congress to encourage "thought over memorization." The article provided the following "top-rated" solution for a sample problem on the United States National Achievement Test. Can you top this top-rated solution with a better rule, table, and statement of justification?

EXCERPT FROM ACHIEVEMENT TEST PROBLEM:

Dear Problem Solver,
We have decided to sell laces ... We will sell different lengths for shoes with different numbers of eyelets (4 to 18) ... You have to figure out what lengths to make and which lengths go with which shoes, based on the number of eyelets... We collected some data from store customers ... It is confusing because there haven't been very many lengths available. That means that sometimes the customers have had to use lengths that are too short or too long... We want a unique length for each number of eyelets. Write your decisions about lace length so the advertising people can understand it. They want a table... They also want a rule... You better explain how your decisions make sense ... Thanks, Your Boss, Angela

DATA FROM STORE CUSTOMERS WITH SPORTS SHOES

| Lace Length (inches) | Eyelets (numbers) | Lace Length (inches) | Eyelets (numbers) |
| --- | --- | --- | --- |
| 45 | 8 | 54 | 12 |
| 54 | 10 | 24 | 4 |
| 26 | 4 | 72 | 14 |
| 63 | 14 | 54 | 12 |
| 63 | 12 | 72 | 16 |
| 36 | 8 | 72 | 18 |

TOP-RATED SOLUTION:
The rule is $L = 3(E - 1) + 20$, where $E$ is number of eyelets and $L$ is length of lace. Thus, the length of each lace allows enough for 3 inches between each eyelet, plus 20 inches for the bow. Of course, many people

use more than 20 inches for their bow, but most don't use a whole 3 inches for each eyelet, so there should be plenty. My table also pretty much corresponds with the data from the customers... Sincerely, The Problem Solver

| Eyelets | 4 | 6 | 8 | 10 | 12 | 14 | 16 | 18 | |
|---------|---|---|---|----|----|----|----|----|--|
| Lace Length | 29 | 35 | 41 | 47 | 53 | 59 | 65 | 71 | inches |

ANSWER: This student's rule, $L = 3(E - 1) + 20$, correctly has $L$ as the dependent variable and $E$ as the independent variable but the principle by which this student obtained the slope, 3, and intercept, 17, was not specified. Thus, the sense in which this rule is "desirable" is unknown. Its negative properties, however, can be demonstrated. First, the within sample prediction errors do not sum to zero; they sum to 35, as seen in the "$L - R$" column in the table below. This implies that on average the predicted lace lengths are too short (by 2.92 inches). Second, the error sum of squares for this rule (461, in the $(L - R)^2$ column) is not as small as that achievable by fitting an ordinary least squares (OLS) regression to the 12 records. The equation of the ordinary least-squares regression is

$$\text{Predicted } L = 11.7704 + 3.74057E$$

The intercept (11.7704) and slope (3.74057) are obtained with the Microsoft Excel commands "=INTERCEPT(A1:A12,B1:B12)" and "=SLOPE(A1:A12,B1:B12)" where the twelve paired lace lengths and number of eyelets are in columns A and B. Table 12.6 (column "$L - OLS$") shows that the prediction errors for this OLS regression sum to zero. The sum of squared prediction errors for this OLS regression is only 242.648, which is far less than the 461 for the rule found in the "top-rated" solution. Thus, the preferred eyelet and lace length solution, based on the least-squares principle, is

| Eyelets | 4 | 6 | 8 | 10 | 12 | 14 | 16 | 18 | |
|---------|---|---|---|----|----|----|----|----|--|
| Lace Length | 27 | 34 | 42 | 49 | 57 | 64 | 72 | 79 | inches |

Before I published this activity, I asked students to determine a formula to predict shoelace length based on the number of eyelets in the shoes. (The most common techniques involved drawing a line through the scatter plot or using a "high-low method" learned in accounting classes.) Based on the sum of prediction errors and the sum of squared prediction errors, students were then asked to compare their predictions with the "top-rated" answer. Finally, they see how even the "top" answer can be improved using a regression that minimizes the sum of squared errors. When students learn that regression analysis is traceable to Adrien Marie Legendre (1752-1833), Carl Friedrich

## Table 12.6: The Superiority of Least-Squares Regression

| Lace $L$ | Eyes $E$ | Predicted by Top-Rated Rule $R$ | Error $L-R$ | Error Square $(L-R)^2$ | Predicted by Least Square Regression OLS | Error $L-$OLS | Error Square $(L-$OLS$)^2$ |
|---|---|---|---|---|---|---|---|
| 45 | 8 | 41 | 4 | 16 | 41.6950 | 3.3050 | 10.923 |
| 54 | 10 | 47 | 7 | 49 | 49.1761 | 4.8239 | 23.270 |
| 26 | 4 | 29 | -3 | 9 | 26.7327 | -0.7327 | 0.537 |
| 63 | 14 | 59 | 4 | 16 | 64.1384 | -1.1384 | 1.296 |
| 63 | 12 | 53 | 10 | 100 | 56.6572 | 6.3428 | 40.231 |
| 36 | 8 | 41 | -5 | 25 | 41.6950 | -5.6950 | 32.433 |
| 54 | 12 | 53 | 1 | 1 | 56.6572 | -2.6572 | 7.061 |
| 24 | 4 | 29 | -5 | 25 | 26.7327 | -2.7327 | 7.468 |
| 72 | 14 | 59 | 13 | 169 | 64.1384 | 7.8616 | 61.805 |
| 54 | 12 | 53 | 1 | 1 | 56.6572 | -2.6572 | 7.061 |
| 72 | 16 | 65 | 7 | 49 | 71.6195 | 0.3805 | 0.145 |
| 72 | 18 | 71 | 1 | 1 | 79.1007 | -7.1007 | 50.419 |
| | | | 35 | 461 | | 0.0000 | 242.648 |

Gauss (1777-1855), and Sir Francis Galton (1822-1911) they ask: "why isn't it being used?"

Making use of popular press articles that provide academic references demonstrates that academics have thought about issues before the general public see analysis in the news media. In addition, the data can usually be retrieved. This approach makes use of a reporter's ability to identify newsworthy work and the researcher's expertise as a statistician. It may also yield the instructor great data sets. For example, *The New York Times* (April 11, 1994) reported that Federal District Court Judge Clarence Newcomer turned to Orley Ashenfelter to help him decide whether to order a new election in Pennsylvania's Second State Senatorial District in Philadelphia or declare the losing candidate Bruce Marks (Republican) the winner in the 1993 November election. In this special election to fill a Senate vacancy, Marks received 19,691 votes on voting machines and his Democrat opponent, William Stinson, received 19,127. In absentee ballots Stinson received 1,391 to Marks' 461. The Republicans charged that many of the absentee ballots were falsified by the Democrat-controlled County Board of Election. The scatter plot of absentee and machine ballot differences in the previous 21 elections that accompanied the *NYT* article (Figure 12.1) makes clear the role of regression analysis. Marks was awarded the seat. An advantage of this data set for classroom use is that it is small and yet provides a meaningful estimation of a simple regression model.

Another example, consider Ashenfelter's study with Krueger (1994) on returns to schooling. This study was highly publicized in the popular press both

## Figure 12.1: Looking for Fraud in Philadelphia

The dots show the margin of victory or defeat for the democrats, by both absentee ballot and voting-machine ballot, in 22 elections in Philadelphia's senatorial districts over the last decade. The plot of absentee and machine votes shows a rough relationship between the two: the bigger the Democratic majority on machine votes, the larger their margin on absentee ballots. The 1993 election and a few others produced results that are far from typical. The probability that the unusual results of the 1993 election were simply caused by random variations in voting patterns is just 6%.

Difference between Democratic and Republican tallies

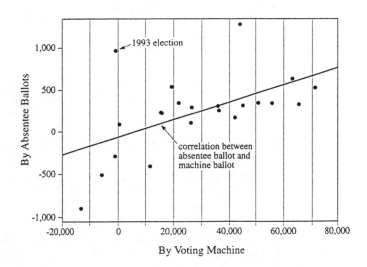

By Voting Machine

Source: Data and figure provided by Orley Ashenfelter, as appeared in *The New York Times*, April 11, 1994

for it use in U.S. Congressional debate and in discussions of Herrnstein and Murray's (1994) controversial book on IQ (e.g., *The New York Times*, November 9, 1994). The fixed-effect, least-squares estimates for the difference in identical twins' earnings as a function of differences in years of schooling involve only 149 observations and, like the Pennsylvania election data, provide another example of a meaningful simple regression. Unlike the Pennsylvania election data, however, this data set can be used to demonstrate problems caused by selection effects and measurement error, with generalized least squares used to correct these problems.

## VI. SAMPLE SELECTION BIAS

The press is rich in articles showing sample selection problems. Greene (1997, 683), for example, introduces the effect of truncation with a story from the *New York Post* on "affluent Americans" having average income of $142,000 per year. He shows how the income of the "typical American" can be estimated from this information on the top 2 percent who make at least $100,000 per year. Similar examples of truncation appear regularly in the press. One of my favorites had the headline "Sears Is Accused of Billing Fraud at Auto Centers." This *Wall Street Journal* (June 12, 1992) article reported on a study by the California Department of Consumer Affairs in which "its agents were overcharged nearly 90% of the time, by an average of $223."

QUERY: What happened to charges the other 10 percent of the time?

ANSWER: If $Y$ is a normal random variable of over, under, and exact charges, then

$$P(Y>0)=0.9 \rightarrow P\left(Z>\frac{0-\mu}{\sigma}\right)=0.9 \rightarrow \frac{0-\mu}{\sigma}=-1.282$$

The department's findings imply that

$$E(Y|Y>0)=\int_0^\infty yf(y|y>0)dy=\mu+\sigma\frac{\phi(\alpha)}{1-\Phi(\alpha)}=223$$

where $\phi$ is the probability density function and $\Phi$ is the distribution function; thus,

$$\mu+\sigma\frac{0.175847}{1-0.1}=223$$

because $\phi(-1.28155) = 0.17550$ and $\Phi(-1.28155) = 0.1$

Excel cell A1:   −1.28155   =NORMSINV(0.1)

Excel cell A2:    0.17550   =NORMDIST(A1,0,1,0)

Solving for $\mu$ and $\sigma$ yields $\mu=193.55$ and $\sigma=151.03$

Excel cell A4:   151.03    =223/(−A1+(A2/0.9))

Excel cell A5:    193.55    =−A1*A4

Finally, the mean of under and exact charges is $71.50.

$$E(Y\,|\,Y\leq 0)=\int_{-\infty}^{0} yf(y\,|\,y\leq 0)dy = \mu - \sigma\frac{\phi(\alpha)}{1-\Phi(\alpha)}$$

$$= 193.55 - 151.03\left(\frac{0.1755}{0.1}\right) = -71.5$$

Excel cell A6: −71.50   =A5 − A4*(A2/0.1)

Unlike the standard presentation of a Heckman adjustment for sample selection in least-squares regression estimation, the above example makes clear what the selection problem is and what the adjustment is doing.   The mathematical symbols, conditional statements and algebra become intuitive with actual and meaningful calculations.   The role of the hazard function in the calculation of the expected value of $Y$ conditioned on a range of $Y$ values is made obvious. Neither the equations nor the computer calculations are "black boxes."

## VII. ENGAGING STUDENTS

To engage students individually and in group work with computers, small classes are needed.   In the business and economics statistics class at Indiana University approximately 800 students per semester are allocated to some 32 computer-lab sections.   Computer-lab instructors have weekly staff meetings to review what students are to do, and to learn what problems to expect.   Two lab activities that students seem to like require them to go to the World Wide Web in search of information.   For the first, students are to find a news item for which a multiple-choice question can be written.   Students are encouraged to use the Web and a search engine (Yahoo) to find the major news and data sources.   Although all students attempt this, they quickly learn the frustration of the "World Wide Wait."   Most assignments are handed in with an original hard copy source and not a printout from the Web.   In the honors section of the course, students must find a data source that can be used throughout the semester for data analysis.   At the beginning of the semester students are told to find data on several variables for which they suspect a relationship.   Students are encouraged to search the Web.   Students learn, as discussed by Sosin in this volume, that all the major government agencies and news services maintain Web sites where data can be accessed.   They also learn that the most comprehensive listing of these sites is at < http://econwpa.wustl.edu/EconFAQ /EconFAQ.html> where Bill Goffe's opening page has over 44 links to resources for economics.   For current information, students no long need visit the reading room or government documents section of the library. We can make teaching statistics and econometrics timely and relevant right in our computer labs.

## VIII. DO'S AND DON'TS

To implement the popular press-based short case study approach outlined here it may be helpful to keep the following Do's and Don'ts in mind:

- Do read the *Wall Street Journal*, *Business Week*, *The Economist* and similar publications on a regular basis.
- Do let your colleagues know of your interest in clippings; they will often share their discoveries with you.
- Do look for small data sets that can be used easily in hand calculations and with easy-to-use computer programs.
- Do keep an electronic and/or hard copy file folder of your clippings.
- Do mark the relevant text of the clipping and note how it might be used.
- Do show students direct quotes that capture the essences of the issue in the clipping.
- Do encourage students to look for clippings.
- Do require students to make use of news clippings in assignments, but also require them to mark the few relevant sentences in the clipping.
- Do estimate (or approximate) missing values, but state that this has been done.
- Do edit lengthy material to provide students with the essence – only a few sentences.
- Do check and double-check the wording and calculations to make sure they are correct.
- Don't use features that cannot be tied to economics or business examples.
- Don't wait until the time of a test or needed homework or class activity to look for news releases.
- Don't fake newspaper cites, make up names, or create erroneous data sources for hypothetical or contrived problems.
- Don't change numbers to suit your needs; if the real values do not fit your needs find something that does.
- Don't get involved in copyright problems – you don't have to provide students with the entire article.
- Don't ridicule the popular press for errors, just don't use those bad articles.
- Finally, don't assume that students can learn software on their own; work with the software and with the students in a computer lab.

## IX.  CONCLUDING COMMENTS

Introducing headline grabbing situations into my undergraduate teaching of statistics and econometrics has facilitated the exposition of statistical concepts. Students no longer ask: "how is this stuff relevant?" There are variable costs associated with this approach because you must stay up on current events and invest time to prepare new cases. The additional time commitment to prepare the cases is trivial for anyone who is already reading the popular and academic publications. Furthermore, the identification of problems can add to one's research agenda with problems and issues that truly have social importance. Analysis of these issues should add greatly to our students understanding of the applications involved as well as the quantitative methods employed in analysis.

## NOTES

* Indiana University. This work is supported by grants from the National Science Foundation (DUE 955408 and DUE 9653421) and a grant from the Calvin Kazanjian Economics Foundation. Parts of this chapter were prepared at the University of South Australia where W. E. Becker is an adjunct professor, in residence for the period of May through August 1997. Suzanne Becker, George Bredon, Peter Kennedy, and Michael Watts provided constructive criticism on earlier drafts.

1. Fisher's negative view toward the contribution of the social sciences to the development of quantitative methods is traceable to the first version of his book in 1925 and is shared today by many scholars in the natural sciences and departments of mathematics. Econometricians, psychometricians, cliometricians, and other "metricians" in the social sciences have different views of the process by which statistical methods have developed. Given that Fisher's numerous and great contributions to statistics were in applications within biology, genetics, and agriculture, his view is understandable, although it is refuted by sociologist Clifford Clogg (1992) and the numerous commentaries on his article.

2. Nobel Laureate Gary Becker also adds "students have unnecessary difficulties learning economics because textbooks generally do not have enough good examples of real-world applications."(*Business Week*, October 21, 1996, 19)

3. Outside an exam setting, data to make this book pricing example real can be obtained by having students go to the book store and acquire price and page length information. Alternatively, this information can be obtained from book reviews in local papers or national papers such as *The New York Times*. Using the news media as a source provides the student with a means for documenting that the data are not bogus. Students can also retrieve information on variables other than page length that might explain price (e.g., the number of books previously published by the author, paper or cloth binding, number of competing books, and other market features). Examples involving price determination have the added caveat that they require students to consider the specification of the equation estimated – is it a demand curve, supply curve, reduced form or what?

## REFERENCES

Angelo, T. A. and P. K. Cross. 1993. *Classroom assessment techniques: A handbook for college teachers*. San Francisco: Jossey-Bass Publishers.

Ashenfelter, O. and A. Krueger. 1994. Estimates of the economic return to schooling from a new sample of twins. *American Economic Review* 84(December): 1157-73.

Becker, W. 1997. *Statistics for business and economics using Microsoft Excel 97*. Bloomington: SRB Publishing.

_____ and M. Watts. 1996. Chalk and talk: A national survey on teaching undergraduate economics. *American Economic Review* 86(May): 448-53.

Bernstein, P. L. 1996. *Against the gods: The remarkable story of risk*. New York: John Wiley & Sons.

Clogg, C. 1992. The impact of sociological methodology on statistical methodology. *Statistical Science* 7(May): 183-95.

Crossen, C. 1994. *Tainted truth: The manipulation of facts*. New York: Simon & Schuster.

Fels, R. 1974. Developing independent problem-solving skills in economics. *American Economic Review* 64(May): 403-7.

Fisher, R. 1970. *Statistical methods for research workers*. New York: Hafner Publishing Company.

Gal, I. and J. Garfield, eds. 1997. *Assessment of challenge in statistics education*. Amsterdam: IOS Press.

Georges, J. and T. Craire. 1995. Generalizing Monty's dilemma. *Quantum* 5(March/April): 17-21.

Greene, W. 1997. *Econometric analysis*. 3rd ed. Englewood Cliffs: Prentice Hall.

Hansen, M. and W. Hurwitz. 1946. The problem of non-response in sample surveys. *Journal of the American Statistical Association* 41(December): 517-29.

Herrnstein, R. and C. Murray. 1994. *The bell curve*. New York: Free Press.

Huff, D. and I. Geis. 1954. *How to lie with statistics*. New York: Norton.

Light, R. 1992. *The Harvard assessment seminars*. Cambridge: Harvard University Graduate School of Education and Kennedy School of Government, Second Report.

Maxwell, N. L. and J. S. Lopus. 1994. The Lake Wobegon effect in student self-reported data. *American Economic Review* 84(May): 201-5.

Morgan, J.P., N. R. Chaganty, R. C. Dahiya, and M. J. Doviak. 1991. Let's make a deal: The player's dilemma. *American Statistician* 45(November): 284-7.

Scheaffer, R., M. Gnanadesikan, A. Watkins, and J. A. Witmer. 1996. *Activity-based statistics*. New York: Springer-Verlag.

Siegfried, J., R. L. Bartlett, W. L. Hansen, A. C. Kelley, D. N. McCloskey, and T. H. Tietenberg. 1991. The status and prospects of the economics major. *Journal of Economic Education* 22(Summer): 197-224.

Snell, J. L. and J. Finn. 1992. A course called "chance." *Chance* 5(3-4): 12-6.

Thaler, R. 1993. *Advances in behavioral finance*. New York: Russell Sage Foundation.

_____. 1995. Behavioral economics. *NBER Reporter*, National Bureau of Economic Research, Fall: 9-13.

Tufte, E. 1983. *The visual display of quantitative information*. Cheshire, CT.: Graphics Press.

Tversky, A. and D. Kahneman. 1981. The framing of decisions and the psychology of choice. *Science* 211(January): 453-8.

_____. 1982. Belief in the law of small numbers. In D. Kahneman, P. Slovic and A. Tversky, eds. *Judgment under uncertainty: Heuristics and biases*, pp. 23-31. New York: Cambridge University Press.

_____. 1992. Advances in prospect theory: Cumulative representation of uncertainty. *Journal of Risk and Uncertainty* 5(4): 297-323.

Utts, J. 1991. Replication and meta-analysis, *Statistical Science* 6(November): 363-78.

Von Neumann, J. and O. Morgenstern. 1944. *Theory of games and economic behavior*. Princeton, New Jersey: Princeton University Press.

# Index

# S